Practices of Wonder

Practices of Wonder

Cross-Disciplinary Perspectives

Edited by
SOPHIA VASALOU

☙PICKWICK *Publications* • Eugene, Oregon

PRACTICES OF WONDER
Cross-Disciplinary Perspectives

Copyright © 2012 Wipf and Stock Publishers. All rights reserved. Except for brief quotations in critical publications or reviews, no part of this book may be reproduced in any manner without prior written permission from the publisher. Write: Permissions, Wipf and Stock Publishers, 199 W. 8th Ave., Suite 3, Eugene, OR 97401.

Pickwick Publications
An Imprint of Wipf and Stock Publishers
199 W. 8th Ave., Suite 3
Eugene, OR 97401

www.wipfandstock.com

ISBN 13: 978-1-61097-216-1

Cataloging-in-Publication data:

Practices of wonder : cross-disciplinary perspectives / edited by Sophia Vasalou.

xii + 254 p. ; 23 cm. —Includes bibliographical references and index.

ISBN 13: 978-1-61097-216-1

1. Wonder (Philosophy). 2. Philosophy. I. Vasalou, Sophia II. Title.

B105.W65 P73 2012

Manufactured in the U.S.A.

To the aspiring and unwitting authors of Archimedean points

Contents

List of Contributors · ix
Acknowledgments · xi

Introduction by Sophia Vasalou · 1

1 Wonder: Toward a Grammar · 16
    —Sophia Vasalou

2 From Biology to Spirituality: The Emotional Dynamics of Wonder · 64
    —Robert Fuller

3 Wonder and the Beginning of Philosophy in Plato · 88
    —Sylvana Chrysakopoulou

4 Wonder, Perplexity, Sublimity: Philosophy as the Self-Overcoming of Self-Exile in Heidegger and Wittgenstein · 121
    —Stephen Mulhall

5 Heidegger's Caves: On Dwelling in Wonder · 144
    —Mary-Jane Rubenstein

6 Wonder and Cognition · 166
    —Derek Matravers

7 The Microscopic Glance: Spiritual Exercises, the Microscope, and the Practice of Wonder in Early Modern Science · 179
    —Claude-Olivier Doron

8 Literary Wonder in the Seventeenth Century and the Origins of "Aesthetic Experience" · 201
    —Alexander Rueger

9 The Conception of *Camatkâra* in Indian Aesthetics · 225
—MICHEL HULIN

10 Wonderment Today in the Abrahamic Traditions · 235
—DAVID B. BURRELL, CSC

Index of Authors · 251

Contributors

David B. Burrell, CSC, is Professor of Comparative Theology, Tangaza College, Nairobi, and Hesburgh Professor Emeritus, University of Notre Dame. He has worked widely on comparative issues in philosophical theology in Judaism, Christianity, and Islam. Recent publications include *Faith and Freedom: An Interfaith Perspective* (2005), *Deconstructing Theodicy* (2008), *When Faith and Reason Meet* (2009), and *Learning to Trust in Freedom: Signs from Jewish, Christian, and Muslim Traditions* (2010).

Sylvana Chrysakopoulou is a researcher at the Hellenic Parliament Foundation in Athens, Greece, and has taught ancient Greek philosophy at the Universities of Patras and Crete. Her main research interests focus on the pre-Socratics; Plato and the pre-Platonic thinkers; Aristotle and the pre-Socratics; ancient Greek philosophy and poetry; and ancient Greek philosophy and religion. Her publications include an English translation of Plato's *Parmenides* (2010), and her *La naissance de la théologie dans la poésie présocratique* will be published in 2012 by Peeters (Leuven).

Claude-Olivier Doron is currently a doctoral student at the University Paris-Denis Diderot (Paris VII). His research interests and recent publications range over the history of the natural sciences and psychiatry in the eighteenth and nineteenth centuries, contemporary criminology and psychiatry, and the philosophy of Michel Foucault.

Robert Fuller is Professor of Religious Studies at Bradley University. Specializing in the psychological study of religion and American religious history, his two most recent books are *Wonder: From Emotion to Spirituality* (2006) and *Spirituality in the Flesh: Bodily Sources of Religious Experience* (2008).

Michel Hulin is Professor Emeritus of Indian and Comparative Philosophy at the University Paris-Sorbonne (Paris IV). His works deal with classical Indian philosophy and with the epistemological and metaphysical problems raised by the confrontation of the European and Asian intellectual traditions. Recent publications include: *La mystique sauvage* (1993), *Qu'est-ce que l'ignorance métaphysique (dans la pensée hindoue)* (1994), *Classical Indian Philosophy Reinterpreted* (with V. Lysenko; 2007), *Comment la philosophie indienne s'est-elle développée* (2008), and *La Bhagavad-Gîtâ, avec des extraits du Commentaire de Shankara* (2010).

Derek Matravers teaches philosophy at the Open University. He is also an Affiliated Lecturer at Cambridge, where he is a Fellow of Emmanuel College. In addition to *Art and Emotion* (2008), he is the author of many articles in aesthetics, ethics, and political philosophy. He is currently working on an introduction to the Philosophy of Art to be published by Acumen, and a monograph titled *Fiction and Narrative*, to be published by Oxford University Press.

Stephen Mulhall is Professor of Philosophy and Fellow of New College, Oxford. His research interests include Heidegger, Wittgenstein, Sartre, and Nietzsche, as well as the relationship between philosophy and the arts. His most recent publication is *The Wounded Animal: J. M. Coetzee and the Difficulty of Reality in Literature and Philosophy* (2009).

Mary-Jane Rubenstein is Associate Professor of Religion at Wesleyan University, where she teaches primarily in the intersections of continental philosophy and philosophy of religion. She is the author of *Strange Wonder: The Closure of Metaphysics and the Opening of Awe* (2009) and of numerous articles and chapters on negative theology, relational ontologies, and the postcolonial Anglican Communion. She is currently writing a new book about "multiverse" cosmologies.

Alexander Rueger is Professor of Philosophy at the University of Alberta. He has published widely in the philosophy and history of science and, more recently, on the history of aesthetics, especially on Kant. He is now working on a book on the *Critique of Judgment*.

Sophia Vasalou is Junior Research Fellow at Gonville and Caius College, Cambridge. Her first book, on classical Islamic theology, is *Moral Agents and Their Deserts: The Character of Mu'tazilite Ethics* (2008), and she is currently preparing a study of Ibn Taymiyya's ethics. Her research interests in philosophy include Wittgenstein and Schopenhauer, and she is currently at work on a longer study of wonder and a monograph on Schopenhauer titled *Schopenhauer and the Aesthetic Practice of Philosophy*, to be published by Cambridge University Press.

Acknowledgments

IT IS A PLEASURE to be able to thank those involved at the different stages of this project's lifespan—a lifespan that passed through still-unshapely ideas, to the conference organized in Cambridge (June 2008) as a stage for pursuing them, and finally to the present collection of essays. At the first stage of its lifespan (though also at others), I would like to thank David Jennings, whose evening conversations about the role of wonder in science in St. John's helped water sleeping seeds, just as I would like to thank Emmanuel Halais, with whom our philosophical preoccupations have often followed mysteriously parallel tracks, and wonder has been one of these. Etienne Roesch was often a conversation partner willing to offer his knowledge of emotion and to bite into ideas to test their worth in the most geographically divided places, through Bath, Thessaloniki, Sifnos, and beyond.

At the next stage, I would like to thank the Centre for Research in the Arts, Social Sciences and Humanities at the University of Cambridge for their support both financially and logistically—and here I'm particularly grateful to Michelle Maciejewska and Philippa Smith—in helping the conference take form, and also the British Society of Aesthetics for likewise lending a much-needed financial hand, and Derek Matravers for helping this happen. I would also like to thank Jane Heal, Brad Inwood, and Patricia Fara, whose presence contributed greatly to the character of the event.

I am also grateful to John Marenbon, who as usual shadowed virtually every stage of the way, though perhaps most memorably in the skill and zest with which he squeezed every ounce of our resources to extend the warmest hospitality to attendees of the event. My gratitude to Olivier Doron must likewise cut across lifespan stages, as he was an invaluable partner not only in helping ideas take shape, but also in many of the organizational aspects that took us door to door.

Acknowledgments

And in this rather permeable striation of this project's stages and debts, I am happy that I can only thank Agis Marinis in the last, for offering a sharp gaze and punctilious taste for detail to parts of the text where it was most needed.

Last, but not least, and as the almost unthankable presupposition to every activity in the last four years, I am grateful to Gonville and Caius College, whose support made such intellectual excursions beyond narrow disciplinary bounds possible.

Introduction

SOPHIA VASALOU

WONDER IS A FACE that we have known very well. It is the face we recognize in the gaze of children, turned upward and outward toward a world that consists of a concatenation of first-time experiences and exposures to historical firsts. In this face, the look of wonder has often shaded into others, as in a look of open humility and artless vulnerability confronted with the visible world.

This wonder is one we may call natural twice over: in sharing the naturalness we ascribe to childhood, and in being a wonder that often appears to be torn from the outward-looking gaze with the spontaneity of a sudden, effortless gasp. It is a gasp that will accompany many of the moments, even in later years, when we are confronted with something extraordinary beheld or experienced for the very first time: our first sight of a rainbow or of snow, our first vision of the solemnly silent crystalline interior of a long-undiscovered cave, of the pummeling descent of a powerful waterfall or the swirl-colored underwater, of the world below seen from an airplane window.

Yet if wonder has had a natural place in our lives, it has also occupied another kind of role in a series of activities and pursuits that we may call "practices," not only in the loosest sense that may be drawn out of the Greek root of this term (*prattein*, to act)—an iterated, organized activity; a doing (*praxis*) disciplined by reflection—but also in the thicker terms that Alasdair MacIntyre made available to us in one of his works, emphasizing that such disciplined acting has a history, a tradition, internal standards of excellence and conceptions of its internal goods. By the term *practice*, in MacIntyre's words, we may understand

> any coherent and complex form of socially established cooperative human activity through which goods internal to that form of activity are realized in the course of trying to achieve those standards of excellence which are appropriate to, and partially definitive of, that form of activity, with the result that human powers to achieve excellence, and human conceptions of the ends and goods involved, are systematically extended.[1]

Tic-tac-toe and throwing a football with skill do not count as practices on this definition, though the game of chess or the game of football do. Planting turnips and bricklaying are not a practice, but farming and architecture are. The inquiries of scientists and historians, and the activities of philosophers and artists, offer themselves as paradigmatic examples of this term's scope.

Using these terms, we may say that wonder has occupied a special and significant place in many of our most valued practices, including those that MacIntyre makes central to his account. Its place in philosophy was marked early on by Plato's oft-rehearsed words in the *Theaetetus* that named wonder as the beginning of philosophy, which were later rehearsed by Aristotle in his *Metaphysics*, and were due to echo throughout the length of philosophical history—a history that was not, of course, exclusively philosophical but was shared by other disciplines, including science, that remained for a long time intertwined, sharing their textual and conceptual inspirations. In religious or spiritual practices, again, wonder—along with its associated concepts, such as awe—has sometimes been seen as the religious passion *par excellence*. In art, similarly, wonder has at different times figured prominently in the ideals for the aesthetic experience that works of art should aim to (re)produce.

The appearance of wonder at so many important locations in our practices serves, on the one hand, as a testimony to the inherent complexity of this emotion. For if, in many of our philosophical, scientific, and other intellectual inquiries, wonder has often been cast as the passion of inquiry and connected with the desire to know and understand, its presence in other practices, as in spiritual or aesthetic contexts—if indeed we may draw these boundaries with sufficient distinctness—brings to the fore its character, not merely as a questing or inquisitive, but more importantly, as an appreciative response. And if this consideration attunes us to one source of complexity, we should also be prepared to be attuned to another. For this plurality of appearances across different practices should not mask

---

1. MacIntyre, *After Virtue*, 187.

important differences—differences subject to historical evolution—in the exact nature of each appearance, even in what (with some license) we may permit ourselves to call a "single" practice.

The kind of differences in question are already visible in one of the examples listed above: for if wonder was jointly claimed as the beginning of philosophy by both Plato and Aristotle, this should not make us overlook the difference in both location and content that define these kinds of wonder—the latter outward-looking, directed to natural phenomena, and positioned at the beginning of inquiry with the assumption that explanation should purge it, the other inward-looking, toward conceptual phenomena, and positioned not only at the beginning of inquiry but also as its pursued end. And such different understandings, as several papers in this volume suggest, are ones that have continued to be elaborated and developed throughout the history of philosophical conversation. Here, MacIntyre's terms afford us useful ways of expressing these differences, for they may be rephrased as ones that contest the place wonder should occupy in the standards of excellence and epistemological ideals that govern philosophical inquiry. And armed with those terms, one may go on to make other fruitful statements about the changing place of wonder in the standards and ends governing other practices, as several papers in this volumes suggest. Change, for example, is the implicit context for the paper by Olivier Doron, which focuses on the place of wonder in scientific practice, and more specifically in the use of the microscope, in a period between the seventeenth and eighteenth centuries in which the epistemological ideals of scientific inquiry—and the position of wonder within them—were tied to the spiritual and religious ends that the study of the natural world was understood as serving. Yet this position, and the understanding of wonder it imported, registered not only a change from attitudes in the preceding period, but also provided the measure for changes still to come, as not only the place of passion among the epistemological ideals (or standards of excellence) of scientific inquiry, but also the view of the ends science served, came to be revised.[2] Speaking in the context of aesthetics, and working in a similar time frame though with a stronger anchor in the classical literary tradition, Alexander Rueger likewise calls our attention to the changes affecting the place of wonder in literary works and, later on, in conceptions of aesthetic experience. The story of these changes, his account suggests, can partly be told in terms of a distinction, and debate, concerning the exact place that wonder should occupy in the artistic process, and more

---

2. For the broader context of these changes, see Daston and Park, *Wonders*.

specifically whether it should figure as part of its means (in the context of the classical view that rhetorical and literary art aims at persuasion, and emotions may serve as means for achieving it) or as its intrinsic end (as asserted by the Baroque art theorists Rueger focuses on).

The contrast, of course, between a natural wonder and a practiced wonder is not meant to be drawn too sharply. For after all, it is often the natural wonder of first-time experiences—the spontaneous gasp torn from our lips as we confront something that strikes us as extraordinary—that often coincides with the wonder that has historically offered, and continues to offer, to practices their beginnings, and the sources of their continued reflection. Yet if this contrast is worth drawing, and preserving, it is partly because of the way it helps widen our understanding of the kind of relationship in which we may stand to this emotion, and makes available to us a broader notion of its nature and content. For in many of those practices in which wonder has been claimed as an important passion, wonder has often been, not so much the spontaneous and effortless reaction to something novel and unexpected—to the "extraordinary" considered as what naturally stands out of the ordinary and arrests our attention (wonder as an effortless beginning, natural in the second sense identified above). Wonder has often presented itself, not as a given, but rather as a passion to be mastered, often requiring an effort on our part to see something *as* extraordinary where we did not do so before. For, after all, isn't the process of learning to philosophize or to think scientifically or to experience the world in certain aesthetic ways at the same time a discipline initiating the learner to the capacity to wonder at things not wondered at before, introducing a wonderment that, while in some respects no doubt recovering, or partaking of, an earlier child-like spontaneity, is the product of a deliberately and purposefully wielded technique?

And to lay stress on the nature of wonder as a product dependent on discipline and learning involves, as may be readily seen, giving a different account, incorporating different stresses, of the objects that impart to it its content. For in the plurality of practices in which wonder is a willfully cultivated response, one's effort is often turned upon the task of enthralling one's attention to the wondrousness, not of what is extraordinary, abnormal, or irregular in our experience, but indeed of what is most ordinary and most regular, in order to see it under its aspect—in its very orderliness—as an extraordinary thing. This extension of the account seems to be urged most compellingly by scientific inquiry, with its defamiliarizing attention to the regularities in nature that underlie our capacity to simply get on with our practical relationship with the world and whose pervasive orderliness makes the ordinariness of an everyday world possible. For here isn't it precisely the most self-evident things—the apple that falls when one releases one's grip and the water that boils when placed on the fire, the magnet that raises the paper clip from the desk or the next step we take as we put our foot forward, as much as solar eclipses and rainbows (or monstrous births or newly discovered species)—that one *ought* to be able to meet with fruitful perplexity and see as though for the first time, at some stage or other of the history of the science or of the individuals who absorb its history and take it forward?

Religious practices could be interestingly compared and contrasted with the sciences in their tendency to encourage a habit of estranging the ordinary by valorizing a perception of the world (and the self) under its aspect as a gift or extraordinary given. In those practices organized around the notion of a creative deity, the contingency of this given can be evoked by considering it as the product of a creative act that might not have taken place, inflaming the imagination with the sharp dichotomy of a "nothing" that preceded this act and a "something"—an "everything"—that immediately succeeded it. (And this initial miracle, which establishes nature, is the ground for the subsequent possibility of miraculous acts that disrupt nature and provoke spontaneous wonder.)

A similar task of estranging the ordinary has been assigned at different times and in different ways to art, whose aim has sometimes been described as that of recovering and renewing our capacity to ("really") perceive the objects surrounding us, which have retreated into a jaded invisibility by force of habitual use and encounter. The formulation of the Russian Formalist literary critic Viktor Shklovksy about the role of art in "estranging" objects to rescue them from "automatized perception" and to replace mere "recognition" with "sight"[3] has much to divide it but also much to unite it, especially in its concern with recovering sight, with the project to which writers belonging to the broader Romantic movement and American Transcendentalists gave voice. Emerson echoes Carlyle and Coleridge echoes Wordsworth (in a train of echo that has a longer and wider life) when talking about the importance of restoring the wondrousness of ordinary things from the "lethargy of custom" and of recovering the child's sense of wonder and the "miraculousness of daily-recurring miracles."[4]

---

3. Shklovksy, *Theory*, ch. 1.
4. Abrams, *Natural Supernaturalism*, 377–84; cf. Tanner, *Reign*.

Practices of Wonder

In philosophy, finally, the dialectic between a natural and a learned capacity to wonder is deeply embedded in the conception of the subject by which philosophers guide themselves. Both as a stage in the development of the discipline and as an episode in the history of the individual apprenticing in it, philosophy may be grounded in a reaction of wonder that forms its natural point of departure. Yet this reaction—and the capacity to experience it—survives as an internal good of philosophical inquiry and as a constituent in the intellectual excellences that govern its practice, as one pursues a critical reflectiveness that dissolves the givenness of the most ordinary things and yields a lesson in surprise that is ceaselessly rehearsed. Rousseau, in his *Discourse on Inequality*, gives voice to many when he speaks of philosophy as that "which man must have to know how to observe once, what he has every day seen." Even those who censure the particular way in which traditional philosophy goes about its task of being surprised by familiar things—such as the later Wittgenstein, who, among other things, questioned the roots of a specific kind of philosophical amazement at the mind—still appear to engage in a reflective practice oriented around wonder, though with a changed conception of its content and point. It would be a wonder produced by replacing false perceptions about what is "queer" (which correspond to a false sense of the "sublime") with a truer perception of what is remarkable ("The aspects of things that are most important for us are hidden because of their simplicity and familiarity"[5]). This truer perception will be directed towards the language games we play with words and the forms of life that support the possibility of meaning within which philosophy must curb its ambitions, content with describing them and renouncing the ambition to explain, animated throughout by a sense of wonder at the very existence of language itself as the ultimate given.[6]

The presence of wonder in many of our most highly valued practices, in this light, turns out to be a complex one in more ways than one, and there is a host of interesting questions to be raised in tracking it. Questions, certainly, inviting more fine-grained accounts of the position wonder has occupied in the standards and ideals governing different practices; questions concerning the nature of wonder and its peculiar objects as these have been variously understood; and questions, likewise, about the value that we attach to a capacity for wonder.

---

5. Wittgenstein, *Philosophical Investigations*, §129.
6. See Cavell, *Claim*, 15.

For the status of wonder as a beginning and motive force of inquiry would suggest that, in asking about the value of wonder, we might be able to answer this question most intuitively in instrumental and utilitarian terms. Wonder, on these terms, would be as valuable as its capacity to stimulate inquiry and lead us to an understanding of things we had previously not held in our grasp. Yet even there, could the note of utility be sounded exclusively and without ambivalence? Is wonder, as this would imply, only justified so long as explanation has not been attained? Is our right to wonder—as the juridical tones of "justification" would have it—fully abolished once explanation has been secured? (Do we still possess the right to wonder at what would seem to be the most dizzying fact—that there is something instead of nothing—only because scientists have not *yet* provided us with a satisfying answer to the question "why"?) And if the function of wonder is to be liquidated by explanation—as Aristotle himself suggested in the *Metaphysics*—then what sense is one to make of a scientist's claim to find in wonder "a deep aesthetic passion" that "makes life worth living" or of his project of composing a book on science that aims to arouse wonder and that of course communicates, not what science does *not* know, but what it *does*?[7]

If an instrumental view of wonder should here be questioned, it is challenged even more strongly when we turn to the role of wonder in other domains, including theologically or spiritually motivated practices. For wonder, here, might seem to have the character of a devotional exercise whose end exhausts itself in the perpetuation and celebration of a particular way of perceiving the world—in many theistic practices, as a radically contingent given—considered as a form of knowledge in its own right. When this spiritually motivated attention is turned towards the givens that define one's individual existence, the training in modal perception is revealed at the same time as a training in moral perception, as when one is taught that one *could* have been born into poverty, or into blindness, or into madness, or not at all. The ethical culmination of this habit of foregrounding the ordinary (one's riches or vision or reason or existence) by an eliciting background of counterfactual possibility reveals an order of means and ends in which wonder would attract its value under its aspect as an instrument in the service of moral formation. Yet another domain—that of art—would seem close to the spiritual or theological in assigning to the experience of wonder a greater degree of evaluative finality, according to it the intrinsic value of an aesthetic response divorced

---

7. See Dawkins, *Unweaving the Rainbow*.

from the imperatives of action. (Though here again one might ask: how clean is the distinction between wonder as an aesthetic and as a scientific response?[8] How clear-cut is the distinction between wonder as part of an aesthetic ideal and wonder as part of a spiritual one?) Questions of value and motivation will clearly be raised in more pressing terms when what is at stake is the disciplined wonder directed to what is most ordinary and familiar. For the order of the ordinary world, after all, is something to which the roots of our attachment run deep, and the need to motivate its disturbance would seem in direct proportion to its power to emotionally disturb. Why strive to acquire awareness of the "enraging wonder of the everyday"?[9] Why live in rage, or in the need that a sense of mystery—of the "sudden uncanniness" of everything one thought one knew—creates for one who tastes it? Why live with a sense of one's contingency? Why wonder?

To the extent that such questions are considered with an awareness of the historicity of the emotions, it is clear that they will demand attention to the historically changing character of the answers they have received in different schemes and different periods. One would do well here to follow the lead given by Lorraine Daston and Katharine Park and look toward larger narratives of change and development in which particular conceptions of wonder may be situated. And such a form of attention will be tightly bound with another; for to the extent that one aspires to place on speaking terms experiences of wonder drawn from different historical contexts, one cannot avoid asking: What makes it possible to track the subject of our interest across variegated histories and lends us the certainty that we have identified what can claim to constitute a single subject? What makes it possible in the first place to hold up Plato's *thaumazein* next to Kant's *Bewunderung*, Descartes' *admiration* and Wordsworth's or (the English-speaking) Wittgenstein's *wonder*? And if part of the answer lies in tolerating the tension between the essentializing conviction that one can recognize the emotion through its unchanging objects, and the more cautious acknowledgment that the boundaries of these concepts cannot be drawn with perfect clarity and set against each other in terms of conceptual equivalence, one should aspire to finer-grained responses to such strategic conceptual questions.

---

8. It is a key part of Fisher's aim, in his *Aesthetics of Rare Experiences*, to question this distinction.

9. Rubenstein, "A Certain Disavowal."

The considerations set out above, and the questions that run through them, no doubt stand in need of enrichment attuned to the perspectives of different disciplines and domains—even as they should prepare us for the discovery that the boundaries between these prove permeable once the place of wonder in them is considered more closely. Taken together, they map out a broad horizon against which to seek to bring the experience of wonder into focus, and it is in this larger horizon of questioning in which the papers of this collection can be situated. Let us trace out the main lines of inquiry of the studies that follow.

Focusing the editor's opening paper is a larger question—"what is wonder?"—that takes its point of departure from the relatively elusive and neglected place that wonder has occupied in contemporary research on the emotions. Outlining some of the most familiar analytical approaches to the emotions, it suggests several aspects of wonder that place it in an awkward relationship to such approaches. Having drawn on a broadly Wittgensteinian perspective to propose a general account of wonder, the essay then turns to Daston and Park's reading of wonder's history, which would seem to shed light on this account, supplement it, and potentially contradict it. The key focus falls on a question about the felt experience or affective tone of wonder, and more specifically about its connection to pleasure or delight—a connection that is central to Daston and Park's account of the historicity of wonder and forms the backbone for important questions about its historical identity. Working through this question involves giving closer consideration to Adam Smith's understanding of wonder, and leads to an effort to bring together Daston and Park's historical reading with the one recently articulated by Rubenstein, who, taking us from wonder's beginnings in Plato to Heidegger, calls attention to the darker elements (the dreadful, or the terrible) in wonder and helps further nuance the questions about its affective tone that are central to considering its identity.

A concern with the elusive place of wonder in contemporary emotion research and with questions about the boundaries between concepts of the emotions are also background themes of the paper by Robert Fuller, who argues for the need to consider wonder under its aspect as a biological phenomenon, in the context of a view of emotions as biological systems shaped by natural selection. Wonder, here, is considered as a response to the unfamiliar, and more specifically to what strikes us as intensely powerful, real, or beautiful. Fuller's proposal for locating wonder in an evolutionary framework, though one that still reveals wonder to be an unintended byproduct rather than an adaptation, focuses on the character of wonder (and awe, to which it is related) as a response to new stimuli that exceed our existing cognitive structures and require us to accommodate them anew to the world. Connected with this character are a variety of functions that can be ascribed to wonder, above all, its tendency to enlarge our field of perception, widen our world of empathy or concern, broaden our cognitive capacities, and—significantly for Fuller's argument but also for bridging the distance from a naturalistic view of emotions to their cultural context and roles—build higher-order patterns of thought capable of stimulating philosophical and religious reflection. These functions of wonder, in turn, form the core of Fuller's reading of wonder as an emotion of special importance for the development of spirituality, a reading that he pursues in the context of a larger preoccupation with the value of wonder.

The latter question is likewise a shared theme in the essay by Derek Matravers, which is formed out of the intersection of two main strands of questioning, one concerning the relationship between wonder and cognition, and the other concerning the value we ascribe to wonder. In the background of broader questions about how the relationship between affective and cognitive elements should be written in a philosophical account of the emotions, Matravers considers three approaches for grounding the value of wonder, which respectively refer us to distinct accounts of the relationship of wonder and cognition. Having identified what he takes to be the thought at the heart of wonder—it is provoked by objects profound and impressive with respect to ourselves—he suggests that this should be read in terms of an account of emotions as "cognitively penetrated." When we believe an object is profound or impressive, we experience it *as* profound or impressive. Yet any judgment we then go on to make concerning the value of wonder would have to take into account, crucially, questions concerning the truth of the beliefs on which the response of wonder is founded.

Sylvana Chrysakopoulou's essay takes us to the earliest beginnings of philosophy's preoccupation with wonder, offering a study of wonder in Plato's works. Passing through a close reading of the *Theaetetus*, this study expands to bring into its scope a richer set of texts that include the *Symposium*, the *Phaedrus*, and the *Republic*. Placing these texts into conversation creates an unexpected set of relations, connecting the passion of wonder (*thauma*) to the passion of love (*eros*), which share their suffering quality and orientation to wisdom, and then placing this suffering quality into relationship with the maieutic metaphor that governs the Socratic art. These connections, in turn, help deliver a re-reading of Platonic wonder as a response to the beautiful—to wisdom under the aspect of its beauty—just as they reveal wonder as the product, not so much of sight, as of insight, that is, as a response to invisible realities perceived with the eyes of the soul. In an understanding articulated in the backdrop of a rich mythical legacy, wonder turns out to provide philosophy, not only with its beginning, but also with its end, understood as an initiation to the mysteries beheld by the soul in its prenatal existence. As Chrysakopoulou shows, this understanding betrays strong debts to pre-Socratic philosophical texts, as also to the Homeric literary tradition. At the same time, and significantly, these debts reveal groundbreaking revisions, particularly in the Platonic construal of the response to wisdom in passionate terms, and in the rewriting of the heroic character in terms of a philosophical ideal.

Turning from these earliest beginnings of philosophical wonder to some of its more recent episodes, Stephen Mulhall focuses on Heidegger and Wittgenstein, two twentieth-century philosophers who have exhibited particular concern with the governing mood of philosophical inquiry. Having identified bewilderment or perplexity as the inflection of this mood that both philosophers share, he considers the question whether this is a condition that inquiry is understood as transcending. With Heidegger—whose question about Being, in *Being and Time*, invites a perplexity that seems to endure unpurged at the close of inquiry—this mood is one whose enduring character, Mulhall suggests, is tied to the fact that it mirrors (or is attuned to) fundamental aspects of Being; of the discourse of philosophy that thematizes it; and of human being, internally related to mystery by being related at every moment to that which makes no sense—namely, the possibility of non-being. This inevitability reiterates itself, though in different terms, in Wittgenstein, who preoccupied himself intensely with our seemingly inveterate tendency to remove ourselves from our linguistic home, and to be "bewitched" into an exile—an exile to metaphysical uses of words that is a state of nonsense—that leaves us bewildered. Addressing the notion of the sublime as it figures in Wittgenstein's critique of this habit of linguistic self-exile, Mulhall explores a specific instance of our subliming tendency—the idea that demonstratives are the only true names—by placing it in two mythological contexts, Wagnerian and Socratic, which suggest the reflection that if there is a true sublime, it is to be found in the creativity of language. The way we continue to sublime even those tools deployed against our subliming tendency, however, suggests that this is a self-exile of perplexity in which we are fated to dwell.

It is in the same shadow, of a question about wonder as a dwelling and abode, that Mary-Jane Rubenstein's essay is written, now focusing on Heidegger more narrowly and drawing on a number of later Heideggerian texts in which wonder comes up for more systematic discussion. At the same time, it is written in another and rather longer shadow, that of Heidegger's disastrous political decisions: were these, perhaps, the result of an excess of star-struck wonder? This provides the setting for asking whether wonder is a location in which we should (and could) dwell, which in turn involves asking what wonder is (or should be). As articulated elusively in Heidegger's later writings, what stands out in his conception of wonder is its feeling tone and its objects—the tone of shock and awe that characterizes the attunement of wonder, not to the new and unfamiliar, but to that which is most ordinary and familiar: the "that" of being, *that beings are*, which is presupposed in everything we do and say. Passing through a study of Heidegger's developing readings of Plato's allegory of the cave, one closely connected to his developing views of the notion of truth, what emerges is an understanding of Heidegger's political choices as a failure to assimilate his own insights about the occurrence of truth and the nature of wonder. For wonder does not dwell in the extraordinary—above the clouds—but in the extraordinary seen through the ordinary, in the space between the everyday and the clouds—suggesting, likewise, that talk of wonder as a "dwelling" should not obscure the fact that wonder constantly needs to be reconquered through the dialectic that generates it.

A concern with the ordinary as an object of wonder plays a similarly governing role in the paper by Olivier Doron, which studies the place of wonder in the scientific work of microscopists in early modern science, in the period from the end of the seventeenth century until at least the middle of the eighteenth, among whom the microscope became a means—in the stronger sense of a technical instrument—for the cultivation of wonder at ordinary things transfigured into marvels under the lens. This programmatic courting of wonder, Doron argues, needs to be situated in an understanding of science that would align it with the notion of a spiritual practice, one that aims not merely at truth, but at wisdom, and aims at a radical self-transformation that, in the case of these scientists, can be specified in ethical and religious terms. To see the glory in the fly: this spiritualized idiom, which echoes similar topoi among the poets of the broader Romantic movement (Wordsworth: the "splendor in the grass" and the "glory in the flower"), invites us to perceive a wondrousness that returns to God as a token of His glory. As Doron's account shows, the notion of science revealed in this practice of wonder stands at the seams of changing conceptions of scientific inquiry—including the place of objectivity among its intellectual virtues—and of its key terms, such as the notion of experience and fact, and the means capable of producing the latter.

The essay by Alexander Rueger emerges from the same historical background as the one that provides this scientific episode with its roots, at a time when, as Daston and Park have suggested, changes in scientific notions found their reflection in changes in aesthetic sensibility, and when aesthetic standards were in flux in more ways than one. Rueger's concern, in this period of shifting standards, is with the seventeenth- to eighteenth-century literary critical debates about the place of wonder or the marvelous in literature and about its legitimacy as an artistic tool. The relationship of wonder to the traditional rhetorical framework, and particularly the notion of literary decorum to which art had to answer, had already been marked by important tensions. But the adoption of wonder as the headline of an aesthetic ideal by Baroque art theorists—one that went hand in hand with an emphasis on the poet's ingenuity with formal devices—provoked a heightened tension with the Neoclassicist literary canon that, on Rueger's account, set the stage for the seminal translation by Boileau of Longinus' treatise on the sublime, in a move that looked back to ancient rhetorical resources to establish a form of wonder that could take over from the marvelous as a legitimate literary heir. These debates, and the reformulated notion of the sublime they injected into literary discourse, played a crucial role in the emergence of the notion of aesthetic experience in the eighteenth century, and in the emergence of a new mode of experiencing nature, as an object of awed wonder that was provoked by the terrible, the vast, and the disordered.

Michel Hulin's concern, located in a rather different context than the one that situates the other studies, is with the notion of wonder in Indian aesthetics, developing from the fourth and fifth centuries CE onward from an initially dramaturgical focus into a larger theory of aesthetics. Wonder plays a central role in this theory, particularly in accounting for the aesthetic pleasure that works of art afford us. More specifically, it is involved in the transfiguration or sublimation of ordinary emotions into their aesthetic counterparts, and in conferring to our aesthetic reactions the "as-if" quality that removes their practical tendency. Wonder, in this account, marks the dissociation from the individual egoistic perspective to a supra-individual level on which our sole identity is that of conscious beings capable of wondering who are, as such, free, and above the suffering caused by the egoistic perspective of the individual, and who use their freedom for the embrace of universal necessity. And while this account may be anchored in a very different context from the previous studies, its terms might evoke several affinities with views of aesthetic experience familiar to readers of Western philosophical texts. Not only in construing the aesthetic moment in terms of a transcendence of the perspective of practical, egoistic interest (as Kant, most notably, understood it), but also in involving a discovery of freedom that may remind us both of Kant's notion of the rational embrace of moral law, but also, and perhaps more strikingly, of Schopenhauer's understanding of aesthetic experience as an ascent to the supra-individual that offers reprieve from the suffering caused by the will.

David Burrell, in his contribution, takes his point of departure from Charles Taylor's recent analysis of the secular age, cast in terms of the emergence of a self-sufficient humanism productive of social imaginaries that disembed society from the cosmos and reject inherent hierarchies, involve a transformed conception of uniform and controllable time, and exclude notions of an outside source for the reception of power such as characterize an authentically religious outlook. Responding to the Hegel-like inevitability that this account seems to import, Burrell turns to Taylor's account of "conversions" to develop it as a way out of this seeming "iron cage"—the "outside" of a conversion that is glossed as a form of wonder—taking as his focus the diaries of Etty Hillesum, a young Jewish woman in Holland during German occupation, and examining the expressions of her spiritual awakening. This spiritual awakening, issuing in the face of the greatest odds with no "because" and many "despites," emerges as a developing sense of wonder before life and the world. For all its apparent spontaneity, it is an awakening to wonder that, Burrell suggests, is structured by the grammar made available by religious tradition even as it enriches itself with the grammar of traditions other than her own.

Bibliography

Abrams, Meyer H. *Natural Supernaturalism: Tradition and Revolution in Romantic Literature*. New York: Norton, 1973.

Cavell, Stanley. *The Claim of Reason*. Oxford: Clarendon, 1979.

Daston, Lorraine, and Katharine Park. *Wonders and the Order of Nature, 1150–1750*. New York: Zone Books, 1988.

Dawkins, Richard. *Unweaving the Rainbow*. London: Penguin, 1999.

Fisher, Philip. *Wonder, the Rainbow, and the Aesthetics of Rare Experiences*. Cambridge: Harvard University Press, 1998.

Fuller, Robert. *Wonder: From Emotion to Spirituality*. Chapel Hill: University of North Carolina Press, 2006.

MacIntyre, Alasdair. *After Virtue*. 2nd ed. London: Duckworth, 1985.

Rubenstein, Mary-Jane. "A Certain Disavowal: The Pathos and Politics of Wonder." *Princeton University Theological Review* 12 (2006) 11–17.

Schopenhauer, Arthur. *The World as Will and Representation*. Translated by E. F. J. Payne. New York: Dover, 1969.

Shklovsky, Viktor. *Theory of Prose*. Translated by Benjamin Sher. Elmwood Park, IL: Dalkey Archive Press, 1991.

Tanner, Tony. *The Reign of Wonder: Naivety and Reality in American Literature*. Cambridge: Cambridge University Press, 1965.

1

Wonder
Toward a Grammar

SOPHIA VASALOU

Since every reflection needs a stimulus, and every quest a beginning, even a quest for the wonder that often supplies beginnings to reflective quests, and since to think deep one must peer close, let me propose to take the following definition of wonder as the axis of our concern. "Wonder: a sudden experience of an extraordinary object that produces delight."[1] Not a dictionary definition, but for all that we may peer close to locate the joints:

With SUDDEN we might ask: and does wonder always *strike* or might not wonder also need to be *hunted*? With EXTRAORDINARY we might ask: and is the extraordinary something that always reveals itself or something that may also need to be dis-covered? And if we twice converge on the notion of a hunt, or quest, aren't we also querying whether wonder PRODUCES or whether it may not also demand to be produced? And that, in the same breath, is to consider: what would be the OBJECT—in the double sense of *content* and *intent*—of such wonder? Would DELIGHT offer the self-sufficient answer? And what, finally, probing deeper into the unobtrusiveness of grammar, is the meaning of that present tense which relates delight to wonder as its cause (producES) with all the stability of the eternal that grammar places at its disposal?

---

1. Fisher, *Aesthetics of Rare Experiences*, 55.

Even with these questions braking our words, this is already moving too quickly, and too far, with a momentum whose movement our present stage would not be large enough to exhaust. So let us here pause over two of the main joints we have picked out—wonder's SUDDENness and wonder's DELIGHT—to consider more closely: What is wonder?

SUDDEN: On Being Struck; Or: An Emotion Unlike Others?

It has been hailed as the beginning of philosophy, as the end philosophy tends to, and a state philosophy aims to expunge by explanation; as the essence of art, as the aim of art, and as the means that art uses to accomplish its aims; as the origin of scientific quests; as the result of scientific quests; as the religious experience *par excellence*, the only proper response to a created world, and the only possible response of those whose eyes have been opened to see the glory of God in a blade of grass and every created being. It has been acclaimed as a form of redemption, and identified with consciousness itself. Inflected as awe; cadenced as bewitchment; transfigured as the sublime—a sense of wonder has claimed a key presence in a variety of practices of knowledge, activities and pursuits.

Yet for an emotion fêted so widely across a broad range of human practices, wonder appears to register as a rather elusive presence to those who would seek to understand it. This elusiveness, Mary-Jane Rubenstein, expounding Heidegger, suggests to us, may possess a special kind of inevitability—the elusiveness of an investigation whose subject is the very ground that sets it into motion, or, otherwise put, the special difficulty attaching to the self-defeating project of "thinking the condition of thinking's own possibility." For to ask "what is wonder?" is only possible once wonder has already set up the question as an object of (wondering) reflection. So how, she asks, "is philosophy to go about seeking the very wonder that sets it into motion?"[2] And we might say the same about any inquiry that claims wonder as the origin of its motion.

This deeper difficulty may lie in the shadows; but in the daylight lies something simpler to remark, yet no less surprising for that, and that is the widespread neglect of wonder in contemporary research on the emotions. It is a neglect that appears to unite psychologists and philosophers of the emotions otherwise divided by important methodological and philosophical differences, on questions such as what emotions are, how the respective roles of cognition and physiology should be understood,

2. Rubenstein, *Strange Wonder*, 3.

what the respective roles of culture and biology consist in, or what to name as the basic or primary emotions (and on what grounds). And it is one that extends, not only to wonder, but also to related members of the emotion family to which it belongs, such as awe.[3]

Why might that be? Remarking the neglect of wonder in his pioneering book-length account of it, Robert Fuller named one reason for it by pointing to an important feature of contemporary theories of emotion: their preoccupation with an evolutionary paradigm for the study of emotion and with the adaptive significance of emotions considered as biological phenomena. It is true that evolutionary psychologists have warned that this preoccupation should not be understood too narrowly—in terms, for example, of a concern with immediate physical survival.[4] Yet it is clear that some emotions lend themselves to rewarding analysis more readily within this frame than others, and it is not surprising that, within the terms of this paradigm, biologists and psychologists have tended "to emphasize those emotions that lead to the performance of adaptive behaviors such as withdrawal, avoidance, mating, or aggression."[5] More generally, Fuller argues, the focus cultivated by this framework has fallen on emotions that are short-lived; that orient people to concrete aspects of the immediate physical environment; and that are associated with specific facial expressions or gestures. Emotions such as fear and anger—which can easily be tied to behaviors with strategic adaptive importance—are perhaps the strongest exemplars of the analytical promise of such a scheme. By contrast, and unsurprisingly, wonder presents itself as a more awkward fit.

The problem of fit, as one of the elements of Fuller's argument intimates, begins from the moment wonder is sought in the body. It is significant, in this connection, that those working from within an evolutionary or biological paradigm who have joined in the neglect of wonder have included the heirs of the particular evolutionary perspective on emotions developed in Darwin's 1872 *The Expression of the Emotions in Man and Animals*. This work, which studied the regularities of human expressive

---

3. This neglect is certainly foregrounded in Peterson and Seligman's discussion of wonder in chapter 23 of their *Character Strengths*, where they consider it under the rubric of "strengths of transcendence" together with a family of attitudes that include awe, admiration, and elevation and are involved in the appreciation of beauty and excellence—an account the authors signal is still rife with unknowns. This neglect is also a theme in Keltner and Haidt's account of awe in their "Approaching Awe," and is a theme likewise in Fuller's overview of the literature, in his *Wonder*.

4. As pointed out by Tooby and Cosmides in their "Evolutionary Psychology," 115.

5. Fuller, *Wonder*, 11.

behavior and their biological roots, has become the starting point in recent decades for an investigation of the universality of facial expressions corresponding to basic emotions. Notwithstanding the promise held out by Darwin's remarks on admiration in his work, wonder has failed to figure among the emotions which this tradition has concerned itself with; it is excluded, for example, in the list of basic emotions produced by Paul Ekman—one of the best-known exponents of this view— which includes sadness, happiness, fear, anger, disgust and surprise.[6] This exclusion must be taken in part as an avowal of the difficulty of pinning an unambiguous expressive profile to wonder, which might help restate the difficulty with wonder as one that concerns the elusiveness of its embodiment.[7] Among emotion researchers, in fact, those who have included wonder among primary or basic emotions have represented a quaint minority, and even those who have accorded it a place in their taxonomies, such as the Dutch psychologist Nico Frijda (whose work was clearly located in the Darwinian tradition) and the early British psychologist William McDougall, have not always done so in a way that seems sufficiently mindful of the differences—subtle yet not to be dismissed in advance—between related

---

6. For a helpful overview of different accounts of basic emotions, see the list produced by Ortony and Turner, "What's Basic," 316. Yet as Ekman's reply to Ortony and Turner suggests, a lot depends here on how one construes the scope of a given emotion. Ekman's complaint that Ortony and Turner have exaggerated the degree of disagreement among researchers over the identity of basic emotions (Ekman, "Basic Emotions," 550) implies that apparently divergent emotion words should be read in terms of larger categories. This is a point Ekman had already referred to as an important conceptual concern in his key piece (with Friesen and Ellsworth), "Emotion Categories," where, having identified a set of chief emotion categories emerging from the work of previous researchers, he had raised a question about how the "boundaries and inclusion rules for defining each category" should be determined (44–45). His conclusion that happiness, surprise, fear, anger, sadness, disgust/contempt, and interest emerge from this work as recurrent categories had implicitly involved a decision to group divergent individual emotions under these broader categories—including, significantly for our purposes, amazement, bewilderment, or awe, which all appeared in the research considered and seem to have homogenized under the category of surprise.

7. For a suggestion of this kind with regard to one of wonder's conceptual siblings, see Keltner and Haidt, "Approaching Awe," 301–2, where scientific neglect of awe is linked to its lack of a distinctive facial expression. But compare Shiota et al., "Prototype Displays," where the case is made in favor of a distinctive expression. A distinctive expression has, however, been ascribed to emotions to which wonder has been considered to be related, such as joy or surprise. What is at issue, of course, is partly what counts as an adequate or legitimate scientific method for establishing the distinctive expressive profile of a given emotion. A useful overview of recent views on the topic is provided by Matsumoto et al., "Facial Expressions."

Practices of Wonder

emotional concepts (such as surprise and wonder, or wonder and curiosity) in ordinary language.[8] (A point, of course, which suggests that the issue raised here could not be tackled without addressing the fractious question of our ability to identify and individuate emotions.)

These two aspects—the relative obscurity of the adaptive value of wonder and the relative indeterminacy of its expression—are not unconnected, and together they point to a further reason—linked with other methodological tendencies of current emotion research—for this programmatic neglect of wonder. For both difficulties in turn reveal an underlying embarrassment in producing distinct statements about what, falling into line with recent terminology, we would call the action tendencies of wonder, the inbuilt motion of this emotion—or, put more simply still, what wonder makes us *do*. For if fear makes us freeze or fight or flee, if anger makes us rear for confrontation, if envy prepares us for a bitter revenge, if love makes us seek out, and contempt eschew—action tendencies that can be used to build theories about the adaptive value of these emotions in human history, and that are directly related to the repertory of expressive behavior associated with them—what might one say of wonder that would hold with equal force?[9]

For wonder, it seems, can make us do everything or nothing. Even our doing, as this has often been understood (in the history of philosophy, certainly, but not only) has been a species of non-doing, or whatever else we might understand by contemplation. It is striking, for example, and of direct relevance to this point, that some of the emotion researchers who have given their attention to wonder and committed themselves to placing it within their taxonomies have presented a picture of wonder whose most remarkable feature is that of passivity. In Frijda's account, this passivity is manifested both on the level of physiology—marked by suspension of

---

8. In Frijda's discussion (*Emotions*, 18–19), amazement, surprise and wonder, appear to shade into one another without distinction. "Insufficiently mindful" might, at the same time, be too coarse-grained a way of putting the matter. For while, for example, McDougall opens his discussion in his *Introduction to Social Psychology* with the caveat that science may need to do violence to words in adapting them to scientific usage (41)—a caveat that then seems borne out by the rather artificial-sounding, linguistically revisionary proposal that construes curiosity as an instinct, and then identifies wonder as the emotion that corresponds to this instinct—he is at the same time careful to indicate the points at which his account departs from common usage (see, e.g., 49–50, in discussing the relationship between wonder and curiosity).

9. See Elster, "Emotion and Action," for a succinct account of the action tendencies of emotions that bears an open debt to Frijda's work. The distinction between actions and expressive behavior (such as facial or bodily expression) that was implied in the above is, after all, a relatively tenuous one, as Frijda suggests in *Emotions*, 11–12.

breathing and general loss of muscle tone, which "causes the mouth to fall open, and may make the subject stagger or force him to sit down"—and of expressive behavior more narrowly defined—open eyes, raised eyebrows, open mouth, a forgetful relaxation of the body. This passivity—to which Frijda relates the functional significance or meaning of the family of emotions comprising amazement, surprise and wonder, which would appear to consist in the enhancement of contact—is more broadly reflected in "the arrest of locomotion and instrumental action."[10]

And it is precisely this accent on instrumentality, or its lack, that we need in order to give yet a deeper account of the occlusion of wonder we have been trying to track, and perhaps the most accurate diagnosis yet of the difficulty that has made of wonder such a conspicuous absentee from contemporary taxonomies of the emotions. For not evolutionary rationale; not universality of distinct facial expression; nor yet only action-tendencies—it has rather been judgment or cognition that has come to figure as a salient analytical element in recent views of emotion, in both psychology (most markedly since its methodological comeback from behaviorism) and philosophy. An account of emotion whose natural adversaries have ranged broadly from behaviorists, proponents of a physiological James-Lange theory of emotion, to empiricists of Hume's ilk, this is a view that comes in different forms and with different construals of its constituent elements (what is cognition? Is cognition or judgment identical with the emotion, its cause, or a constituent part? Is it necessary or sufficient for emotion?). But whether in psychology or philosophy, such theories share a stress on the role of what, varying with the idiom, we may call the person's (organism's) goals or values, interests or projects, or more broadly, the elements entering a person's well-being. My fear as I cross a dark road registers my safety and integrity as an object of value presupposed by anything else I might desire; my grief over a loss traces out the halo of value around the person I have lost; my joy at good news about an unlooked-for success registers my attachment to a certain kind of achievement; my guilt registers a breach between an ideal I had treasured and now feel I have let down. In its philosophical guise, in which it has emerged out of a combat with dismissive views of emotions as dangerous or irrational or physiologically brute, the cognitive view of emotions has often been parsed as a claim that emotions tell us something about

---

10. Frijda, *Emotions*, 18–19.

the world; they tell us "how things are"—a knowledge of the world that is fundamentally evaluative, and so a knowledge of *our* world.[11]

One of the most suggestive views of this kind is the one recently articulated by Martha Nussbaum in her *Upheavals of Thought*, where she presents a "neo-Stoic" account that stresses four aspects of emotions: their aboutness (emotions have objects); their intentionality (emotions have intentional objects that embody ways of seeing); their basis in beliefs (emotions embody sets of beliefs about objects); and most crucially for the "eudaimonistic" view Nussbaum wants to defend, their connection with value (emotions see objects as invested with an importance that makes reference to an agent's own flourishing). Emotions, on this view, are judgments about external things to which we attach value and which we see as intimately involved in our flourishing; which are vulnerable and beyond our control; and which thus involve an acknowledgement of passivity before the world.[12] Nussbaum is at pains to stress that to describe emotions as eudaimonistic is not to describe them as egoistic, and that we may value things intrinsically and for their own sake (if not impersonally) even though we will always value them as part of *our* life and projects, and thus from an inalienably self-referential perspective. Yet even this broader understanding of value seems to come under strain when it comes to accommodating wonder, which Nussbaum herself describes as the emotion most strikingly subversive to this scheme. "[A]s non-eudaimonistic as an emotion can be," wonder is an emotion that, according to Nussbaum "responds to the pull of the object, and one might say that in it the subject is maximally aware of the value of the object, and only minimally aware, if at all, of its relationship to her own plans. That is why it is likely to issue in contemplation rather than in any other sort of action toward the object."[13]

Weakly connected to action; unconnected to self-referential goals and plans; thus breaching every category that emotion theorists bring to bear when approaching individual emotions. And it is Nussbaum once more who affords us the leverage for yet another addition to this enumeration of wonder's unlikenesses, and for finally resuming our starting point

---

11. For a brief statement of this understanding formulated in these terms, see Goldie, "Emotion" (99: emotions enable us to "see things as they really are").

12. See generally Nussbaum, *Upheavals*, ch. 1, for an outline of her view. And while Nussbaum articulates this view in a philosophical context, it is one she considers to be fundamentally in accord with cognitivist accounts of emotions as articulated by contemporary psychologists, such as Richard Lazarus, Keith Oatley, and Anthony Ortony—see ibid., 106–13.

13. Ibid., 54–55.

or rallying point (the SUDDEN-ness of emotions, or: on being struck). For a feature of emotions that has often recurred in theoretical analyses—and which cognitive theories like Nussbaum's have been considered challenged to accommodate—is one that concerns the passivity with which we typically experience them. Speaking with her own experience of grief as exemplar, she writes of the "feeling of terrible tumultuousness, of being at the mercy of currents that swept over me without my consent or complete understanding . . . the feeling that very powerful forces were pulling the self apart, or tearing it limb from limb," which is an instance of "the terrible power or urgency of the emotions . . . the sense one has that one is passive or powerless before them."[14] This fact—that we experience emotions as uncontrollable, and ourselves as passive with regard to them; the fact that emotions *strike*—lies at the root of much traditional hostility toward emotions in philosophical history, and it is one that, it has likewise been suggested, we can read off the very grammatical evidence of our language.

That emotions are "passions"—in the literal sense of "states produced by one's being *acted on* in certain ways"—is suggested, Robert Gordon writes, "by the fact that the great majority of adjectives designating emotions are derived from [passive] participles: for example, 'amused,' 'annoyed,' 'astonished,' 'delighted,' 'depressed,' 'embarrassed,' 'frightened' . . . 'overjoyed,' 'pleased' . . ."[15] It may seem remarkable, then, that in this respect wonder once again presents itself as an anomaly, and only conveys passivity when encountered in compound ("wonderstruck"). This is an anomaly that our own experience of frequent struggles with paroxysms of anger, fear and grief, and rare encounters with a wonder that overpowers and we seek to repulse, might confirm, and that once again bespeaks a weaker anchor in the body and a more ambiguous (thus less overpowering) kind of embodiment.[16] And this, in the light of Nussbaum's analysis, should not surprise us, if the intensity of emotion is analogous to the degree of importance with which its object is invested among our goals or projects,[17] so

14. Ibid., 26.
15. Gordon, *Structure of Emotions*, 112.
16. This, however, is to simplify somewhat more complex matters. For what we perceive as overpowering, or what we experience as a struggle, is not fixed by natural facts (including facts about the nature of a given emotion), but depends on an underlying set of value judgments about the emotion and its effects—value judgments that affect our views concerning what we *ought* to experience as a struggle, and are situated in a larger cultural context. This is certainly a reflection pressed by the history of wonder (see next section), which attests that wonder has indeed at other times been seen as a potentially overpowering emotion against which struggle may be required.
17. This is suggested in *Upheavals*, 55.

that an emotion weakly connected to my plans would be one that strikes weakly, if at all—and one too weakly connected to patterns of vital human interests to have been written into the body by the evolutionary process as a *striking* one cannot repulse.

With our attention to the linguistic idiosyncrasies of wonder sharpened, we should now be well prepared to remark another, which unseats wonder from among the passions in a different though closely related way. For with many of the emotions, the emotion terms often appear to be employed in the expression of the emotion itself ("I'm angry with you," "It leaves me feeling so sad" or "Frankly, I'm scared"). With wonder, by contrast, that seems to be the exception rather than the rule: "how remarkable," "how extraordinary," or just "*wow*"—the expression of wonder often appears as an attribution to the object rather than an emotion ascribed in the first person to oneself ("I wonder" and "it fills me with wonder" are rarities in our speech). Writers on the emotions have pointed out that in responding emotionally to an object, we typically find ourselves ascribing a quality to the object or perceiving it "as having the emotion-proper property."[18] To be disgusted at something is to perceive it as disgusting, to hate a person is to see them as hateful or despicable—a fact that Peter Goldie suggests is closely tied with our experience of emotions as being justified or reasonable. Yet what seems remarkable about wonder is that, in the language games we play with it, an explicitly attributive mode seems to be the dominant form of our expression.

What this would seem to share with the grammatical point marked just before (concerning the passivity ordinarily enshrined in our language) is a tendency to draw emphasis away from the emotion as an experience, and channel it toward the object that excites it. Even to those convinced of the depth of grammar, however, this peculiarity might not seem sufficiently significant or striking until it is joined to another observation, which develops Goldie's emphasis on rationality and justification—and with which we can finally bring to a close the long list of credentials establishing the uneasy membership of wonder in traditional taxonomies. For in focusing on judgment or cognition, cognitivist theories of emotions have taken themselves to be concerned with an element that plays a cardinal role on two different levels of our thinking about emotions: in our ability to identify and distinguish emotions, and in our ability to justify and explain them. The judgment, implicit in my fit of anger, that someone has harmed something I care about, or the

---

18. Goldie, "Emotion," 99.

judgment, implicit in my access of grief, that something or someone I loved is lost to me, are central to what identifies these emotions as anger or as grief. And it is again these kinds of judgments that would in great part figure in our attempts to justify our emotional reactions and defend them as rational or fitting. With wonder, however, we may well find ourselves stumped for words when we reach out to identify the tissue of judgments and beliefs that form its rational core. "How remarkable!" What more can we say of wonder's judgments and wonder's justice than that it responds to a perception of an object as remarkable, extraordinary, unexpected? And this observation may well leave us feeling that, while emotions may be judgments of value, this judgment is too naked a postulation of value (and is it *value*?) to merit the name—more an exclamation than a judgment, and too much *feeling* to be even dignified with words.[19] It is, perhaps, this sense of wonder's nudity—its deficient or fluid rational core—that seems to be expressed in the psychologist Richard Lazarus's reluctant retreat before "states like awe, wonder, and faith-trust" which "can be used in more than one sense," rendering their meaning one about which it is "difficult to know what to say."[20]

This last point is one we are scheduled shortly to revisit. But for now, we can draw this list of wonder's eccentricities to a close and merely turn the page over to remark that this singular position of wonder among the emotions, far from being the preserve of contemporary theories, has been mirrored in the position wonder has occupied in other phases of its history, particularly in its philosophical trajectory. It is perhaps Descartes, in his landmark work on the emotions, *The Passions of the Soul* (1649), by whom the reasons for wonder's occlusion in modern taxonomies are most loudly echoed. For Descartes, the passions "dispose our soul to want the things which nature deems useful for us"—useful, that is, *qua* embodied

---

19. In search for something that could be more easily dignified with words, and with the status of a judgment, it might seem attractive to embrace a proposal that would account for the judgment of wonder in modal terms. To wonder at *x*, on such an account, would involve something akin to the judgment that "it was possible for *x* not to have existed." This account would dovetail interestingly with Nussbaum's analysis, which also draws us toward modal notions; for if emotions are often directed to entities or states of affairs under the perception of their vulnerability and our lack of control over them (*Upheavals*, 42–43)—and thus under the perception that they are subject to change or might be/have been different than what they in fact are—this introduces a modal element into their heart. But this analysis of wonder would seem problematic in its normativity, and would seem to fail as an account of all varieties of wonder, whose diversity Ronald Hepburn instructively calls attention to in his "Wonder."

20. Lazarus, *Emotion and Adaptation*, 295.

beings. Yet wonder (*l'admiration*) is a passion we experience "before we know whether or not the object is beneficial to us," which is the ground for Descartes' naming it as the first of the passions.[21] This disconnection from interest is in turn related to a diminished embodiment; for given that the sole object of wonder is knowledge, wonder is "not accompanied by any change in the heart or the blood, such as occurs in the case of the other passions," but is only related to the brain.[22]

And while, notwithstanding these two forms of elevation, Descartes himself would still treat wonder as a passion requiring criticism and correction,[23] it is indeed the fact that the passions have often figured in philosophical history from its earliest origins as objects of suspicion, to be critiqued, disciplined and corrected, that provides the most illuminating insight into the unusual position wonder has occupied in this history. Emotion, as Robert Solomon notes, "has almost always played an inferior role in philosophy, often as antagonist to logic and reason."[24] Yet wonder has repeatedly emerged among philosophers as a codicil to this blanket distrust. This is certainly the case with the Stoics, well known for their jaundiced view of the passions as false judgments of value, and for whom—as for many of the ancient schools—philosophy was conceived as a therapy for the passions.[25] Yet wonder, for many of the Stoics, appears to attract none of these strictures, and the spirit that had made of wonder— for both Plato and Aristotle—the philosophical passion *par excellence*, a passion to be prized and not to be repulsed, continues to breathe through their writings.[26] Leaping ahead to a more recent philosophical episode—in

21. Descartes, *Passions of the Soul*, 349–50 (art. 52 and 53).
22. Quote from ibid., 353 (art. 71).
23. See ibid., 354–56 (art. 73–78); and see also below.
24. Solomon, "Logic of Emotion," 41.

25. This is an orientation often stressed in accounts of Stoic, and ancient, philosophy, though perhaps by few as strongly as by Pierre Hadot in his works; see particularly his *Philosophy as a Way of Life*.

26. I owe a big part of my understanding here to a comment paper presented by Brad Inwood at the conference "A Sense of Wonder: Cross-Disciplinary Perspectives" (Cambridge, 2008), which highlighted a crucial distinction between two kinds of wonder in Stoic thought—one negatively, the other positively valenced. Negative, in a sense we may recognize from the Stoic maxim *nil admirari* (*ouden thaumaston*), in which wonder is aligned with the ability of external events to take us by surprise and engage our emotions, and distrusted as such. Yet this distrust coexists with a positive appreciation of wonder as a response to the natural world, and with a conception of nature as an object of legitimate wonder among Stoic writers, including Seneca and Cicero. Inwood gives context to the latter in his account of the place of physics in Stoic philosophy, which focuses especially on Seneca, and in which wonder surfaces at

what is meant to be an indicative and not an exhaustive enumeration—we may say the same of Kant, who shares many of the ancient philosophers' affinities and sources of distrust, and whose ethical viewpoint has often been construed (not always rightly, it has been argued) in terms of a sharp depreciation of emotion in morality and a strident emphasis on reason. Yet it is Kant who, closing the *Critique of Practical Reason*, left us with one of the most eloquent and enduring expressions of wonder when he wrote: "Two things fill the mind with ever new and increasing admiration (*Bewunderung*) and awe (*Ehrfurcht*), the more often and steadily reflection is occupied with them: the starry heaven above me and the moral law within me"—thus tying wonder to the heartland of his ethical theory. And it is Kant, likewise, who made of the sublime—that strain of wonder that became a centerpiece of Romantic experience—one of the most telling moments of his aesthetics, and in which, once more, the separation from selfish interest or purpose is a defining aspect.

Wonder, then, emerges as an emotion unlike others in almost every way, and one calculated to fall through the cracks in taxonomies of emotion; hence, we may conclude, its programmatic neglect in contemporary theories, which have shrugged it off as too slippery to be responsibly handled. An apophatic view of wonder if there ever was one—and not a view at which we could allow ourselves to stop. Because this would surely be to ignore the ways in which we *succeed* rather than fail in recognizing this experience. For bracketing the methodological doubts and well-meant scruples of those claiming a more-than-ordinary expertise on familiar phenomena, what, after all, could be closer to us than wonder? What, to briefly grasp at another of the joints of the Ur-text to which we looked to impart structure to our thought, could be closer to us than that emotional experience that, it has been suggestively claimed, is identical to nothing less than EXPERIENCE itself?

For if the ordinary, as Wittgenstein suggested, is not experienced as such, and we only notice something insofar as it is unexpected or unfamiliar, then surprise, and *mutatis mutandis* wonder, "become[s] the very heart of what it means to 'have an experience' at all," in Philip Fisher's

---

several points as a theme; see his "Why Physics?" This distinction—or tension—would seem to mirror the one found in Aristotle's work, influential over the Stoics in both regards, for Aristotle's apparent depreciation of wonder in the *Nicomachean Ethics* (describing the great-souled man: *oude thaumastikos*, 1125a1–5), coexists with the remarks at the opening of his *Metaphysics* (982b10–20) that enshrined wonder as the opening of philosophical inquiry.

words.[27] The texture of ice cream, the look of snow, the sound of a waterfall, the pleasure of holding a book in one's hand, of standing up unsteadily on one's skates and gliding, of the first look of love one sees returned—everything (everything of which there was ever a *first* in experience) would have been filtered through wonder into one's world. This, too, would seem to be the implication one might draw out of Descartes' view as we have outlined it and which Deborah Brown, commenting, does us the service of bringing out more clearly when she remarks that, for Descartes, to the extent that all "other passions presuppose some knowledge of the object," all "presuppose the prior effects of wonder."[28] To take that reflection seriously would be to be surprised into the view that wonder must lie at the historical root of every object that has entered our experience and has come to form part of the unexperienced furniture lining our world that we navigate around without bumping into, sharing in the invisibility of all we take for granted. Wonder would then be the gatekeeper of experience. And don't we imply as much when we keep coming back to children as the paradigm in which wonder must be thought?

That might be going too fast, forming certainties about the proper objects of wonder (and its inescapable fate of being extinguished) that might seem too quick to be trusted, and which would require closer probing to be judiciously endorsed.[29] But it is sufficient to give us pause, and sufficient to make us turn a half-doubting, half-confident look inward to ask: what is it then we know about wonder? And isn't wonder something we know intimately well? To turn inward for discoveries like these is a move that philosophers have learnt to distrust in many of its philosophical forms, and here we may side with those who, with Wittgenstein and his interpreters, have concluded that one of the few inward turns that legitimately remain to us is a linguistic one. And that is a turn that is simultaneously outward in at least two ways. One, because it is a turn to an "I" that participates in the "we" of the linguistic community to which one belongs as a competent speaker of one's language with authority to judge what can and cannot be said. And the turn to the first person plural is additionally a turn outward to the body, through which language must

---

27. Fisher, *Aesthetics of Rare Experiences*, 20.

28. Brown, *Descartes*, 147.

29. I have in mind the implicit assumption imported by such a view that wonder attaches to what is extraordinary in the specific sense of the new and the unfamiliar—an assumption that Fisher explicitly embraces. This is certainly a key question to take to a "grammar" of wonder, and one that several papers in this volume provide rich material for reflecting on.

pass to reach us—without which the competent speakers who formed my authority as a child could not have taught me to speak, and which still provides me with the criteria for ascribing psychological concepts to others. This was the viewpoint expressed pithily in Wittgenstein's rich if not immediately penetrable aphorism that "the human body is the best picture of the human soul,"[30] which encapsulated a larger effort to call attention to the natural expressions and reactions that language builds upon, grafts itself on and replaces. Aphoristically again and *in medias res*, yet suggestively enough: "The verbal expression of pain replaces crying and does not describe it."[31] And so, *mutatis mutandis*, with the verbal expression of anger, or fear, or surprise.

If this story is correct in outline, it must also be one we can tell about wonder. It will mean that we know wonder as intimately as any other emotion we have learnt to recognize in others and been taught to express, and as intimately as any word we have mastered the ability to use, a mastery we exhibit when we spot looks of wonder on another's face and describe ourselves as having being filled with wonder at a sight. (And thus, returning to the earlier remark that wonder is a state about whose meaning it is "difficult to know what to say" (Lazarus), this perspective would count as a counterclaim that, in another—if not scientifically rigorous—sense, we do know what to say, and when to say it.) This would be in part the intimacy of something we have once known—if one may figuratively speak of "intimacy" or of "knowing"—through our own natural (bodily) reactions, which language replaced and gave us access to. For the fact that we have this knowledge—a knowledge of how to use a word that, as Wittgenstein was keen to stress, resists reduction to sharp definitions—is one that will be genealogically connected to the fact that we had once been offered the words of wonder to replace our exclamation, our open countenance, our dropped jaw—the natural expression of wonder—by those with a mastered relationship to language. That I know what to call wonder, in myself and in others, will therefore be a mastery that has first passed through the body. In this narrative, the child will figure as hero twice over, not only in constituting the archetype or paradigm in which wonder must be thought, but in forming the historical root of anything we can say about wonder as speakers of our language.

To remark this, of course, is to engage and qualify one of the points mentioned above in our enumeration of wonder's ("apophatic")

---

30. Wittgenstein, *Philosophical Investigations*, 152.
31. Ibid., § 244.

unlikenesses—its enigmatic relationship to the body, and the ambiguous expression in which it finds embodiment, which seemed to shut it out of the universalizing perspective of modern-day Darwinians. For if we have ever learnt to (speak of) wonder, wonder must be something we must be able to see (recognize) expressed. But this remark only has a partial reach unless nuanced further. Because even on Wittgenstein's terms, the relationship between language and our natural reactions is not a simple one, and the form of "seeing" just invoked not one in which the biological provides the only system of signs. To the bodily or biological, Wittgenstein's interpreters have added two other contexts that must be taken into account in tracing the pathways of our linguistic learning. One of these is the cultural context that conditions our expressive possibilities, while the other is the narrative context that conditions our interpretation of behavior. The latter is what is cryptically alluded to in Wittgenstein's question: "Why does it sound queer to say: 'For a second he felt violent grief'?"[32]—to which Cavell's words come as interpretation: "What I call something, what I *count* as something, is a function of how I *recount* it, tell it." Elsewhere, Cavell uses the term "logical history" to refer to these kinds of recounting ("a passion, one might say, has a history, as an action has; a logical history").[33] And "logic," here, refers us to the notions of intelligibility that are deeply enmeshed in the ways we apply psychological concepts to ourselves and others. For to identify a given bodily manifestation as a particular emotion, as Stephen Mulhall points out, directly depends on our ability to regard it as an "intelligible human response to the circumstances embodied in the relevant background."[34] It is to such background that you would need to refer to understand my outburst of weeping as one of rage, or grief, or pain, or relief, and the words you would teach me are the words in terms of which my natural expression is one you can understand and make sense of.

And it is likewise in this context—where another's capacity to make sense of my reactions comes up as a stage and condition for my capacity to be taught—that notions of normality and abnormality enter our view, as an indispensable adjunct of intelligibility. It is Cavell, again, who spells out the hold of such notions most compellingly, illuminating the extent to which our ability to (learn to) communicate with each other in language

---

32. Ibid., 148.

33. See respectively Cavell, *Claim of Reason*, 94 and 107.

34. Mulhall, *Seeing Aspects*, 63, and see 62ff. for his broader discussion of the importance of context.

depends on the sheer contingent fact that as human beings we tend to react to certain things in certain ways we take to be normal. To imagine a person who reacts differently—who, for example, expresses suffering by laughing, who could be comforted by whipping, who "laughs at rejection or physical pain the way we laugh at a joke," who screams in pain when touched with affection, who is "bored by an earthquake or by the death of his child or the declaration of martial law" or who gets "angry at a pin or a cloud or a fish" —is to imagine a kind of person of which we may have to say: "such people do not live in our world" and to whom, whether we can still respond as persons, comes into question.[35] Is the language of wonder one that could be taught to a child that reacted to rainbows or kites or its first vision of the world under snow or the modern-day Disneyland designed for enchantment (or any of the other everyday sources of wonder to which children are exposed) with tears of rage or boredom or distress? Such a child, we might say, does not form part of our shared world. (An apophthegmatic remark; and one to which we are certainly fated to return.)

If we began with a half-hopeful look inward, the line we have just drawn out threatens us with the strongest outward-moving thrust. Because to speak of intelligibility and its constraints (including constraints of normality) is by the same stroke to introduce the language of possibility and necessity into our use of words, and to begin to trace a ring around wonder that would bound off what "can" be (called) wonder from what "cannot," and would distinguish between what we can and cannot wonder at. But—leaving aside the characteristic dudgeon provoked by a linguistic "must" that gets between me and mine, as a philosophical drama we must presume defused—just how tightly can this ring be drawn? To restate it in terms we have only freshly employed: if passions have a logical history, what logic belongs to wonder?

To put it in these terms is to return to the thick of a question we passed earlier without pause. For approaching the issue we just raised with the kind of sensitivities Wittgenstein has encouraged us to develop, we might want to programmatically abjure the expectation that an emotion (or any concept *simpliciter*) should respond to a single logic that one could identify and spell out in crystalline terms applicable to every one of its instances. Ronald Hepburn's extraordinary essay on wonder,

---

35. Quotes respectively from Cavell, *Claim of Reason*, 89, 111, 90, and for these themes, see generally ch. 5. See also Mulhall's commentary on these themes in *Cavell*, 114–22.

in which the relation of wonder to elements of cognition or rationality forms a key running theme, could be read as supporting evidence for this view, for it carefully outlines different varieties of wonder in a way that suggests that it would be an aggression on the phenomena to treat wonder as a single thing.[36]

Yet what we saw earlier is that wonder may be an unusual case in a more specific respect, one that might create a special resistance to proposed regimentations of its logic, by virtue of lacking the distinguishable rational core that appears to characterize most other emotions. "How remarkable!"—"How marvellous!" and—"Wow!" To say this, of course, is not to suggest that there are no judgments or beliefs we could ever adduce to explain or justify our wondering response. The person wondering at the existence of life, or the birth of a child, or the ability of the human mind to grasp scientific truths—to mention a few of the most striking instances—or the person standing in wonder before the night sky—to take one of the best-known philosophical topoi—might well be able to formulate the thoughts or beliefs that feed into this emotional response.[37] Yet any such thoughts would seem to be *expressions* of wonder in a way that seems to hold with greater truth than it does for other emotions when their justifying content is expressed ("It was possible that life should never have arisen!" "A whole new human being!"). Hepburn makes a telling remark when he points out that wonder "can indeed by challenged and deflated"—can *always* be challenged, we may add—"by the question, 'What else would you expect?'"[38] In echoing the tones of a jaded cynicism and the refrains of reductivism ("it's *just* . . ."), what this deflationary question—or its permanent possibility—would seem to reveal is the extent to which what is at stake is a reduction of value, and to which a judgment—all too naked—of value is involved.

---

36. See Hepburn, "Wonder." Hepburn's enumeration includes both cases in which a cognitive element is clearly present, as when we lack an explanation for a given phenomenon, as well as cases in which this element seems to be largely absent, as when wonder is the product of sensory impressions, e.g., the view of a vivid blue ocean or a dazzling sheet of mountain ice, where the object of our wonder is "not the genesis of the phenomenon . . . but the phenomenon itself" (139).

37. See Derek Matravers' essay in this volume (and his comments on work by Malcolm Budd) for more on this "feeding" role of thoughts and beliefs.

38. Hepburn, "Wonder," 136. I interpolate "always" because Hepburn's context is rather more specific: he is speaking more narrowly of mathematical or logical truths, where the appropriateness of wonder would seem to come under even stronger challenge given the necessity with which these truths hold.

This observation, which thematizes the relationship of wonder to explanation and the necessity of its liquidation, points ahead to questions we will be meeting again in the following section ("DELIGHT"). But here, and for the purposes driving our thinking, it brings to the fore what appears to be a key question for the issue—concerning the logic of wonder—that we are interesting in clarifying. For it would suggest that, within this logic, the ascription of value to the object of one's wonder could at the very least be identified as a central component. This is an assumption explicitly expressed by Nussbaum, who, as we saw above, described wonder as an emotion responding to "the pull of the object" in which "the subject is maximally aware of the value of the object."

It is a view whose image we may recognize in many of the experiences of wonder we are familiar with in our different capacities, as laymen, as scientists, as philosophers—the prototypical case of wonder before a rainbow seen for the first time, the stunned beholding of a glistening underground cave, the wonder at the miracle of birth, the scientific wonder at the capacities of the mind.[39] The astonishment we experience at such events, thoughts, or discoveries is one that seems inseparable from the experience of beauty or positive significance that accompanies them. On such a view, it is this positive element that would help to distinguish wonder from other emotions such as astonishment or amazement, which would appear more neutral to the value of the objects that provoke it.[40]

This analysis of the logic of wonder might not hold with watertight stability; and with a Wittgensteinian sensitivity to the rough-and-tumble nature of our linguistic practices and the blurred edges of our concepts, we should probably not expect it to. We should accept, that is, that concepts like surprise, astonishment, amazement, wonder, and awe, belong to a family of terms that cannot always be sharply distinguished. And the difficulty of picking the boundaries between related concepts would explain why wonder has often been allowed to shade into its conceptual siblings in the discussion of the handful of contemporary writers who have shown a concern with the emotion. But if we were to agree that this

---

39. Compare Fuller's suggestion that wonder attaches, not merely to what is novel and unexpected, but within this category, to what strikes us as "especially powerful, real, true, and/or beautiful." *Wonder*, 33.

40. "More neutral," though it has in fact been questioned whether emotion could wholly lack an evaluative cadence. In Frijda's words: "What is interesting about the emotion is the emotional. Feeling is not cognition, it is feeling—it is responding 'yes' or 'no'" (*Emotions*, 5). Cf. Ortony and Turner, "Basic Emotions," 317, in the interesting context of an argument against counting surprise as an emotion.

account answers for many of the phenomena,[41] here, it seems, would be the hesitant outline of the ring we had been seeking to draw, fixing (if in a less-than-watertight way) the boundaries of what we "can" and "cannot" wonder at.

Less-than-watertight perhaps—yet to some, it must now be granted, and even with these caveats and concessions, this may still seem a notch too tight for comfort. For talk of logic, of the "can"s and "must"s our concepts must conform to—with a necessity endued with all the eternity of logic—may seem talk condemned to remain brashly ignorant of its history, which often provides the quickest solvent to such necessities. And although a view like Wittgenstein's, which replaced talk of logic with talk of grammar, and sought to undercut the eternal necessities of logic with more finely tuned attention to ordinary language as a "temporal phenomenon,"[42] may seem less liable to this kind of neglect, this is an attention that always needs to be cultivated afresh and case by case.

This attention, in our case, would be invited once we agree to draw a connection between two things that would after all appear to form natural cohorts: the value ascribed to an object in an emotional response, and what (with Daston and Park) we might call the "felt experience" or (with Derek Matravers, in this volume) the "hedonic tone" of that emotional response—by which I simply mean the tone of pleasure or displeasure an emotion involves. Ordinarily, these two aspects would seem to go together, so that the pleasurableness of the swell of joy I experience at good news is inseparable from my thinking the news good; the unbearableness of the indignation that makes me squirm with discomfort is inseparable from the fact that something I consider deeply wrong and unwanted has occurred. Similarly, it would seem, a wonder directed to things of value would be a wonder that would be experienced with pleasure. And this,

---

41. This account is thus meant to be ecumenical, and to allow for the fact that the vocabulary of wonder may appear in reference to states of affairs bearing negative value—as when we might say: "I wonder at his cheek," or "I wonder at his imprudence" (and compare some of the examples s.v. "wonder" (v.), in the *Oxford English Dictionary*, e.g., Thackeray's (1840) remark: "The drawing is executed in a manner so loose and slovenly that one wonders to behold it"). I would want to argue, however, that in such cases the negative state of affairs is often such that it does not directly affect us—or, one's statement implies an intentional cultivation of distance—in a way that ties in with the understanding of wonder in disinterested ("non-eudaimonistic") terms. I find McDougall's discussion of related emotions like curiosity, wonder, awe, and reverence, which presents these as falling on a continuum and brings out their interrelationships yet at the same time proposes markers for their individual seams, a helpful steering wheel for the topic. See *Introduction to Social Psychology*, 110–16.

42. Wittgenstein, *Philosophical Investigations*, § 108.

indeed, seems to be an assumption that is embraced by many writers on wonder, including many of the contributors to this volume. It is one explicitly spelled out by Fuller, for whom the intrinsic delight of wonder ("immediate luminousness") provides a Jamesian argument for granting it a crucial place in the architecture of our spiritual lives.[43] And it is, of course, this assumption we found enshrined in the Ur-text from which we began, in which wonder was claimed as an experience that "produces delight," prompting a question about the present tense codified in this remark ("with all the stability of the eternal").

Yet if this view is correct—or correct for the most part, allowing for the jagged boundaries of the phenomena—it would seem that we should be on our guard against assuming ourselves to have discerned wonder's timeless essence. Or this, it seems, would be one lesson that Lorraine Daston and Katharine Park's unsurpassed narrative of the history of wonder is designed to teach us. The question or doubt of eternity has thus finally caught up with us, offering an obstacle that is truly a blessing in disguise, braking our thinking just when it was going too quickly and delivering a new joint to move it forward. And going forward here means going backward, though we will find that these may not quite be the right terms to characterize the movement required of us. Having considered why wonder cannot be easily known, having discovered what we intimately know about wonder, we are again ready to doubt ourselves. Braking on the "IS" of our logic, let us turn to wonder's history.

DELIGHT: Histories of Wonder, Or: The Rainbow versus the Harpies

That the passions have a history is indeed one of the cardinal lessons that Daston and Park's magisterial volume, *Wonders and the Order of Nature*, might hope for a reader to take away. Tackling a period of several centuries from the High Middle Ages to the Enlightenment (roughly 1150–1750), this is a narrative that tracks the changing histories of two topics that its

---

43. It is also a view shared (in this volume) by Matravers; and lest we think this is an assumption confined to our own cultural experience, it is one we also encounter in the Indian understanding of wonder, as Hulin's discussion of Indian aesthetics attests. It is also a presupposition in Rueger's account of the changing place of wonder in the traditions of literary criticism, for the embrace of wonder as an artistic end by Baroque art theorists would not be comprehensible without it—though of course this account is directly related to the context of Daston and Park's narrative and stands at the crossroads of some of the historical transformations they intend to chart.

Practices of Wonder

authors take to be indissolubly linked: wonders as objects of natural inquiry and wonder as a passion of inquiry, or what they call "the two sides of knowledge, objective order and subjective sensibility." In following its subject, it catches in its searchlights a rich landscape that includes courts and cloisters, nobles and philosophers, and brings into view changing patterns of wealth and power—patterns affected by moments of seismic historical significance, like the conquest of the New World—as well as changing patterns of the scientific and philosophical ethos, and changing views of the natural order.

It is a history marked by several reversals of fortune and near-cyclical vicissitudes, and on Daston and Park's telling, one that both opens and closes on a moment of philosophical distrust. The first of these takes place on a cultural stage marked by the gradual proliferation of wonders and the wonder that tracks them. In noble courts across Europe, collections of wonders have become a widespread presence, serving as symbols of wealth and power, and an appetite for *mirabilia*, which existing traditions of Greek and Roman paradoxography had already fuelled and provided material for, has begun to be reflected in a growing body of writings that includes encyclopedias, travel narratives and the literature of romance. The wonder answering to these wonders—the response these extraordinary particulars are calculated to provoke—is a wonder tinged with pleasure and delight, visible in the exclamations with which a thirteenth-century encyclopedic writer like the Dominican friar Vincent of Beauvais could greet the comparison of animals (the elephant to the gnat, the tiger to the turtle) in his *Speculum Naturale*, as in the ones with which Marco Polo would effuse about the natural wonders of far-flung countries in his *Travels* ("everything there is different from what it is with us and excels in size and beauty").[44]

On this stage, natural philosophers stand apart and aloof, by treating wonder with ambivalence and suspicion. This ambivalence looks backwards and forwards, and betokens a passion that has changed, and is set to change again. Backwards: to Aristotle, from whom philosophers take their vision of philosophical inquiry and ideals of rational explanation. Knowledge, on this philosophical ideal, takes the form of universal and necessary truths that can be known with absolute certainty, and the syllogism provides the stock in trade. Experience, and the study of contingent particulars—particulars like the ones forming the objects of delectating wonder for the philosophers' contemporaries—has little place

---

44. Daston and Park, *Wonders*, respectively 44–45, 32–33.

here. Backwards, too: to Augustine, this time not as a hero but as supposed opponent of rational ideals, as the advocate of a wonder in which Latin philosophers, emerging in the twelfth century from a prolonged intellectual slump, saw philosophical inquiry opposed, insofar as it "elevated wonder at the mighty works of God above the causal explanation of natural phenomena." Wonder, for many of the philosophers of the thirteenth and fourteenth centuries, comes to be associated with ignorance—and in turn often associated, not with pleasure, but with fear—and is dismissed as a passion unfitting to philosophers—it becomes taboo, "the mark of the ignorant, the non-philosopher, the old woman."[45]

And yet these backward looks simultaneously yield tokens of important changes. For Aristotle, as Daston and Park point out, had spoken praisingly of wonder as the passion of philosophical inquiry in his *Metaphysics*, and significantly, had presented a view of wonder and its proper objects that was at odds with the one assumed by medieval philosophers in their disavowal of wonder. Not the unusual, the atypical, the strange— the extraordinary particulars represented by medieval *mirabilia*—but in fact natural regularities, and thus the usual and the regular, were for Aristotle the proper object of wonder. Similarly, while Augustine had indeed claimed wonder as a "highly salutary passion" and as "the proper expression of humility before the omnipotence of God," considering it a religious duty to wonder at creation and its Creator, his had been a wonder in which the medieval delight over *mirabilia* would not have recognized its image.[46] For Augustine had refused to concede any special distinction between the usual and the unusual, or the commonplace and the extraordinary as proper objects of wonder, deeming all things created by God equally wondrous. And far from connecting wonder exclusively with pleasure, he had framed his remarks on wonder by a discussion of God's power to subject the unfaithful to eternal torture, thus bequeathing to his readers an image of wonder tinged with fear.

In marking these changes (or divergences), this brief fragment of Daston and Park's larger narrative already brings into view elements that will play a crucial role in their account of wonder's history. For their claim that the passions in general, and wonder in particular, have a history, is a claim about changes that can be marked on several levels, which include, on the one hand, the objects of the emotion, and on the other, what they refer to as its "affective content" or "felt experience." In naming the contrast

45. Ibid., 111, 118.
46. Ibid., 122.

Practices of Wonder

between the ordinary and the extraordinary, we have already glimpsed part of the changes to which wonder is open at the former level—and here, this is not a level (and aspect of wonder's grammar) will be considering in greater detail. But with the second element, we have found the beginning of a thread that will guide us through this section. Because it is indeed, as it turns out, partly as a vicissitude in delight that the history of wonder as a passion of inquiry, on Daston and Park's account, needs to be written.

In charting this sequence, we will need to leap quickly over many of the developments that prepare the ground for the reversal of wonder's fortunes among the philosophers, from opprobrium to approbation—past the moment in the fourteenth century when Italian medical writers serving at princely courts begin to explore the therapeutic powers of particular marvels, instigating the slow entry of wonders into natural philosophy, past the accomplished ascendancy of wonders in natural philosophy from the mid-sixteenth and especially in the seventeenth century, when "marvels, described in words and displayed as things, saturated early modern European culture, thrusting themselves into the consciousness of nearly everyone, from prince to pauper to philosopher," and in the form of "strange facts" come to preoccupy philosophers, creating a new community of inquirers (the "curious" or "ingenious" of Europe) and a new category of scientific experience (the fact), and establish themselves at the vanguard of a changing scientific ethos, embodied by Francis Bacon, in which the taste for universal certainties and distaste for particulars typical of Aristotelian philosophy are abandoned for a concern with the anomalous and the particular that heralds the empiricist ethos of modernity.[47]

Leaving all this somewhat breathlessly behind, we may leap ahead to the moment when, the infiltration of wonders into philosophy complete, the passion of wonder—the subjective face of this development—similarly comes into its own in the sensibility of inquiry, and thereby embarks on one of the most interesting phases of its history—one of the most interesting, and one of the most rapid, leading to a downfall as fast as a *coup* after its meteoric rise, and one that, if correct, would put us in the mind of cycles and the cyclical as the best description of the history it has been fated to follow.

As the mid-seventeenth century comes into view, it is here, Daston and Park argue, that we can observe a crucial transformation in the passion of wonder, exemplified in Newton's writings but recurrent in the writings of the generation before him. A "minuet" of emotions comes to constitute

---

47. For these final developments, see broadly ch. 6, of which 217–18 quoted.

the sensibility of inquiry as natural philosophers understand it, one that is fashioned as a passage between "musing admiration, startled wonder, then bustling curiosity." Wonder, longtime pariah of the intellectual passions, now appears as the staple of inquisitive sensibility. What has happened here? A change, it is argued, so radical that Daston and Park contest whether the passion that emerges from it retains its identity, and whether we preserve our entitlement to speak of it as a single thing. "Although there is a kinship of descent," they write, "and, no doubt, some resemblance of feeling between the wonder praised by Augustine and blamed by David Hume, or between the curiosity castigated by Bernard of Clairvaux and that celebrated by Hobbes, they are not of the same emotional species." A large claim—and one that, fresh from a discussion about what wonder is or can be, will have a captivating grip on our attention. What are its grounds? At the most basic, they consist in "a premise that the felt substance of an emotion depends to a significant extent on the company it keeps." And it was the relocation of wonder and curiosity relative to each other, and their relocation individually on the map of the "vices and virtues, passions and interests," that therefore changed their substance and "emotionally restructured both."[48]

Long considered separate from wonder and either ignored in this connection—as by Aristotle and his Latin commentators—or disparaged—as by Augustine, who associated it with pride and lust—curiosity, in this period, comes to be reinterpreted and relocated amongst the passions. At the hands of Hobbes, the foremost artisan of its new meaning in the seventeenth century, curiosity rises to become the quality that separates human beings from animals, and, in Hobbes' desire-centered psychology, acquires the status of the archetypal desire—an insatiable desire fated never to be at rest, whose objects are the obverse of the useful and range over the novel, the extravagant, the rare, and as such, a passion understood as a "refined form of consumerism" and associated with greed in the map of the virtues and vices.[49] It is with this newly interpreted curiosity that wonder enters into alliance, and, in opposition to the Aristotelian understanding of wonder as a response to the regular, follows the bent of this "refined consumerism" and succumbs to the fascination with the rare and the unusual with which the world outside philosophy had for a long time been awash, to make of the rare and the extraordinary wonder's proper object.

48. See ibid., 303–5.
49. See particularly ibid., 307–10.

Practices of Wonder

Yet let us follow this story through, to have it before us in full before grappling with the grain of its detail. For what happens, then, that, after this brief efflorescence, sees wonder again banished from the passions of inquiry only a few decades later, at the end of the seventeenth century, in a process that the middle of the eighteenth century sees through to its conclusion? On this account, it would appear to be in part, and precisely, the feeling tone of wonder—its delightful character, or intrinsic "sweetness"—that brooked the grounds for the unstable relationship between wonder and inquiry, threatening to sever the two asunder. This sweetness seemed to be exhibited in a tendency of wonder to reduce to a stupefied stare—to mere gawk—and thus to freeze inquiry rather than to motivate it, which was reflected in the descriptions of philosophical writers on the passions in this period who spoke of the tendency of wonder to arrest rather than move—to leave the "whole body . . . immobile as a statue," in Descartes' words, later echoed by Spinoza—in a way that indicated a willing abandonment to its charms.[50]

But the severance of wonder from inquiry, when it happens, has a more complex foundation. Part of it reflects a worry for which the seventeenth-century natural philosopher Robert Boyle became an important mouthpiece, in suggesting that wonder directed to nature was wonder drawn away from God. This is a worry that leads, not so much to the eclipse of wonder, as to its displacement and rechanneling into a theological passion, so that wonder acquires a strongly theological orientation in seventeenth- and eighteenth-century natural philosophy, one accompanied by a displacement of focus from extraordinary particulars to the ordinary and to the natural order. This development, Daston and Park

---

50. Descartes, *Passions of the Soul*, 354 (art. 73); cf. Daston and Park, *Wonders*, 316ff. In this passage, Descartes is in fact speaking directly, not of wonder, but of astonishment, but astonishment is in turn understood as an excess of wonder. Keeping in mind the relation between these two notions—in which astonishment is construed as a modification of wonder—we would seem to be left with a view of wonder that is bound to be paradoxical. For if wonder moves to inquiry, *and* wonder stalls (or, in Spinoza's view, leaves the mind "without motion" and "transfixed": *Ethics*, 129 [III Def. of the Affects IV]), this would seem like a puzzling set of claims to be faced with—for how could both be true? And how, more importantly, could such a dispute be settled? (Would it be enough to simply draw a distinction between wonder and astonishment, resolving the dispute by means of definition?) What is arguable, at the very least, is that this view of the tendencies of wonder would not appear to constitute another lesson in historicity, for the disagreement is one that divides near-contemporaries, and indeed a single writer against himself.

suggest, had an important result: for "wonder proved intractable to such a dramatic orientation and ceased to be a philosophical passion."[51]

But the trend that led to the marginalization of wonder among European intellectuals in the eighteenth century—the rejection of the marvelous that came to typify "the new, secular meaning of the enlightenment as a state of mind"—had its roots in two even broader transformations—transformations of both "metaphysics and sensibility." One of these was a distrust of wonder that was the product of the grueling civil strife of the sixteenth and seventeenth centuries, to the extent that wonder was associated with enthusiasm (*Schwärmerei* in German) and superstition and its destructive effects in religion and politics. The other concerned a new understanding of the natural order, which revealed nature as governed by immutable laws that expressed themselves in the rigid uniformity and regularity of natural phenomena everywhere. Nature, on this revised understanding, was expected to behave with a cool, measured dignity in which marvels and the marvelous could have no place. It, too, obeyed a kind of *decorum*—a term familiar to us from literary criticism (see Rueger's paper in this volume), which thus reveals an emphasis on the regular, the uniform, and the proportionate, and a distaste for the marvelous, that is shared by both views of nature and aesthetic ideals of the period. This account of wonder's demise, it should be noted, involves a rejection of the simple narrative of the "disenchantment" of the world associated with Weber, according to which it was the development of science and of an increasingly rational stance toward nature (combined with the processes of secularization) that vacated nature of its mystique.[52]

But vacant, certainly, is how Daston and Park suggest we find it by the end of this process. By the time this transformation is complete, wonder and curiosity have been decoupled, curiosity has been bequeathed to the next generations of naturalists as the principal motor of inquiry—an impulse of sober industriousness free from wonder's sentimentalities—and wonder has been relegated to mere gawk and to a vulgar, "bumptious form of pleasure" scorned by the intellectuals and reserved for the "unlettered

---

51. Daston and Park, *Wonders*, 328. It is a remark, however, that would imply rather too restrictive a view concerning what wonder requires in order to constitute a properly philosophical passion—a view that is undermined by Daston and Park's own reminders about the concern with the natural order, and the orderly and regular, enshrined in Aristotle's wonder, and a view that several papers in this volume, in highlighting the history of philosophical concern with the ordinary, would further place in question.

52. See ibid., ch. 9.

masses." Thus, we may add, returning it to the origins from which it had descended, so that the curtain of this long history of wonder falls on a distrust bearing a more than passing resemblance to the suspicion on which our stage had opened.

A "grand narrative" indeed—the kind of narrative we need to find our bearings in this long, fractious history and one that illuminates our topic from every angle. A narrative, too, that is grainy with overturnings and reversals. Yet one question we will need to raise is: are these entirely to be read as *reversals*, or might there be another way of reading them? To get to this question, however, we first need to return to the opening claim that gave us our direction, planting itself in the ground below our feet as a first spade to unsettle it when it seemed too steady and stodgy with unquestioned "is"s and "ought"s linking wonder with delight. Daston and Park's focusing claim, we will recall, had been framed as the suggestion about changes in the "affective content" or "felt experience" of wonder that result from the relocations of the passions, virtues, and vices relative to each other and that establish wonder's historicity. So where do we stand with this claim? The evidence for it in fact has not yet come into view, and when it does so, it is the philosopher Adam Smith that appears to serve as a linchpin witness.

He is a witness, certainly, that cuts a lonely figure on the stand, for with the relegation of wonder to mere gawk by the mid-eighteenth century among the learned, Adam Smith is one of few to retain wonder as a philosophical passion. Yet this, Daston and Park argue, is no ordinary retention, for it testifies to the demotion of wonder from its former status as a source of delight, to a passion now experienced with a very different affective tone. They write:

> Smith composed a history of astronomy in which one cosmological system succeeded another by allaying or exciting philosophical wonder, so that wonder became the engine of progress in that science. Yet he found the passion an uncomfortable one, inducing "confusion and giddiness" in small doses and "lunacy and distraction" in large. The naturalist confronted with a "singular plant, or a singular fossil" must somehow classify it "before he can get rid of that Wonder, that uncertainty and anxious curiosity excited by its singular appearance . . ." Gone was Malebranche's *sentiment de douceur* . . . Smith's wonder resembled not so much fear, as it had for the scholastic philosophers, as a nasty hybrid of seasickness and toothache.[53]

53. Ibid., 326–27.

It would seem to be this passage that bears the onus of the argument concerning the shifting experiential tone of wonder and its decline from pleasure to distress. Now without a doubt, one must acknowledge, on the one hand, the importance played by what Daston and Park call the "neighborhood" of emotions in determining their identity and the mode in which we experience them. This is a suggestion that, articulated in a general form, has commanded assent by several other writers on the emotions. It is defended, albeit in a different language, by Nussbaum, when she remarks the impact the value judgments we place on emotions have on the way we experience them, a claim she illustrates by the case of anger. In societies in which anger figures as an object of moral disapproval, its experience is one that will often be inflected with shame; contrast this with the experience of anger in Roman society, where its connection to honor meant that anger was "hooked up to a feeling of manly pride, and to a quasi-erotic excitement." In Greek and Roman taxonomies, as a result, anger was—we may thus be surprised to find—described a "pleasant emotion directed at the future, because of the pleasure of contemplating revenge."[54]

And yet in the present case there are grounds for resisting this reading, though it requires some care to articulate one's misgivings in a judicious way. "A wonder that feels like giddiness and anxious confusion, like distress?" One might be tempted to respond to this in the way one would to the person that turned to us glowingly to exclaim "I feel such *envy*—every time I look at my wife standing and talking with her handsome colleague, I want to run up to him and embrace him with my two arms," or to the person who turns to say to us while furiously scratching his feet: "I'm dying from curiosity—the soles of my feet are burning with tingling sensations all over." You have it wrong, we might like to say here; what you're feeling simply isn't what we call "envy" or "curiosity"; and as for your tingling feet, whatever the physical experiences that might contingently accompany your use of particular words, this isn't how the meaning of words is established. To Smith's tooth-ached apprehension of the singular appearance, one would similarly like to respond by saying: you have it wrong; whatever it is you are feeling, this isn't wonder. For wonder is not anxious, is not distressed. Reaching back to the language-learning perspective we set out earlier in accounting for our intimate knowledge of wonder, we might say: a Smith-like child that responded to the first ("singular") sight

---

54. Nussbaum, *Upheavals*, 159–62. See also Rorty's relevant remarks ("Enough Already," 273–74), stressing the interrelationships between emotions and other attitudes, which affect the way we identify and individuate emotions (forming what Daston and Park might have called an emotion's "emotional neighborhood").

of rainbows, of waterfalls, of snow, or of an *aurora borealis*, with all the symptoms of nausea or with groans of distress would be one that would never be given the language of wonder to replace its natural reactions. It would be a child that would not "live in our world." And conversely: we would be unable to understand why a child greeting singular appearances with all the signs of distress would then seek out such experiences instead of shunning them as one shuns toothaches, hunger, and the cold ("what are our criteria for saying that a person has toothache or experiences distress?"). Ascending from the child to the philosopher, we might continue by questioning whether, if wonder still counts as philosophy's beginning, we could ever desire anything other than to bring philosophy to the swiftest end.

But to put it this way—with an unabashed appeal to a linguistic "we"—would be to express ourselves in the very terms that Daston and Park's argument is designed to interrogate, calling into question whether there is indeed a single linguistic community in place—a single "we"—whose intuitions could be expected to coincide. And while the language-learning perspective outlined above is one that proposes itself as a description of a community that is not local or historical but human—the "our" of "our world" the first person plural of human beings—the argument here can be made more compellingly by allowing the possibility of a distinction between linguistic communities and raising a question concerning Adam Smith's relationship to his own. This, indeed, is a question Smith himself brings to the fore in first setting out the meaning of the terms "wonder," "admiration," and "surprise" at the opening of his essay "The History of Astronomy" where he concertedly discusses them, when, in true philosophical fashion, he dismisses the issue of his account's fidelity to common linguistic usage as one of "little importance" and, waving away the imprecisions of language, insists on the distinctness of the experiences aroused by different objects even if "the words made use of to express them may sometimes be confounded."[55]

55. Smith, "History of Astronomy," 34–35; at the same time, Smith suggests that his use is probably faithful to common usage, though he then immediately adduces examples that contravene it. This rather cavalier attitude towards the facts of language would appear to be at home in the broader approach to the relationship between mind and language typical of the Cartesian understanding of the mind and its introspective transparency—an understanding echoed in the remarks with which Descartes himself had earlier prefaced his *Passions of the Soul* (p. 328 [art. 1]: "This topic . . . does not seem to be one of the more difficult to investigate since everyone feels passions in himself and so has no need to look elsewhere for observations to establish their nature.") This type of attitude would seem crucial to take into account in—just as it would seem

This programmatic remark signals that one would need to exercise serious caution in reading Smith's remarks on wonder and using them to draw conclusions about wonder's historical vicissitudes. With Smith's relationship to his linguistic community already in question, we can then observe that the picture of wonder that emerges from the body of his discussion is a far from unified one. For while, certainly, wonder is associated with anxiety and vertiginous unease in the passage cited by Daston and Park, in other passages it is explicitly associated with pleasurable emotion, as when Smith speaks of "the pleasing wonder of ignorance" or, discussing sculpture and painting, of "that pleasure . . . founded altogether upon our wonder."[56] This, of course, should not be surprising in the wake of the narrative Daston and Park have presented to us, for we have heard that wonder is never purged of its delights and is at most ostracized outside the study doors of the learned (a distinction to which the first of our quotes implicitly refers us). Study doors, as Hume once famously remarked, are such that one is always condemned to eventually reopen them; yet what is more relevant here is the question whether there are certain doors—such as those in the face of one's linguistic community—that one may never entirely close behind one.

Even if, however, such a possibility of separating what lies inside and outside the study doors remained open, and the wonder of the learned could be allowed to part ways with the wonder of the ignorant, it would be important here to note that Smith's study doors turned on rather more particular hinges, and swung open to a rather special interior. For if philosophers have often shown a greater than average preoccupation with rule and exception, order and anomaly, normal and abnormal, and the known and the unexplained, Smith's philosophical interior was one marked by an even higher concern with such notions, for which he owed to David Hume's influence a more than superficial debt. The philosophical universe they shared was one in which regularity, under the name of custom, played a crucial epistemological role, in Hume's view accounting for basic operations of the mind, such as the formation of abstract ideas—a role best known perhaps to philosophical readers through its place in Hume's account of the connection between causes and their effects, where it was invoked as the principal source of our causal reasoning. In this picture, the primary tendency of the mind confronting the world was one of classification—of establishing patterned order out of disjointed

---

to complicate—any effort to write the history of particular emotions.

56. Smith, "Imitative Arts," 185.

phenomena—and a desire for a state of rest and equilibrium that serves as a baseline against which change and disturbance emerge as disruptions, and as threats to be quickly repulsed so that order may be restored. Such a picture of the mind, sharing with the comfortably established bourgeois a love of peace and established order, would seem to heavily determine the attitude that could be taken toward the unfamiliar and the new, which appear as assaults upon what we have been accustomed to think and expect.

That the familiar was something we incline to with greater pleasure was something Hume had already intimated in his *Treatise of Human Nature*, when he remarked the effect of custom and repetition in "bestowing a *facility* in the performance of any action or the conception of any object; and afterwards a *tendency* or *inclination* towards it," the facility produced by repetition forming "an infallible source of pleasure." By contrast, when "the soul applies itself to the performance of any action, or the conception of any object, to which it is not accustom'd, there is a certain unpliableness in the faculties, and a difficulty of the spirit's moving in their new direction." And closing in on the objects of our specific concern: "As this difficulty excites the spirits, 'tis the source of wonder, surprize, and of all the emotions, which arise from novelty."[57]

Our natural love of order is likewise articulated in clear terms by Smith, who remarks that "the mind takes pleasure in observing the resemblances that are discoverable betwixt different objects."[58] It is in this context that Smith's remarks about wonder should be understood. For wonder, when it arises, presents itself as a problem of classification and as a disruption of the smooth customary grooves followed by our thoughts.[59] Confronted with the new and the singular,

> The imagination and memory exert themselves to no purpose, and in vain look around all their *classes* of ideas in order to find one under which it may be arranged. They fluctuate to no purpose from thought to thought, and we remain still uncertain

---

57. Hume, *Treatise*, 422–23. The continuation of this passage, however, suggests that taking this view was not inherently incompatible with acknowledging that surprise and wonder should nonetheless constitute pleasurable experiences ("this difficulty . . . is in itself very agreeable, like every thing, which inlivens the mind to a moderate degree")—a judgment that would not only accord with the view of wonder "outside the study doors," but also with Hume's remarks elsewhere, as in his essay "Of Miracles," in his *Enquiry Concerning Human Understanding* (*Enquiries*, 117).

58. Smith, "History of Astronomy," 37.

59. In this, it would seem to evoke the account of wonder presented by Fuller drawing on a Piagetian model, in which the experience of wonder marks the stress fractures of the cognitive structures through which we process the world. See *Wonder*, ch. 6.

and undetermined *where to place it*, or what to think of it. It is this fluctuation and vain recollection, together with the emotion or movement of the spirits that they excite, which constitute the sentiment properly called Wonder . . . What *sort* of a thing can that be? What is that *like?* are the questions which, upon such an occasion, we are all naturally disposed to ask.[60]

Wonder, then, exhibits all the painfulness of disorientation. If the mind loves stability, and wonder marks its fault lines, little wonder then that wonder should be experienced as a burden to the soul.

Indeed, for a passion that belongs to the free—philosophy, itself cast as a wonder-driven attempt to remove "seeming incoherences" and "render the whole course of the universe consistent and of a piece," arises once material necessities have been satisfied and is explicitly opposed to practical need—wonder appears as a distinctly unfree passion, and one that shares with suffering more than a superficial grammar.[61] Textured by his philosophical conception of the mind's operations, Smith's wonder becomes reminiscent of the suffering anxiety with which an obsessive-compulsive might survey their room upon finding it in a state altered from the way they last left it. This suffering tone is suggestively revealed in some of the examples Smith appeals to in ascribing to wonder the dangers of lunacy and distraction, inviting us to imagine "a person of the soundest judgment, who had grown up to maturity, and whose imagination had acquired those habits, and that mold, which the constitution of things in this world necessarily impress upon it, to be all at once transported alive to some other planet, where nature was governed by laws quite different from those which take place here" and who "would be continually obliged to attend to events, which must to him appear in the highest degree jarring, irregular, and discordant." Or again, on *terra firma* this time, consider what it is like to "look over even a game of cards, and to attend particularly to

---

60. Smith, "History of Astronomy," 39 (emphasis added).

61. Quote from "History of Astronomy," 50. That wonder shares the grammar of suffering is suggested by a striking turn of phrase Smith employs, speaking of a person who sees another wonder at what he no longer wonders at himself, and who (Smith writes) may often be "disposed rather to laugh at, than sympathize with our Wonder" (ibid., 44). Such a remark, however, would not suffice as sole evidence of the negative or suffering quality of wonder, given the once again particular philosophical understanding Smith brings to the notion of "sympathy." For sympathy, in the terms set out in the *Moral Sentiments*, is not confined to negative emotions or experiences, but can rather be taken "to denote our fellow-feeling with any passion whatever," including the pleasant along with the painful, and joy and happiness no less than pain and sorrow (*Moral Sentiments*, 10).

every single stroke, and if he is unacquainted with the nature and rules of the game; that is, with the laws which regulate the succession of the cards; he will soon feel the same confusion and giddiness begin to come upon him."[62] Alighting on another planet and being bombarded with confusing phenomena; looking on while others play a game answering to unfamiliar rules—images of a struggle with incomprehensible phenomena that falls back in frustration, claimed by Smith as images of wonder. "But is it wonder?" This doubt is one that, standing outside his philosophical study doors, Smith's contemporaries may also have recognized as their own.

What I have been suggesting is that it is a particular philosophical view of the mind that underpins the negative terms in which wonder is characterized by Smith.[63] And if the argument is correct, we should be cautious about reading this characterization as a reflection of wonder's historical transformations, and as unambiguous support for questioning the identity of the wonder experienced by Smith and his contemporaries to the wonder that opened our history. Where are we, then, with the thread of our argument? For if our thread began from a willingness to abandon the smug certainties of an "is" that would tie wonder to delight as its eternal essence, then the suggestion that this reading of wonder's passage into something more saturnine be revised might seem to leave us free to embrace, with more rightful complacence this time, the certainties of our own grammar.

Yet this would once again be moving too quickly. For if this particular reversal of feeling tone and value sign, from delight to something more tenebrous, falls into question—explained away partly as an abstention from linguistic community and as an insulation behind the doors of an especially well-ordered philosophical universe—one thing seems clear,

---

62. Smith, "History of Astronomy," 43–44.

63. This proposal might seem, in another respect, dissatisfying; for the claim that *fear* should constitute the basic reaction to the unknown seems intuitively plausible for reasons articulated by Fisher when he writes that "in a world not yet sufficiently familiar, the predictable response to the extraordinary is a feeling of alarm that the novelty will turn out to be dangerous to the fragile order that maintains the self" (*Aesthetics of Rare Experiences*, 48)—words that may indeed remind us of Smith's own remarks about the reaction of primitive human beings to their surrounding world, predominantly one of "terror and consternation" ("History of Astronomy," 48). (Cf. the earlier association between wonder and fear in Daston and Park's remarks about the scholastics.) Yet the most relevant point to make in this connection is that the negatively valenced reaction to the new is articulated here in general terms, without regard for the specific circumstances that give context to the experience; and considered as a philosophical response, wonder—as Smith himself suggests—emerges in a context where immediate danger should be of little concern.

and that is that this is by no means wonder's first brush with darkness, nor the first time that the thread of delight has been pulled in the length of its history. For as we have seen, the curtain opened on this history from the High Middle Ages to the Enlightenment with a moment in which wonder was linked with fear by scholastic philosophers approaching it with distrust, even as a wonder of pleasure was taking root in cultural milieus all around them. If the inside and the outside of philosophical doors afforded different experiences or interpretations of wonder in the eighteenth century, then, this was not for the first time in wonder's history. And in juxtaposing the "inside" and the "outside" as alternatives to the "before" and "after" of historical narratives, this observation raises a question we already posed above but passed without pausing, namely: should these different feeling tones of wonder be read as reversals taking their place in a forward-moving historical narrative, or is there a different way of reading these possibilities?

Not consequents and antecedents, but contemporaries—this would be one of several ways of rewriting the distinction that is offered by another recent account of wonder, Mary-Jane Rubenstein's *Strange Wonder: The Closure of Metaphysics and the Opening of Awe*, which at certain points competes with, but at many others reinterprets in new terms, the historical narrative we have been working with. Competes: for the transformations of wonder, as Rubenstein reads them, are cast in terms of the triumph of one kind of wonder over another which certainly involves a progression of before and after, including an "after" that Daston and Park had written as one of decline (and of which we will have more to say). Reinterprets: for this involves a new typology of wonder in which different kinds of wonder—and the different affective tones that specify them—are identified as immanent possibilities. It is a narrative in which the experience of seasickness Smith had complained of provides a key joint—but in terms that we will find very different from those in which Smith had understood it.

For seasickness, or a species of it, is the moment on which Mary-Jane Rubenstein's eye-opening story of philosophical wonder opens and ends—though with this, we find ourselves already *in medias res* in a dialogue that has been in progress for some time. Socrates, having met the precocious youth Theaetetus, has been conducting a dialogue about the nature of knowledge, when the youth's head begins to spin with a vertigo (*Theaetetus* 155c) that Socrates instantly recognizes as the "sense of wonder" that is "perfectly proper to the philosopher" and that is philosophy's sole foundation. Preceding this sense of vertigo has been a stretch of philosophical thinking in which, responding to a first hypothesis that would identify knowledge with perception, Socrates has prestidigitated before Theaetetus' wondering eyes a dizzying stream of examples—a set of six dice is more in relation to a group of four, and less in relation to a group of twelve; Socrates now is bigger than Theaetetus but smaller in a year despite having undergone no change—that would seem to leave a basic and seemingly self-evident premise shaken: that nothing can be anything other than what it is. It is this vertiginous loss of certainty, in which "an everyday assumption has suddenly become untenable" and "the understanding cannot master that which lies closest to it—when, surrounded by utterly ordinary concepts and things, the philosopher . . . finds himself surrounded on all sides by aporia" that Rubenstein identifies as the heart of Socratic/Platonic wonder, tracing out what will become the first term of her typology.[64]

It is clear already that the feeling tone of wonder and the objects of wonder are indissolubly connected; for if this wonder is "a profoundly unsettling pathos," as Rubenstein suggests, it is because of the way in which it directs itself to what is most ordinary and familiar, and renders "uncanny the very ground on which the philosopher stands." And it is this, again, that creates its instability, because, faced with the "open sea of endless questioning, strangeness, and impossibility" and the "frightful indeterminacy" of wonder, the experience of seasickness makes one pine for firm ground.[65] Wonder, thus, contains the seed of its own undoing, in bringing on an urge for closure and for quick resolution that would lift the sense of being at loss and the vulnerability of uncertainty, and that one must struggle against as a temptation. Restated in the terms of a familiar Socratic ideal: what must be fended off is the anxious desire to see the maieutic stance transcended through the birth of firm philosophical positions and conclusions, the critical stance shed and replaced by positive theses.[66] Wonder is thus a passion to be endured; and the possibility of enduring wonder, and of remaining with it, is indeed a key theme in Rubenstein's account.

---

64. Rubenstein, *Strange Wonder*, 4, 3.

65. Ibid., 4, 5, 7.

66. The account of wonder in Plato's works developed by Chrysakopoulou in this volume clearly supports and dovetails with Rubenstein's accent—drawing mainly on the *Theaetetus*—on the negative feeling tone and suffering quality of Socratic/Platonic wonder. Where the two accounts might appear to differ concerns whether the labor pangs can and should be embraced as harbingers for the birth of positive knowledge.

It is this image of wonder that next becomes, in Rubenstein's narrative, the key term for a dichotomy that is given more than one name. It becomes, on the one hand and crucially, a dichotomy between Platonic and Aristotelian wonder. "For it is owing to their wonder that men both now begin and at first began to philosophize," wrote Aristotle in the *Metaphysics*, and "they philosophized in order to escape from ignorance" (982b10-20)—forging a connection that would recur throughout much of philosophical history, between wonder and ignorance, and wonder and the desire for explanation. A wonder directed to what we do not understand, and paradigmatically to the unfamiliar, it presents itself as a temporary irritant to be cured by explanation, and only valuable for its instrumental role in stimulating inquiry—offering a bridge that is then to be burnt behind one, and generating an inquiry whose aim is to liquidate its beginning or, in the words of Daston and Park, "to make wonders cease." For, bringing the two narratives together, it is here that Rubenstein offers a new set of terms for recapitulating wonder's history, which she reads as one in which Aristotle's wonder comes to displace Socrates' in Western philosophical and theological understanding. It is Aristotelian wonder we find among the medieval scholastics; it is similarly, and more recently, the one we find in one of the best-known spokesmen for early modern wonder, Descartes; and it is similarly this kind of wonder, we can now say, that we find mirrored in Smith, for whom wonder constitutes but a passing frustration to be quickly purged.

And it is perhaps Smith who helps us characterize this wonder more precisely, in a way that allows us to distinguish two kinds of vertigo of very different texture, and significance. For in making wonder mark the fault lines of an orderly universe in which order is the default state and incoherence a contingent, temporary entropy to be swiftly cleaned up and compulsively cleared away, Smith displayed a feature of Aristotle's wonder that becomes one of the most crucial and illuminating conceptual woofs of Rubenstein's narrative—that is its relationship with the pleasures of mastery and control. It is not an accident that Smith, in discussing the wonder of the philosophers as they are confronted by "seeming incoherences," describes them as "stopped and *embarrassed*" by these incoherences.[67] Embarrassment might strike us as a surprising inflection to introduce into the experience of wonder, but it is this very turn of phrase that reveals the connection in which philosophical understanding stands to a sense of pride and achievement, pointing to the way in which the unfamiliar

---

67. Smith, "History of Astronomy," 50 (emphasis added).

or incoherent is experienced as a limitation of one's own power, and more specifically of the power one wields through the ability to explain. And it is in fact a preoccupation with these notions—of power, mastery, and control—that Rubenstein sees expressed in the cultural fascination with wonders throughout the period Daston and Park examine, in which wonders are obsessively collected, cataloged, and possessed, acting as emblems of power. With their infiltration of natural philosophy, the wondrous becomes an object of scientific comprehension, to be mastered through explanation—a mastery at the same time directly correlated to notions of self-mastery (taking on the meaning, Rubenstein adds, even of self-divinization).

Not vulnerable, then, or at loss, but in command and control, assimilating all strangeness, one's vertigo that of one only momentarily peering into the abyss of one's impotence and one's wonder the kneejerk reaction of one obsessed with order and intent on establishing it—a confident posture that Rubenstein counts as a refusal of the vulnerable uncertainty that Socrates' wonder invites us to remain open to, despite the vertigo of anxiety with which it makes our head swim.[68] Aristotle's wonder seeks resolution where Plato's wonder avoids it as temptation. And this is a contrast that signals that the triumphal procession of the former through philosophical history would be disfigured by being read solely in terms of a forward-moving contingent historical progression. For this movement forward, it now appears, would simultaneously have to count as an evasion of wonder's immanent possibility.

"Evasion," indeed, is a notion that recurs even more strongly in the second dichotomy Rubenstein maps on to the one just outlined, now in terms that we will recognize as our own, for it is a dichotomy precisely in

---

68. In these terms, Fisher's account of wonder would align itself roundly with the second pole of Rubenstein's typology, in connecting wonder to explanation not only forwards—in terms of its self-dissolving aim—but also backwards, by grounding the very experience of wonder when confronted with the new or extraordinary—wonder constituting a pleasurable experience opposed to the negative response of fear—in a history of successful explanation and experiences of mastery: "that we do not find ourselves for the most part defeated by the unusual, left baffled in an unresolvable way so that we 'give up' and think of something else, provides the experiential base for pleasure in the sudden, the unexpected and the extraordinary" (*Aesthetics of Rare Experiences*, 48). Compare the remarks by Josef Pieper (whose perspective is clearly aligned with the first pole of Rubenstein's typology): "to wonder is to be on the way, *in via* . . . wonder reveals itself as having the same structure as hope, the same architecture as hope . . . We are essentially *viatores* . . . beings who are 'not yet.'" (Pieper, *Leisure*, 136–37). Yet Pieper later adds: this is a perpetual "not yet"; for philosophy can never fully comprehend its objects (ibid., 142).

terms of a more lighthearted wonder, a wonder of pleasure and delight, and a wonder that falls under a longer shadow. Rubenstein's starting assumption, here, is that it is the former wonder in which we will have least difficulty recognizing ourselves—a "sugarcoated" wonder of sweetness and light, or the wonder of "white bread, lunchbox superheroes, and fifties sitcoms." But dig a little deeper into the history of wonder packed geologically within it, and a very different set of facts comes to the surface. Scratch beneath the connection of wonder with "smiling" in the Latin *admiratio* and the connection with "seeing" in the Greek *thauma* and you find a connection with "fear" in the very same Greek root. Follow the knots up the obscure genealogy of "wonder" and you should be prepared to entertain the German *Wunde* or "wound" as one of its possible ancestors. Even in the English history of the word, its descent is overlaid with darker overtones, and in rising to its modern usage it passes through the evil, the horrible, the terrible. And it is indeed to the "terrible" that we need to look in order to begin bringing into view another strand of that family of concepts in which wonder finds kinship—and that is awe, in its different inflections: from the dread of *yir'ah* in the Hebrew Bible that is also Augustine's wonder, to the sublime of the Romantic poets and philosophers, to Pascal's awe before the twin abysses of minuscule and majuscule, to Kierkegaard's *horror religiosus*. That wonder should have lost these meanings, leaving them "forgotten and repressed," is symptomatic of the difficulty of holding our nerve before the terrible element of wonder. The wonder of delight should thus count as an evasion of its darker other.[69]

Sugarcoated wonder versus awe; or: the wonder of the rainbow versus the wonder of the Harpies. Because, bringing another genealogy into view, this time a mythological one, the sea god Thaumas (to which the term *thauma* is related) gave birth to Iris, goddess of the rainbow—enduring symbol of delighting wonder to our times—but he also fathered the Harpies—symbol of the monstrous and the awesome. And it is in fact by following the rainbow to its end that we may catch a glimpse of one of the most vivid images illustrating the sweet-tasting wonder Rubenstein has in mind. For hardly any image could rival the one found in Richard Dawkins' *Unweaving the Rainbow*, undertaken as an apologia for science and an argument for its contribution to making a "life worth living." In this argument, wonder serves as a capstone, cast as a "deep aesthetic passion" with the rainbow as its paradigm object, and encapsulating the promise of a life in which human beings explore the world around them like children at

---

69. Rubenstein, *Strange Wonder*, esp. 9–11.

play, grass high and sunlight streaming, to giggles of wonder and delight.[70] Parts of the book read like a latter-day *Wunderkammer*, a gallimaufry of wonders held up for display by the scientific gaze, from the outlandish life of octopuses, to the wonders of our own bodily constitution, to the mind-bending marvels of 500-million-year-old trilobites and the mind-boggling attempt to think vast time, adding up to a panegyric to science and the aesthetic feast of wonders it affords. Missing from this festival of wonders is the element of mystery (though its vocabulary makes occasional appearances), or a sense of vulnerability in the human confrontation with the world, or any of the darker elements of a wonder that would be at loss rather than in command, for Dawkins's, like Smith's, is an "orderly universe" in which "everything has an explanation"—and if one has not yet been uncovered, then "we're working on it."[71]

"We're working on it"—the posture of an expectant mastery that would now appear as wonder's evasion. And it is this, to complete this alternative reading of wonder's history, that also forms the key motif for one of the critical philosophical episodes that impart to it its closing seams. For it is this preoccupation with representing and calculating, with treating beings as objects of (scientific) explanation and technological manipulation, that Heidegger departs from in calling for a different way of attunement that would return us to Being—and this is to say: to that which is closest and most familiar to us, the *that* of beings everywhere occluded by being presupposed. Articulating that mode of attunement takes the form of a concerted study of the different senses of wonder or *thaumazein* that is pursued almost *sub rosa*, in unpublished work and deleted passages—inconclusively in Heidegger's 1937–38 Freiburg lectures, more informatively yet still gnomically in his unpublished *Contributions to Philosophy (from Enowning)*—and when it is named, it emerges as a blend of wonder in which the element of the terrible sounds out as a dominant chord. Provisionally named *Verhaltenheit* ("restraint," "reservedness"), it contains as "equiprimordial comportments" shock or terror (*Schrecken/Erschrecken*) before the fact that things cannot be—because Being has withdrawn from beings; because "beings can *be* while the truth of being remains forgotten"—and awe (*Scheu*) at the fact that nevertheless they are.[72]

A terrible wonder before the fact "that things are"—we have certainly come a long way from *Wunderkammern* and medieval *mirabilia*,

70. Quotes from Dawkins, *Unweaving the Rainbow*, xii.
71. Ibid., xiii and 17.
72. See generally Rubenstein, *Strange Wonder*, ch. 1, and also this volume.

following this darker thread of wonder. Yet what we should here observe is that it is then a wonder in the shadows that opens and closes this history—if indeed we can speak of closure (as against its temptations). And to regain our thread yet again, what this narrative suggests is that the relationship of wonder to the lighter and darker elements of its being, to be adequately captured, needs to be written, not merely as a historical concatenation, but as a relationship between immanent possibilities and potential contemporaries. Contemporaries? Yet here, in fact, we should be more precise. Wonder "is inherently ambivalent," writes Rubenstein, using an "is"—what wonder is, what wonder does, as in the remark that "wonder wonders at the strangeness of the most familiar"—that returns us to the language of our starting point, when we first put an ear to the ground of our eternalizing grammar.[73] And yet the "is," which here seems to refer us to factualities of our own present, should not make us disregard the fact that the tenebrous elements of wonder are ones that, after all, and on Rubenstein's own telling, need to be exhumed from the geological substrata of our language in which they are now hidden. The gradual disappearance of the tincture of the terrible from wonder's meanings is amply charted by the *OED*, and the dulcet wonder Rubenstein identifies as its evasion has established itself in contemporary usage and become the pitch we should not be surprised to find on our tuning forks. Its retrieval would thus constitute either a revisionary act or a demand of changed focus on one variant of wonder against another, in what is surely the same part of the dictionary and the same larger conceptual family, marking out the "is" as one in the power of a potentiality.

Yet whether as revision or new intellectual demand, we must also remark that this story clearly contains the seed of yet another re-reading of the grand narrative Daston and Park present us, which is crucial for the understanding of wonder's history we have been pursuing. For in bringing into view a lineage of wonder whose latest philosophical episodes are still unfolding in our own times—Heidegger's *Verhaltenheit* becomes the first thread in a weave that continues through to Emmanuel Levinas, Jean-Luc Nancy, and Jacques Derrida—Rubenstein lends her voice to what should become a polyphony of appeals against telling the later fortunes of wonder as a simple story of decline. This story, we may recall, was intended to characterize the attitudes of the philosophers and intellectual elites in the first instance. Yet Heidegger, in articulating his own version of a wonder in whose clearing the encounter with Being can take place, looked back

---

73. Quotes from ibid., 9, 8.

to a philosophical genealogy in which Plato's wonder was certainly not the only member and which encompassed his own immediate philosophical past, including, most significantly, those of his predecessors sharing the sensibilities of Romanticism. For this, perhaps the best evidence is the one found in his winnowing critique of the competing varieties of wonder, which passes through *Verwunderung, Bewunderung, Staunen* and *Bestaunen* to reject them as inadequate interpretations of *thaumazein*. For it was *Bewunderung* that had figured in Kant's expression of wonder at two objects—the moral law within and the starry sky above—that later reappeared at central junctures in his account of the sublime in the *Critique of the Power of Judgement*. And while Heidegger might have rejected this strain of wonder as implicating the very posture of mastery requiring to be transcended, he shares with Kant—as with Schopenhauer, that maverick heir of Kantian thought—several features of his understanding of wonder.

Certainly the fundamental opposition between the stance of wonder and the stance of interest or utility ("mastery"): for Kant, the sublime in both its forms—as an encounter with nature at its vast, in the mathematically sublime, and with nature at its most powerful, in the dynamically sublime—involves, not only the absence of interest—as is the case with the beautiful, which pleases us "without any interest"—but indeed an opposition to it, arising in "resistance to the interest of the senses." This notion of resistance or opposition is expressed even more strongly by Schopenhauer in the context of his metaphysics of the will, in which the aesthetic moment arrives as an almost miraculous liberation. For the starry skies and crashing waves that typify the sublime are "terrible to the will" and thus require an active struggle with one's will to be experienced in their sublimity, demanding that one "consciously turn away from it, forcibly tear oneself from his will and its relations" to be contemplated.[74] And in sharing this aspect, Heidegger shares with both predecessors an understanding of wonder as the mode or location of one's contact with a higher Being or truer reality, once the relationship of mastery ceases to stand in its light—for Kant and Schopenhauer, a higher reality that is simultaneously a higher aspect of one's own being: one's noumenal status as a rational being with a moral vocation (Kant), or as the world-creating subject of representation (Schopenhauer).

But equally, and more relevantly for our direct purposes, what he shares is a gravitation toward the darker strains of wonder. And it is to

---

74. Respectively Kant, *Critique of the Power of Judgment*, 150 (§29) and Schopenhauer, *World as Will*, 1:201.

these darker strains, and more specifically, to that somber-yet-exulting, humbling-yet-exalting alloy of awe and wonder—that tense amalgam of "delightful horror" and "terrible joy"—coming together in the Romantic sublime, that one might do well to look to locate one of wonder's worthiest heirs and most potent continuants of its later history. Not the sole heir; and not even the sole one to figure in the preoccupations of those sharing the sensibilities of Romanticism. For these also included a wonder of more joyful tincture directed to the most ordinary and mundane (as against the grand) as its proper object. Given paradigmatic expression in the work of Coleridge and Wordsworth but also, as M. H. Abrams shows, in the works of many of their English and German contemporaries whom we identify with the multifarious Romantic movement, and in America, in the writings of the Transcendentalists, this latter wonder left a paper trail through many of the philosophers (such as Merleau-Ponty, Bergson, and others), as well as many of the literary writers and artists, who constitute our immediate past.[75]

This paper trail is a long and important one, and one about which more could be said; yet it is to the shadowy strain of wonder that we should now attend as providing us with the best foothold on wonder's later history. Emerging in the eighteenth century with an intellectual pedigree reaching back to ancient philosophy and rhetoric, the sublime begins life among European intellectuals with the revival of Longinus' *Peri Hypsous* as translated and interpreted by the French critic Boileau (1674) as a development in the rhetorical tradition. In a movement that gathers pace with the contributions of literary critics and philosophers such as John Dennis, Joseph Addison, the Earl of Shaftesbury, Edmund Burke, and others, it spreads outward to become the foundation of a new mode of experiencing nature, responding, in a way that marks a radical breach with previous attitudes, "to the mighty, the majestic, the mysterious aspects of Nature, to a sense of vastness and spaciousness never expressed—and apparently never felt—before the closing years of the seventeenth century."[76] In this discovery of the sublime in nature, as Marjorie Nicolson argued in a work that shares with Daston and Park's account a central concern with the historicity of our passions, the changing experience of mountains— transformed from repulsive objects seen as expressive of divine wrath, to objects experienced with a thrill of joyfulness in which the surviving element of terror betrayed its religious ancestry—formed a linchpin.

75. Abrams, *Natural Supernaturalism*, ch. 7, esp. 375–84.
76. Nicolson, *Mountain Gloom*, 27.

Practices of Wonder

This discovery—which went hand in hand, via the accent on emotion it imported, with the emergence of "aesthetic experience" as a new experiential category—involved a subversion that would seem to be key for stitching the earlier and later fortunes of wonder together at the point where their relationship comes into question. For if it is a new conception of nature that is implicated, on Daston and Park's account, in the declining fortunes of wonder—one conforming to a sober decorum of regularities and uniformities which the literary criticism of the time shared as an aesthetic ideal—it is precisely as an opposition to and revision of these aesthetic standards that the sublime emerges. Not the well-formed, the proportionate, the regular of neoclassicist ideals—not symmetry and order—but rather the disordered, the formless, the vast (a term of dispraise in the neoclassic canon) suggestive of infinity are the proper objects or occasions of sublime experience, paradigmatically embodied in the terrible spectacle of high mountains through which eighteenth-century European travelers experienced their first brushes with the sublime. If the sublime emerges as wonder's heir, it is thus precisely as a reaction to the standards that, on our earlier account, lead to wonder's demise, weeding out the marvelous from the upper strata of intellectual culture. But this, it will be clear, is a wonder with altered tone and object: not the delighted response to marvelous particulars, but the more somber response to grandeur.[77]

As a reaction, and perhaps even, on another telling, as a direct descendant: for on Nicolson's view, it was precisely the new science of astronomy with its novel instruments of observation, which unleashed cosmic vistas of infinite and possible worlds into view and into the imagination, that was partly responsible for the subversion of the older ideals of beauty and order, bursting the dams of a cosmos that had previously born the appearance of a well-ordered world turning in its eternal orbits to the music of the spheres. In a development in which Cambridge Platonists like Thomas More and his circle—fervently embracing the imaginary of infinite space—are allotted a crucial role, the awe "once reserved for God, passed over in the seventeenth century first to an expanded cosmos, then from the macrocosm to the greatest objects in the geocosm—mountains, ocean, desert . . . Scientifically minded Platonists, reading their ideas of infinity into a God of Plenitude, then reading them out again, transferred from God to Space to Nature conceptions of majesty, grandeur, vastness in

---

77. Cf. Rueger's suggestion (in this volume) that it is precisely as a legitimate successor to the gaudy extravagances and ingenuities of the Baroque marvelous—as a respectable marvelous with a pedigree acceptable to neoclassicists—that the story of the sublime's emergence can be written.

which both admiration and awe were combined. The seventeenth century discovered 'The Aesthetics of the Infinite.'"[78] On this account, the developing taste for the infinite and the aesthetic of the sublime would emerge from the very heart of the new science which wore the decorum of proportion and regularity as its other face.[79]

But with or without this particular inflection of the story, what is striking is that this understanding of wonder's most notable heir would offer a double reversion to Daston and Park's account of wonder's decline. For if, once again, it was as an aversion to a religious enthusiasm with pernicious social and political consequences that the intellectual repugnance to wonder had developed, it should nonetheless be noted that the notion of enthusiasm was brought into relationship with the sublime at several key junctures of its history. It appears, early on, in one of the first critical attempts to articulate the sublime in the eighteenth century, in John Dennis's distinction between ordinary emotion and enthusiasm—described by Monk as an attempt to demarcate aesthetic emotion—in which the latter becomes the foundation for the sublime. It reappears in the Earl of Shaftesbury's acclaim of enthusiasm in a context that directly links it with the nascent sublime, describing it as an exalted state of mind faced with majestic beauty which raises above ourselves and which, Shaftesbury significantly adds, forms the basis of virtue itself.[80] Significantly, because it is this link with virtue that recurs in what is perhaps the most important philosophical pairing of enthusiasm and the sublime, in the account of the sublime given by Kant in his *Critique of the Power of Judgement*—an account in which the link with morality plays a key role. Enthusiasm (*Enthusiasm* or *Enthusiasmus*) is a state of mind that Kant characterizes as "aesthetically sublime" and describes as a response to morality—it is "the idea of the good with affect."[81] Kant's stance, it must be admitted, is not one free from ambivalence, not only of the more familiar kind which those attuned to Kant's suspicion of emotion in matters of morality may have been already prepared to see expressed, but also, and returning us to the picture presented by Daston and Park, a suspicion of enthusiasm's

---

78. Nicolson, *Mountain Gloom*, 143.

79. This point is not free from debate, however, inasmuch as Nicolson's account rests on a controversial premise concerning the limited role of the rhetorical tradition—and in particular, Boileau's translation of Longinus—in the genesis of the "natural" sublime, or the sublime as a response to the natural world (see, for example, ibid., 29–33). See Rueger's brief remarks in chapter 8 of this volume.

80. See respectively Monk, *Sublime*, 48–49, and 208–9.

81. Kant, *Critique of the Power of Judgment*, 154 (§ 29).

dangers, one reflected in a terminological distinction between positive and negative variants (*Enthusiasm/us* versus *Schwärmerei*).[82] Yet even with this ambivalence texturing our view, enthusiasm would pose itself not exclusively as opponent but also as partner to the place of wonder—and more specifically of that darker strain represented by the sublime—in intellectual culture.

A history of wonder, then, that would not be a simple story of decline, and one in which its darker strain would occupy a special—if not exclusive—place; a wonder open, and not closed, though one that it may take an effort of self-overcoming to retain open; a wonder, at any rate, that would still be available to us as its heirs. "Wonder"—even with this merely partial grammar, we have come far enough to be wary of the claim of unity this expression offers.

Picking our way through competing narratives of wonder's history, we have carved deep tracks into the Ur-text that provided us with our initial bearings: "Wonder: a sudden experience of an extraordinary object that produces delight." SUDDEN, we asked—yet does wonder strike like other emotions? What kind of knowledge do we have of an emotion so unlike others? DELIGHT, we said, at an object perceived to be of value and positive significance—yet is that the only tone of feeling with which wonder has historically been tensed, and the only one it carries as its possibility?

Not the only questions to ask, and not the only joints held up by our starting point as promises of thinking—but such promises belong to a rather longer grammatical tale.

---

82. For some discussion of this, see Clewis, *Kantian Sublime*.

Bibliography

Abrams, Meyer H. *Natural Supernaturalism: Tradition and Revolution in Romantic Literature.* New York: Norton, 1973.
Aristotle. *Nicomachean Ethics.* Translated by Terence Irwin. Indianapolis: Hackett, 1985.
Brown, Deborah J. *Descartes and the Passionate Mind.* Cambridge: Cambridge University Press, 2006.
Cavell, Stanley. *The Claim of Reason: Wittgenstein, Skepticism, Morality and Tragedy.* Oxford: Oxford University Press, 1999.
Clewis, Robert R. *The Kantian Sublime and the Revelation of Freedom.* Cambridge: Cambridge University Press, 2009.
Daston, Lorraine, and Katharine Park. *Wonders and the Order of Nature, 1150–1750.* New York: Zone, 2001.
Dawkins, Richard. *Unweaving the Rainbow: Science, Delusion, and the Appetite for Wonder.* London: Penguin, 1999.
Descartes, René. *The Passions of the Soul.* In *The Philosophical Writings of Descartes*, translated by J. Cottingham, R. Stoothoff, and D. Murdoch, 1:328–404. Cambridge: Cambridge University Press, 1985.
Ekman, Paul. "Are There Basic Emotions?" *Psychological Review* 99 (1992) 550–53.
Ekman, Paul, et al. "What Emotion Categories or Dimensions Can Observers Judge from Facial Behavior?" In *Emotion in the Human Face*, 2nd ed., edited by Paul Ekman, 39–55. Cambridge: Cambridge University Press, 1982.
Elster, Jon. "Emotion and Action." In *Thinking about Feeling*, edited by Robert C. Solomon, 151–62. New York: Oxford University Press, 2004.
Fisher, Philip. *Wonder, the Rainbow, and the Aesthetics of Rare Experiences.* Cambridge: Harvard University Press, 1998.
Frijda, Nico H. *The Emotions.* Cambridge: Cambridge University Press; Paris: Editions de la Maison des Sciences de l'Homme, 1986.
Fuller, Robert C. *Wonder: From Emotion to Spirituality.* Chapel Hill: University of North Carolina Press, 2006.
Goldie, Peter. "Emotion, Feeling, and Knowledge of the World." In *Thinking about Feeling*, edited by Robert C. Solomon, 91–106. New York: Oxford University Press, 2004.
Gordon, Robert M. *The Structure of Emotions: Investigations in Cognitive Philosophy.* Cambridge: Cambridge University Press, 1987.
Hadot, Pierre. *Philosophy as a Way of Life: Spiritual Exercises from Socrates to Foucault.* Translated by Michael Chase. Oxford: Blackwell, 1995.
Hepburn, Ronald W. "Wonder." In *"Wonder" and Other Essays*, 131–54. Edinburgh: Edinburgh University Press, 1984.
Hume, David. "Of Miracles." In *Enquiries Concerning Human Understanding and Concerning the Principles of Morals*, edited by L. A. Selby-Bigge, revised by P. H. Nidditch, 109–31. 3rd ed. Oxford: Clarendon, 1975.
———. *A Treatise of Human Nature.* 2nd ed. Edited by L. A. Selby-Bigge. Revised by P. H. Nidditch. Oxford: Clarendon, 1978.
Inwood, Brad. "Why Physics?" In *God and Cosmos in Stoicism*, edited by Ricardo Salles, 201–23. Oxford: Oxford University Press, 2009.

Practices of Wonder

Kant, Immanuel. *Critique of the Power of Judgment*. Translated by Paul Guyer and Eric Matthews. Edited by Paul Guyer. Cambridge: Cambridge University Press, 2000.

Keltner, Dacher, and Jonathan Haidt. "Approaching Awe, a Moral, Spiritual, and Aesthetic Emotion." *Cognition and Emotion* 17 (2003) 297–314.

Lazarus, Richard S. *Emotion and Adaptation*. Oxford: Oxford University Press, 1991.

Matsumoto, David, et al. "Facial Expressions of Emotion." In *Handbook of Emotions, 3rd Edition*, edited by Michael Lewis et al., 211–34. New York: Guilford, 2008.

McDougall, William. *Introduction to Social Psychology*. 30th ed. London: Methuen, 1950.

Monk, Samuel H. *The Sublime: A Study of Critical Theories in XVIII-Century England*. Ann Arbor: University of Michigan Press, 1960.

Mulhall, Stephen. *On Being in the World: Wittgenstein and Heidegger on Seeing Aspects*. London: Routledge, 1990.

———. *Stanley Cavell: Philosophy's Recounting of the Ordinary*. Oxford: Clarendon, 1994.

Nicolson, Marjorie H. *Mountain Gloom and Mountain Glory: The Development of the Aesthetics of the Infinite*. Ithaca: Cornell University Press, 1959.

Nussbaum, Martha. *Upheavals of Thought: The Intelligence of Emotions*. Cambridge: Cambridge University Press, 2001.

Ortony, Andrew, and Terence J. Turner. "What's Basic about Basic Emotions?" *Psychological Review* 97 (1990) 315–31.

Peterson, Christopher, and Martin E. P. Seligman. *Character Strengths and Virtues: A Handbook and Classification*. Washington, DC: American Psychological Association; New York: Oxford University Press, 2004.

Pieper, Josef. *Leisure, The Basis of Culture*. Translated by Alexander Dru. London: Faber & Faber, 1952.

Plato. *Theaetetus*. Translated by Robin A. H. Waterfield. London: Penguin, 2004.

Rorty, Amélie O. "Enough Already with 'Theories of the Emotions.'" In *Thinking about Feeling*, edited by Robert C. Solomon, 269–78. New York: Oxford University Press, 2004.

Rubenstein, Mary-Jane. *Strange Wonder: The Closure of Metaphysics and the Opening of Awe*. New York: Columbia University Press, 2008.

Schopenhauer, Arthur. *The World as Will and Representation*. Translated by E. F. J. Payne. 2 vols. New York: Dover, 1969.

Shiota, Michelle N., et al. "The Faces of Positive Emotion: Prototype Displays of Awe, Amusement, and Pride." *Annals of the New York Academy of Sciences* 1000 (2003) 296–99.

Smith, Adam. "The History of Astronomy." In *Essays on Philosophical Subjects*, edited by W. P. D. Wightman and J. C. Bryce, 31–105. Oxford: Clarendon, 1980.

———. "Of the Nature of That Imitation Which Takes Place in What Are Called the Imitative Arts." In *Essays on Philosophical Subjects*, edited by W. P. D. Wightman and J. C. Bryce, 176–213. Oxford: Clarendon, 1980.

———. *The Theory of Moral Sentiments*. Edited by D. D. Raphael and A. L. Macfie. 1976. Reprint, Indianapolis: Liberty Fund, 1982.

Solomon, Robert C. "The Logic of Emotion." *Noûs* 11 (1977) 41–49.

Spinoza, Benedictus de. *Spinoza's Ethics and "De Intellectus Emendatione."* Translated by Andrew Boyle. London: Dent, 1910.

Tooby, John, and Leda Cosmides. "The Evolutionary Psychology of the Emotions and their Relationship to Internal Regulatory Variables." In *Handbook of Emotions, 3rd Edition*, edited by Michael Lewis et al., 114–37. New York: Guilford, 2008.

Wittgenstein, Ludwig. *Philosophical Investigations*. Translated by G. E. M. Anscombe. Oxford: Blackwell, 2001.

2

From Biology to Spirituality

The Emotional Dynamics of Wonder[1]

ROBERT FULLER

THE AIM OF THIS volume is to explore one of the most profound and subtle of all human experiences—the experience of wonder. A truly interdisciplinary approach to this topic requires the integration of insights from the natural sciences, the social sciences, and the humanities. Doing this, however, is not an easy task. It means creating an explanatory model through which different disciplines make different kinds of contributions. The base of this model consists of the contributions afforded by the biological sciences (including biologically based models in psychology).[2]

---

1. Based on *Wonder: From Emotion to Spirituality* by Robert C. Fuller. Copyright © 2006 by the University of North Carolina Press. Used by permission of the publisher. www.uncpress.unc.edu.

2. I have elaborated on the importance of biological insights for the study of topics traditionally thought to be the domain of the humanities or social sciences in my *Spirituality in the Flesh*. See also Edward Slingerland's important contribution to interdisciplinary methods in *What Science Offers the Humanities*. I might also point out that in a previously published study of wonder I suggested that the prototypical characteristics of wonder "can be assessed at any number of levels: the evolutionary-adaptive level, the neurophysiological level, the motivational level, the cognitive level, the attitudinal level, and—perhaps most important—the phenomenological level. No one level of analysis alone can tell us the whole story of the emotion of wonder." See my *Wonder*, 33.

After all, we can only think and feel what our brains permit us to think and feel. Although biology doesn't dictate the full range of human experience, it forms the preconditions of that experience. The first step toward an interdisciplinary understanding of an emotional experience as elusive as wonder is thus to focus attention on its biological substrates.

Biological Substrates of Emotion

Wonder arises in human life as an emotional experience. It is important, then, to recognize that emotions are among the most prominent biological systems shaped by natural selection. Seen from an evolutionary-adaptive perspective, emotions are part of a circular feedback system that connects individuals with their surroundings.[3] We continually scan our surroundings (often unconsciously) in order to identify potential harms or potential benefits. Certain kinds of sensory information trigger emotional programs whose purpose is to mobilize the organism for an appropriate response. Carroll Izard explains that because emotions arouse the neural programs that direct behavior, they "constitute the primary motivational system for human beings."[4] Research indicates that emotions activate such vital activities as prioritizing goals, screening sensory information, retrieving goal-specific memory, regulating physiological processes, and communicating intent.[5] Emotions thus motivate efforts to scan our surroundings while selectively attending to data that appear relevant to our survival or other interests.

It is important that we move past thinking of emotion as a general category and instead isolate the motivational influences of distinct emotions. Joseph LeDoux explained this well when he pointed out that there is no one emotional region of the brain. Instead, "the various classes of emotions are mediated by separate neural systems that have evolved for different reasons."[6] Distinct emotions are aroused by distinct biological processes and perform distinct biological functions. Thus "if we are interested in understanding the various phenomena that we use the term 'emotion' to refer to, we have to focus on specific classes of emotions."[7]

---

3. Robert Plutchik provides an overview of the evolutionary approach to the study of emotions in his essay, "A General Model."
4. Izard, *Human Emotions*, 3.
5. Cosmides and Tooby, "Evolution and Emotions."
6. LeDoux, *The Emotional Brain*, 16.
7. Ibid.

Identifying specific emotions is difficult. Emotions are among the most slippery and variable human attributes. The very first challenge faced when studying specific classes of emotion is that of distinguishing between the biological and the cultural components of emotion. Scholars investigating emotion differ greatly in their views on this important issue. Theoretical orientations range along a continuum that at one far end emphasizes the wholly biological basis of emotion and at the other far end emphasizes the constructive role of culture. Although there is as yet no complete consensus on the relative roles of biology and culture, a survey of major texts in the field indicates that the vast majority of researchers believe that emotions have identifiable biological substrates.[8] A truly interdisciplinary approach to wonder, then, must start by surveying available insights into its biological moorings.

An additional word of caution needs to be interjected into any discussion of discrete emotions. Aaron Ben-Ze'ev calls attention to what he calls the "subtlety of emotions."[9] One implication of this subtlety is that the feeling states we label emotions (as well as their nature, causes, and consequences) are far too variable and complex to be neatly categorized. The very concept of an emotion is what Ben-Ze'ev calls a "prototypical category" based on a preponderance of empirical characteristics. He argues that various feeling states are to be considered emotions according to their degree of similarity to the most typical case. The same applies to the argument for distinct emotions. The existence of distinct emotions is not an all-or-nothing affair; it is, rather, a matter of the degree of similarity to the most typical case. We need to resist premature foreclosure on any one definition of emotion in general, let alone distinct emotions, until we get much closer to understanding the precise mix of biological and cultural factors that make emotions so subtle and variable.

Evolutionary-Adaptive Foundations of Wonder

Many emotions originate in response to unexpected or anomalous sensory information. Our brains are wired to respond to unanticipated events by mobilizing particular kinds of cognitive modules and emotional programs. Evolutionary biologist Richard Dawkins explains the biological substrates

---

8. See Plutchik, *Emotions and Life*; Izard, *Human Emotions*; Davidson et al., *Handbook of Affective Sciences*; Lazarus and Lazarus, *Passion and Reason*; and Lewis and Haviland-Jones, *Handbook of Emotions*.

9. Ben-Ze'ev, *Subtlety of Emotions*.

of wonder by observing that "it is as if the nervous system is tuned at successive hierarchical levels to respond strongly to the unexpected, weakly or not at all to the expected."[10] Fear is the most commonly cited example of an emotional program triggered by some unexpected sound or sight. Fear is perhaps the most biologically governed and evolutionarily oldest of all humanity's emotional programs. Its principal function is to arouse cognitive and behavioral responses that will protect us from threatening agents. Fear focuses attention, restricts our utilization of sensory cues, redirects memory, and prompts communication patterns in an effort to discern the presumed existence of a causal agent threatening our well-being.

Wonder is also an emotional experience triggered by the perception of something novel, unexpected, or inexplicable. Yet wonder differs from other startle-induced emotions in terms of its specific motivational effect on perception, cognition, and behavior. The motivational functions unique to wonder illustrate why some researchers find it useful to distinguish between *positive* and *negative* emotions. Negative emotions (e.g., fear or anger) are those emotional programs triggered when new experiences fall short of expectations, thereby frustrating or threatening the organism's overall well-being. In contrast, positive emotions (e.g., joy, interest, or wonder) are those emotional programs triggered when new experiences exceed expectations. Positive emotions have received less experimental attention than the study of negative emotions. A principal reason for this is that negative emotions are easier than positive emotions to differentiate according to their facial, autonomic, and behavioral components. Barbara Fredrickson argues that although research of positive emotions has lagged behind that of negative emotions, empirical evidence supports what she terms a "broaden-and-build" model that explains how certain positive emotions broaden an individual's thought-action repertoire.[11] As Fredrickson points out, the emotional class to which wonder belongs broadens a person's scope of cognition, increases her or his intellectual repertoire, and builds a more extensive network of social relationships.

It will be my argument here that wonder, as an emotional experience, broadens our cognitive repertoire in ways that facilitate a stance toward life that might be considered broadly spiritual. We can identify at least some of the biological and psychological mechanisms that underlie this broadening and building process. This line of investigation invariably raises the complex question concerning the evolutionary rationale for the existence

10. Dawkins, *Unweaving the Rainbow*, 264.
11. Fredrickson, "Positive Emotions."

of an emotion as seemingly unconnected with physical survival as wonder. It is important in this context to note that evolution constructed brains to solve many adaptive problems other than those ensuring short-term physical survival. Evolution also favored emotional programs designed to solve recurrent problems that are more clearly social or cultural than physical. This is why it is important that we distinguish between the very different emotional systems that exert motivational influences on perception and cognition. Psychologist Jonathan Haidt proposes that evolution favored a distinct set of motivational programs that he calls the "moral emotions."[12] Moral emotions differ from those emotional programs designed to solve problems related to immediate physical safety in that they are designed to serve the interests or welfare of the social group to which a person belongs. Haidt points out that emotions such as disgust, contempt, shame, embarrassment, and guilt promote the long-term interests of a social group by inducing both loyalty and conformity to group activities.

According to Haidt, both awe and wonder are among the moral emotions that contribute to the formation, maintenance, and occasional restructuring of social groups. Haidt has primarily addressed the emotion of awe. He proposes, for example, that awe consists of a biologically based emotional reaction whose principal function is to prompt subordination to a powerful leader. As Haidt and his colleague Dacher Keltner explain, "much as humans are biologically prepared to respond to certain fear-inducing stimuli (e.g., fast approaching objects, darkness), we argue that humans are prepared to respond to awe-inducing stimuli (e.g., large stature and displays of strength and confidence)."[13] It appears that awe is thus a biological response to stimuli that are sufficiently vast (i.e., physical size, fame, authority, prestige) that they diminish our sense of self and challenge our accustomed frame of reference. The cognitive and perceptual changes peculiar to awe remind us that one of the principal functions of emotions generally is that they frequently serve as "place markers" designating individuals' roles and positions within social hierarchies.[14] Awe, as a social emotion, has an important role in the formation and maintenance of social hierarchies. The experience of awe is comprised of biologically based action tendencies that prompt subordination to the dominant individual by displaying passivity, heightened attention towards what is perceived as

---

12. Haidt, "Moral Emotions."

13. Keltner and Haidt, "Approaching Awe," 306. See also Shiota et al., "Awe."

14. See Clark, "Emotions in Everyday Life," and Keltner and Haidt, "Social Functions."

powerful, and imitation. Awe is, incidentally, almost always accompanied by at least some element of fear. It functions to diminish one's own sense of self in relation to that which is perceived as "vast." By diminishing or lowering a person's sense of self, awe is a classic example of a moral emotion in that its principal function is the formation, maintenance, or change of social hierarchies.

Although awe has evolutionary origins in procuring subordination to powerful social others, it can also be detected in experiences triggered by "vast" stimuli arising from nature, art, and certain epiphanic experiences. Indeed, the key elicitors of awe appear to be what Haidt and Keltner describe as "perceptual vastness and the need for accommodation." Vastness refers to anything that is experienced as much larger than the self whether in terms of simple physical size or such socially constructed qualities as fame, authority, or prestige. Accommodation refers to the process described by Jean Piaget whereby humans adjust mental structures that cannot assimilate a new experience. Whereas assimilation involves interpreting new stimuli in terms of existing schemas, accommodation entails revising these schemas or even creating wholly new mental schemas to account for new stimuli that exceed older cognitive structures.

While awe undoubtedly emerged owing to its ability to induce individuals to submit to social authority, it nonetheless serves as a host of other psychological functions that are not directly related to humanity's biological survival. Haidt and Keltner, for example, found awe to be an integral element in a variety of classic religious or epiphanic experiences such as are attributed to Arjuna in the *Bhagavad Gita* or to Paul in the New Testament. Haidt and Keltner found evidence suggesting that "awe can transform people and reorient their lives, goals and values . . . awe-inducing events may be one of the fastest and most powerful methods of personal change and growth."[15] In a follow-up study, Keltner, Michelle Shiota, and Amanda Mossman found that awe often prompts people to see themselves as part of a greater whole, instigating "the sense of being in the presence of something greater than the self and a feeling of being connected with their surroundings."[16]

Wonder belongs to the same family of emotions as awe. Wonder, like awe, is elicited by novel or unexpected stimuli that defy assimilation to pre-existing conceptual categories. Vastness and the need for cognitive accommodation are the principal factors that elicit wonder just as they

15. Keltner, and Haidt, "Approaching Awe," 312.
16. Shiota et al., "Awe," 955.

serve to elicit awe. Indeed, wonder most frequently occurs as a response to something that strikes us as intensely powerful, real, or beautiful. Wonder differs from awe, however, in that it isn't accompanied by fear or submission. Wonder diminishes the sense of self, yet does so without inducing interpersonal submissiveness.

It thus seems probable that humans are capable of experiencing wonder because we have inherited brains shaped by natural selection to respond to novel stimuli, to respond to vastness, and to seek accommodation. Yet wonder itself is in all likelihood an unintended by-product of evolution rather than itself an evolutionary adaptation. True, wonder functions in ways that meet some of humanity's social and psychological needs. But it is nonetheless difficult to see how wonder was itself selected through natural selection (which finally boils down to the capacity to promote reproductive success). It may turn out that natural selection did indeed favor emotional experiences that trigger the broadening and building of our brain's potential for abstract, higher-order thought. The evolution of the human brain was fast and furious. In just 20 to 25 million years, thousands of mutations occurred in the genes that regulate the development and function of the human brain. We are not completely certain how so many changes happened in such a relatively short time, though it appears likely that social structure was the main force driving the evolution of the human brain.[17] Complex social structures put in place mechanisms for selecting intellectually advanced individuals—wonder may be among the emotions that stimulate such advanced intellectual function. Thus we may eventually discern an evolutionary rationale for the biological underpinnings of wonder. Yet, at this point in time, it seems safer to suggest that wonder *per se* is an accidental by-product of psychological capacities that were initially shaped to perform other tasks.

Haidt, Keltner, and others have devoted more attention to awe than to wonder. Haidt has observed that fellow researchers have inexplicably neglected the study of wonder because it motivates response patterns that don't quite fit standard evolutionary-adaptive accounts of emotions. Haidt points out that wonder mobilizes physiological, perceptual, and cognitive changes that "enlarge the field of peripheral vision" and open our attention to a wider field of stimuli than we would ordinarily attend to. Haidt goes further, pointing out that wonder seems to "open our hearts and minds" to other persons in our social group.[18]

17. See Lahn et al., "Evolution of Nervous System."
18. Haidt, "Moral Emotions," 863.

It seems, then, that we can safely conclude that humans have a biologically grounded capacity to respond to vastness (and thus also to the need for cognitive accommodation) in ways that broaden our thought-action repertoire. Though having received surprisingly little attention, wonder is surely among the foremost of these positive emotional programs. And even though it seems likely that the thought-action functions mobilized by wonder are by-products of capacities that evolution selected for other adaptive purposes, they nonetheless meet many distinctively human needs and are therefore worthy of more systematic study in their own right.

Wonder and the Capacity for Higher-Order Thought

The broadly biological functions performed by wonder help us understand its distinctive influence on human cognition. Wonder, like other emotional programs triggered by unexpected sensory events, mobilizes the brain's modules for detecting causal agency. Identifying causal agents is crucial to biological survival. Our brains have consequently been shaped by natural selection to detect agency, particularly in ambiguous or threatening situations.[19] Events that elicit agency detection usually mobilize cognitive processes that assimilate new sensory information into existing mental schemata leading to appropriate action. Wonder, however, is most frequently elicited by vastness and the need for cognitive accommodation. As a consequence wonder typically prompts us to identify agency or intentionality at a more general level of existence. Put a bit differently, rather than leading to immediate defensive action, wonder leads to the relatively passive contemplation of why things are as they are. As such, wonder is the ontogenetic basis for the development of thinking that goes beyond the constraints of the immediate physical environment. It stimulates our efforts to contemplate ever-more general orders of existence. The motivational functions performed by wonder, then, are closely linked with the development of some of humanity's highest cognitive and cultural achievements. Not the least of these achievements is the emergence of humanity's capacities for both moral reflection and philosophical speculation.

The argument here is that wonder performs a special role in stimulating the development of very particular kinds of cognitive abilities—abilities that support humanity's capacity for abstract, higher-order thought.

---

19. Helpful introductions to evolutionary psychology and the brain's modules for detecting agency can be found in Atran, *In Gods We Trust*, 59–63, and Tremlin, *Minds and Gods*, 75–86.

Practices of Wonder

For this reason the work of Jean Piaget is particularly relevant. Piaget's goal was to elaborate a broadly biological explanation of knowledge. Because he viewed knowledge as a form of adaptation continuous with organic adaptation, he set about studying the cognitive development of children as they adapted to ever-expanding environmental perplexities.[20] He closely observed children, particularly his own children, as they learned to make sense of the world about them. Of particular interest to Piaget was the sequential process through which children come to understand such things as causality, the relationship between parts and wholes, and the relationship between change and constancy. He eventually identified three distinct phases in the normal course of cognitive development: the sensorimotor phase (roughly, ages 0–2) during which infants relate to the world largely through reflexes and acquired motor habits; the phase of "concrete operations" (roughly, ages 2–11) during which young children learn to organize experience into fairly static configurations; and the phase of "formal operations" (beginning after the age of 12) when teens gradually learn to construct hypothetical models of reality that allow them to consider and compare ideas and thereby achieve a measure of mental control or direction over their lives. Subsequent researchers have challenged Piaget's argument concerning the universality of these phases and his relative neglect of the role that environmental conditions have upon the way that children learn to construct their reality. These limitations noted, Piaget's essential paradigms have nonetheless generated the bulk of what we know today about cognitive development and thus provide a helpful context for understanding how the emotional experience of wonder contributes to acquisition of specific kinds of cognitive skills.

Piaget studied the way that children tried to solve various problems that arose while interacting with their natural and social environments. Each new problem disrupted the equilibrium that had previously existed between children and their world, thereby motivating them to acquire new cognitive understandings that would once again allow them to interact successfully with their surroundings. Piaget was thus interpreting cognitive development as a form of biological adaptation. He found it useful to explain this ongoing process of adaptation by drawing attention to the two alternating ways that we relate to our world: assimilation and

---

20. There are many fine introductions to the work of Jean Piaget, including Evans, *Jean Piaget*, or Elkind and Flavell, *Studies in Cognitive Development*. In celebration of the centennial anniversary of Jean Piaget's birth, *Psychological Science* published a collection of articles assessing his legacy to the field of cognitive psychology. See *Psychological Science* 7 (1996) 191–225.

accommodation. Assimilation represents our efforts to incorporate new experiences into the existing stock of ideas with which we fashion our goal-seeking behavior. When new experience can't be assimilated into existing cognitive schemata, accommodation occurs. Accommodation refers to changes the individual makes to adjust to the environment. It signifies the way we modify our previous cognitive structures to include those new features of the environment learned through new or unexpected perceptions.

New experience often disturbs the equilibrium that formerly existed between a child's cognitive structures and the surrounding world. Cognitive development occurs as persons struggle to resolve this disequilibrium through some combination of assimilation or accommodation. The emotions of surprise, curiosity, and wonder are therefore critical to the overall course of cognitive development. All three emotions originate as reactions to unexpected events, mobilizing efforts to change cognitive structures in ways that will ensure our overall well-being. Surprise is the most general of these "orienting responses" and may easily combine with curiosity or wonder. William Charlesworth points out that Piaget's entire model of cognitive development hinges around the central role played by the emotion of surprise. Charlesworth explains that the emotion of surprise is a complex orienting response that has an "instigatory effect on attentional and curiosity behaviors" needed if unexpected "stimuli are to become part of and help reshape existing cognitive schemata."[21]

Surprise reactions have a general arousal effect. Surprise mobilizes selective attention to the environment and thereby alters our manner of attending to, and processing, sensory information. The emotion of surprise thereby ensures that the organism behaves in such a way as to produce new knowledge about problematic properties of the environment. Among other things, surprise instigates the process whereby we grow beyond concrete thought and become capable of more abstract, fully operational thought: "Under normal environmental conditions surprise reaction and subsequent attentional and curiosity behaviors are very hard to suppress, and for this reason they seem to be good candidates for the mechanisms that insure that most individuals make the progression from sensorimotor intelligence to formal thought."[22]

Piaget was also aware that curiosity, like surprise, motivates cognitive growth. He frequently observed how curiosity propels children to interact

---

21. Charlesworth, "Surprise in Cognitive Development."
22. Ibid., 308.

proactively with their environment. Piaget often used the metaphor of "little scientists" to capture the way that curiosity drives children to investigate and create in the context of their interactions with the world. His point was that curiosity is rewarding in its own right. Curiosity draws children into sustained rapport with their environment. Curiosity motivates children not just to register experience passively, but to organize and interpret such experience. Of special significance is the fact that curiosity motivates sustained investigation of the relationship between ideas and experience. Curiosity therefore helps individuals refine their conceptions of the world to correspond more closely with the actual facts of experience.

Piaget's research focused primarily upon the developmental acquisition of domain-specific knowledge rather than the ability to think in ways that stretch beyond domains. Thus Piaget, and cognitive psychologists in general, extol the role of curiosity in fostering the assimilation of environmental patterns into our working stock of behavioral strategies, but inadvertently denigrate cognitive activities that seek to make connections between different kinds of things or to put things together in higher-order ways.[23] And these, of course, are the cognitive activities most directly stimulated by wonder. Fortunately, the total context of Piaget's work provide conceptual tools for understanding the developmental link between the emotion of wonder and our capacity for higher-order thought. In his *Language and Thought of the Child*, Piaget noted that the emergence of "why" questions in early childhood is linked with a capacity to think about the existence of an imperceptible reality behind the apparent perceptible world. This observation draws attention to the fact that children are naturally curious about the purposes, intentionality, or teleology of things. Children have a natural tendency to infer the existence of a reality that in some way lies beyond or behind observed reality—and it is this more general sense of reality that enables them to unite objects together or to interpret their purpose or meaning.

This is an important observation. Children are motivated not only to understand local causal mechanisms, but also to understand them in terms of some broader or larger context of meaning. This begins fairly early in childhood when children ponder time before they were born, what life was like in the age of dinosaurs, or what life will be like when they grow up.[24] All such cognitive operations require the construction of

---

23. See the excellent discussion of Piaget and "the world of possibilities" in Harris, "Children's Metaphysical Thinking."

24. See Johnson, "Putting Different Things Together."

larger contexts based upon non-actual, fictional, and meta-physical possibilities of the past, present, or future. This process extends much further in late childhood and early adolescence when we first observe the movement from what Piaget labeled "concrete operations" to "formal operational thought." Formal operations depend upon the adolescent's ability to entertain abstract, possible constructions of reality that then guide hypothetico-deductive reasoning whereby multiple strategies can be entertained and compared. Thus, as Piaget notes, the adolescent differs from the child by becoming "an individual who thinks beyond the present and forms theories about everything, delighting especially in considerations of that which is not."[25] The highest levels of reasoning require the construction of a hypothetical model of existence, a structured whole that can be used to assess the meaning or value of the observed particulars of existence. As Piaget notes, at this important stage "reality becomes secondary to possibility."[26] The existence of higher-order conceptions of reality frees us from sheer necessity and brute survival to consider what our existential and ethical response to life might optimally be.

The point here is that just as curiosity propels children to sustain their inquiries into the workings of physical reality, wonder is a prime ingredient in the emergence of higher-order conceptions of existence. Beginning in childhood, wonder disrupts cognitive equilibrium and prompts us to accommodate to the most general order of thinking possible—an order from which we might contemplate the intrinsic cause or intentionality of things. At least potentially, neither children nor adults have any problem distinguishing between the actual and the possible. The difficulty lies instead in discerning the boundaries of the possible.[27] We lack means of empirically testing our conceptions of the possible. For this reason we typically rely on our own sense of plausibility and, of course, upon the mythic and theological traditions of our community. Beginning with Piaget, developmental psychologists have implicitly denigrated such cognitive processes owing to their frequent connection with theological and mythic thought that strike researchers as forms of prelogical thinking.[28] Developmental psychologists have thus implicitly favored cognitive

25. Piaget, *Psychology of Intelligence*, 148.

26. Piaget, cited in Maier, *Three Theories*, 149.

27. See the excellent discussion of this issue in Johnson, "Putting Different Things Together."

28. This unfortunate slighting of the role of wonder in stimulating metaphysical thought is especially curious given the larger context of Piaget's life and thought. Piaget's godfather introduced the young Piaget to Bergson's descriptions of "creative

processes associated with assimilation (which can be empirically tested in our experience) to those associated with accommodation (which are not always susceptible to such empirical testing).[29]

This brief foray into studies of cognitive development illuminates the fact that cognitive growth is defined by much more than the acquisition of skills for manipulating our external environment. From childhood on, humans are also curious in their own right, eager to accommodate to features of the environment that arouse their interest and that disclose something that strikes them as intensely powerful, real, true, or beautiful.[30] That is, we often find ourselves moved by a state of wonder to approach and make contact with the surrounding world. Moreover we find pleasure or intrinsic reward in uncovering relatedness not just to discrete objects but to something more, some greater whole that connects and imparts meaning to otherwise separate objects. Wonder elicits sustained accommodation

---

evolution" and "*the élan vital*" thereby opening up the budding scientist's sense of wonder. The experience, he recounted, was "a moment of enthusiasm close to ecstatic joy." He was "seized by the demon of reflection" the very moment he entertained the radical and previously unexpected possibility that God can be identified with the whole of life. Piaget now had an experiential template for envisioning the whole of life as a dialectical movement toward some "supreme" or "ideal" reality that in some way lies beyond our observed reality. Thus, in his autobiography, Piaget would claim life has an innate tendency to seek out "the ultimate order of the universe." Although Piaget obviously didn't engage in metaphysics in any traditional sense, the personal meaning or purpose of his life work flowed from the wonder generated by his perception of something intensely powerful, real, and beautiful about the movement of life. See Vidal, *Piaget Before Piaget*.

29. Robert Kegan, a self-professed follower of Piaget, warns that we must be careful to correct for the tendency of Piagetians to be principally concerned "about *cognition*, to the neglect of *emotion*; the *individual*, to the neglect of the *social*; the *epistemological*, to the neglect of the *ontological* (or concept, to the neglect of being); *stages of meaning-constitution*, to the neglect of *meaning-constitutive process*." See Kegan, "Religious Dimensions," 406.

30. See the discussion of perception and creativity in Schachtel, *Metamorphosis*. Schachtel, a psychoanalyst and student of child psychology, argues that psychologists have devoted far too much attention to the child's acquisition of autocentric perception, i.e., perception that guides utilitarian manipulation of distinct objects in the environment, and not enough to the acquisition of allocentric perception, i.e., perception that goes beyond utilitarian interest and perceives an object "not as isolated from the rest of life but as containing in it the *mysterium tremendum* of life, of being ... the relatedness to a particular, very concrete object in fully allocentric perception is also always a relatedness to something more than just an isolated, separate, single object" (83). He adds, "the main motivation in this development toward allocentric perception is not coercion by reality ... [but] rather an insatiable curiosity and wish to approach and make contact with the surrounding world in a thousand different ways, and the pleasure in these contacts" (147).

to the widest possible range of human experience even as it triggers the construction of cognitive categories that make it possible to seek what Aristotle described as "final" rather than "efficient" or "material" causes that affect our well-being.

It is important, too, to note how an emotion such as wonder strengthens our capacity for moral conduct. First, it does so by making it possible to envision general orders of existence in reference to which we might make moral judgments. Second, wonder elicits our prolonged engagement with life. By imbuing life with an alluring luster, wonder sustains our desire to connect with the surrounding world. For this reason the experience of wonder often leads to forms of empathy and selfless concern quite different than would arise in a life shaped solely by the active will. Ethical theorist Martha Nussbaum argues that wonder is the emotion that most clearly enables humans to move beyond self-interest to recognize and respond to others in their own right. Wonder, she writes, is the emotion that responds "to the pull of the object, and one might say that in it the subject is maximally aware of the value of the object, and only minimally aware, if at all, of its relationship to her own plans. That is why it is likely to issue in contemplation, rather than in any other sort of action toward the object."[31]

Insofar as persons remain bound by ego-centered perspectives of the world, their ethical orientation is largely eudaemonistic (i.e., geared toward personal well-being as regulated by rational calculations of self-interest). Yet, "wonder, as non-eudaemonisitc as an emotion can be, helps move distant objects within the circle of a person's scheme of ends . . . seeing others as part of one's own circle of concern."[32] Nussbaum thus contends that no emotion matches wonder in its capacity to evoke true empathy or compassion. The very existence of living beings that appear to us as an ultimate limit to our own egoism awakens wonder at the way in which others embody the ultimate source of all life and vitality. As Nussbaum observes, "wonder at the complex living thing itself" is what mobilizes our compassion and empathy. Wonder redraws our world of concern, establishing true mutuality with a wider sphere of life.

Wonder as a Spiritual Experience

It would thus appear that among the prototypical characteristics of wonder are enlarging our field of perception, motivating accommodation to

31. Nussbaum, *Upheavals*, 54.
32. Ibid., 55.

a wider reality, widening our world of concern or empathy, broadening our cognitive capacity, and building higher-order patterns of thought conducive to philosophical and religious reflection. These characteristics are, moreover, simultaneously among the foremost qualities we typically associate with the concept of human spirituality. The very word *spirituality* comes from the Latin root *spiritus*, or breath. To be spiritual, then, is to be filled with the breath of life—to feel especially close or drawn to the putative source of all that is noble or true in life. The experience of wonder is first and foremost an experience linked with approach and affiliation rather than avoidance. Wonder motivates a quest for increased connection with the presumed source of unexpected displays of life, beauty, or truth. Wonder is thus somewhat rare among the emotions in its functional capacity to motivate persons to venture outward into increased rapport with the environment. Highly regarded psychologists Carroll Izard and Brian Ackerman suggest that wonder is part of a family of emotions that includes joy and interest. They further suggest that wonder, because it seems to be a blend of joy and interest, motivates exploration and learning, guaranteeing a person's ongoing engagement with the surrounding environment. By linking wonder with joy and interest, they draw our attention to how wonder "can sustain long-term constructive or creative endeavors."[33]

A second reason why wonder might be characterized as a spiritual emotion is that it so readily awakens our mental capacity for abstract, higher-order thought. Wonder prompts us to contemplate what might be somehow behind, above, or beyond observed phenomena. Although such higher-order connections rarely contribute to our immediate physical survival, they are indispensable to humanity's chances for obtaining other kinds of satisfaction and fulfillment. Relevant here is the work of Howard Gardner, who has written extensively on the topic of human intelligence. Gardner has proposed that among the many forms of intelligence humans possess is a unique kind of mental ability we might call "spiritual intelligence." Gardner defines spiritual intelligence in terms of our varying capacities to engage "cosmic issues": Who are we? Where did the universe come from? Why do we exist? What is the meaning of love, of life, of death? Spiritual intelligence might thus be defined as "the capacity to locate oneself with respect to the furthest reaches of the cosmos."[34] Wonder, it seems, is an emotional experience particularly capable of fostering this distinctively spiritual mode of thought.

33. Izard and Ackerman, "Discrete Emotions," 257.
34. Gardner, *Intelligence Reframed*, 60.

A third prototypical characteristic of wonder that imbues experience with a spiritual quality is that it temporarily suspends utilitarian striving. Wonder renders us relatively passive and receptive, frequently giving rise to the sensation that we participate in a more general order of life. Psychologists Richard and Bernice Lazarus drew attention to this characteristic of wonder by noting that it often invokes mystery and produces both trust and a sense of belonging. Wonder, they observe, is frequently stimulated by sights of natural beauty or by the sudden recognition that life is a "gift." The sensation of wonder is experienced as intrinsically enjoyable. For this reason they suggest that wonder "can be likened to religious experience." Conceding that wonder is different from most of the emotions typically described in scientific literature, they conclude that it is "an emotional reaction that remains at the frontier of our understanding of the mind."[35]

Assessing Wonder-Driven Religiosity

Exploring the biological and psychological substrates of wonder enriches our understanding of how and why this experience exhibits elements that produce a broadly spiritual approach to life. The greatest promise of an interdisciplinary study of wonder, however, is that it might not only help us to explain wonder, but also to assess its value. This final step of academic inquiry, assessing the value of particular kinds of experience, requires a very different kind of investigation than the natural and social sciences alone can provide. Human beings have a wide range of needs and interests, many of which are fairly independent of measures of biological fitness (which comes down to the ability to produce viable offspring). The failure to recognize this is why someone as astute as Richard Dawkins mistakenly concludes that wonder has value only when harnessed to scientific rationality (in Dawkins's words, "humans have an appetite for wonder . . . which real science ought to be feeding").[36]

The humanities are especially sensitive to the many needs and interests that humans bring to experience. The human brain is not a passive organ. It generates a host of needs and interests that are, in essence, brain-born rather than directly connected with our biological fitness. These, too, must be accounted for in any interdisciplinary explanation or assessment of wonder. For this reason humanistic disciplines are necessarily at the

---

35. Lazarus and Lazarus, *Passion and Reason*, 129.
36. Dawkins, *Unweaving the Rainbow*, 114.

top of the multidisciplinary hierarchy we must use to assess the value of wonder to humanity's overall well-being.

Perhaps the most inclusive framework for evaluating deeply nuanced experiences appears in William James's classic text, *The Varieties of Religious Experience*. The foundations of James's analysis rest in his training both in biology and functional psychology. Yet James recognized that the human brain is not just an organ that passively reacts to sensory information. The brain actively reconstructs its images of the world in ways that are likely to satisfy a host of brain-born needs and interests including what James described as "the social affections, all the various forms of play, the thrilling intimations of art, the delights of philosophic contemplation, the rest of religious emotion, the joy of moral self-approbation, [and] the charm of fancy and wit."[37] Implicit in James's remarks is the observation that the human brain does not simply respond to a world that is already "out there." It actively fashions images of the world that might remake the world in ways that will better satisfy an ever-wider range of our biological and non-biological needs. Assessments of human thought or experience, then, must not only take into consideration our personal biological survival, but also the effect of thoughts and experiences on the satisfaction of a wide range of needs for ourselves and for the wider communities we inhabit. When James assessed religious experiences, he did so on what I earlier referred to as an interpretive hierarchy that rests on insights about the human organism garnered from the biological and social sciences but widens its functional/pragmatic analyses to integrate perspectives about what constitutes distinctively human modes of functioning (thus drawing on such fields as phenomenology, hermeneutics, and—most importantly—philosophical ethics).

James succinctly captured his psychological functionalism and philosophical pragmatism when he suggested that we evaluate subtle experiences such as wonder by relying "on our own immediate feeling primarily; and secondarily on what we can ascertain of their experiential relations to our moral needs and to the rest of what we hold as true. *Immediate luminousness*, in short, *philosophical reasonableness*, and *moral helpfulness* are the only available criteria."[38] Taken together, these pragmatic criteria

---

37. James, "Remarks," 52–53.

38. James, *Varieties*, 51. James, of course, was trained in the biological sciences and brought his Darwinian framework to his study of psychology. James's psychology was functionalist in nature, interpreting the brain in terms of the functions it performs in guiding an organism's adaptive behavior. James's principal philosophical program—pragmatism—was built squarely on his functionalist biological and psychological

permit us to gauge the extent to which the sensibilities elicited by wonder enhance—or constrain—humanity's pursuit of the widest possible range of objective and subjective satisfactions.

That wonder, if even for the briefest duration of time, ushers in "immediate luminousness" is alone warrant for considering it among humanity's most profound emotions. Its value to human life can be justified on this criterion alone much as we would justify the immediate subjective delight of responses to music or art. Experiences of wonder arrest our active will. They make possible the quiet contemplation of a grander scheme of life that strikes us as responsible for life's beauty, order, and vitality. Wonder thereby evokes the subjective sense that we have established a harmonious relationship with the widest possible range of human experience. Wonder is thus accompanied by joy and by feelings of expansiveness. Our lives seem to open up to new possibilities. Experiences of wonder prompt sensations of intimate continuity with sources of beauty, order, and vitality unexpected in a purely rational approach to life. All of this makes for experiences of "immediate luminousness." There can be no question but that they have an immediate subjective feel that strikes us as rewarding in its own right without further need for outside validation.

What further justifies the "immediate luminousness" of experiences of wonder is their ability to make possible certain existential orientations to life that we would otherwise go without. In *Experience and God*, theologian John E. Smith argues that distinctively religious orientations to life arise in those rare moments that "occasion wonder." Smith observes that most of our life is "profane." By "profane" Smith means the taken-for-granted aspects of everyday life. Profane existence is ordinary; because it is ordinary, it fails to evoke consideration of the more-than-ordinary horizons of life that might reveal to us the meaning or purpose of existence. Smith contends that we have an enduring desire to experience, even if only momentarily, an utterly different order of existence that somehow stands beyond the profane, an order of existence that is best termed the sacred or the holy. Smith explains that "the daily round of events is ordinary enough and gives no occasion for wonder or special concern. In the ordinary events there is no question of judgment on life as a whole . . . [they] harbor no mystery, nor call forth the sense that beyond and beneath our life is a holy ground."[39]

---

understandings of the human organism.

39. Smith, *Experience and God*, 60.

Practices of Wonder

Smith's point is that experiences that "give occasion for wonder" provide glimpses of the sacred not available to those less influenced by this emotional response. Wonder-filled experiences take us beyond ordinary events to consider judgments on life as a whole. They harbor mystery, calling forth a sense of what is beyond or beneath ordinary experience. Erich Fromm made a very similar point when he observed that

> One aspect of religious experience is the *wondering*, the marveling, the becoming aware of life and of one's own existence, and of the puzzling problem of one's relatedness to the world . . . Socrates' statement that *wonder is the beginning of all wisdom* is true not only for wisdom but for the *religious experience*. One who has never been bewildered, who has never looked upon life and his own existence as phenomena which require answers and yet, paradoxically, for which the only answers are new questions, can hardly understand what religious experience is.[40]

The second pragmatic criterion, philosophical reasonableness, provides a more complex perspective on wonder-driven orientations to life. Most biological and psychological researchers equate wonder-driven cognition with mistaken notions about cause and effect. Richard Dawkins speaks for many scientifically minded persons when he argues that "real science" ought to be feeding our appetite for wonder, not religion. Dawkins and other champions of the scientific method typically characterize wonder-driven thought as a fanciful diversion from the real facts about existence. This is why many developmental psychologists assume that wonder-driven types of cognition will (and should) gradually be discarded as we make the psychological transition from childish thinking into adult rationality. Yet viewed from another perspective, wonder can be seen as one of the emotional sources of humanity's highest cognitive achievements. Cognitive development requires the construction of realms of possibility. Much of adult life requires our ability to formulate conceptions of more general orders of life in terms of which specific events or behaviors can be assigned meaning and value. Indeed, the highest conceptions of justice, dignity, and worth all require highly developed notions of a general order of existence that in some fundamental way lies "beyond" the observed parts of life. The important point here is that philosophical claims accompanying wonder must be assessed according to standards derived from enhanced accommodation to—not assimilation of—the wider environments we inhabit.

40. Fromm, *Psychoanalysis and Religion*, 94. Emphasis added.

We must acknowledge, however, that wonder-driven cognition is rife with magical qualities. From most philosophical perspectives, magical thinking is an immature and irrational cognitive orientation to the world. Magical thinking thwarts the assimilation of experience into a developing repertory of reality-based conceptions of how the world operates. Insofar as it severs objects of experience from accustomed understandings of causality, magical thinking undermines our long-term abilities to interact productively with our surrounding world. Yet cognitive psychologists have also recognized that magical thinking is potentially valuable when considered from the standpoint of enhanced accommodation to experience.[41] Magical thinking involves a blurring of the usual boundary between the "inner self" and the "external world." This allows persons to feel a basic symmetry between their inner life (i.e., thoughts and desires) and the surrounding world. Wonder, and the magical blurring of distinct boundaries it sometimes occasions, thus promotes certain mental dispositions conducive to psychological well-being: a sense of seamless continuity with the world, felt participation in a larger whole, relatedness to things of meaning, a sense of control over life, and basic trust that the universe is responsive to our needs and desires. Magical thinking therefore has some adaptive qualities. While it is not philosophically reasonable to live permanently in a world with such blurred boundaries, it is nonetheless quite reasonable to strive for a life that periodically benefits from the affiliative nature of wondrous experience.

It appears, then, that even the elements of fantasy and illusion to which wonder often leads have some element of philosophical reasonableness. But this is not to say that abiding in wonder alone is an appropriate existential response to the ultimate context of experience. Wonder, without the balancing emotion of curiosity, will eventually lead to unproductive relationships with the world. As Piaget discovered, curiosity, too, arises amidst unexpected perceptions. Curiosity, however, turns our perception and cognition toward the ever-smaller parts that make up the totality of experience. Curiosity leads to the fine-tuning and adjustment of ideas so that they better correspond with things as they are independent of our desires and wishes. It is the emotion of curiosity, not wonder, that puts us into working touch with reality and ensures the development of productive relationships with the world over the long run. Abiding in wonder alone, therefore, is never an appropriate philosophical response to

---

41. See the excellent discussion of this point in Nemeroff and Rozin, "Magical Thinking." See also Rosengren and Hickling, "Metamorphosis and Magic."

life. Without being balanced by curiosity, wonder runs the risk of leading us only to fantasy and illusion. This, of course, is so often the case with religion. When religion eschews intellectual curiosity it loses its connection with empirical facts and lived human experience. Adaptive strategies based on wonder alone are at considerable risk of steering humans away from the broadest range of experience. The basic danger of religion is that it reifies what "possibly exists." Severed from curiosity, wonder-driven religiosity runs the risk of tunnel vision.

This leads us to one last issue concerning the "philosophical reasonableness" of wonder-driven cognition. While it is true that wonder-driven thought carries considerable philosophical risk, so, too, does thought that is wholly devoid of wonder. This is particularly true of systems of thought that are overtly religious or theological in nature—yet lack any element of wonder. Wonder invests the object of experience with intrinsic value, leading us to seek a closer, more harmonious relationship to our surroundings. Wonder is thus capable of giving religious thought a leading or heuristic quality—a quality that arguably separates mature from immature forms of religious thinking. Wonder instills fascination with its object, yet recognizes that this object in some fundamental way eludes literal designation. Wonder has a tendency to ward off literalism in religious thought (as well as the authoritarianism that so often accompanies literalism). This is a particularly important point because, as Marjorie Taylor and Stephanie Carlson have found, some religious groups actively suppress the kind of cognitive openness generated by wonder.[42] Many conservative religious communities suppress nonlinear thought because it violates their clear bifurcation of the secular and sacred. The gap separating us from the sacred, they maintain, cannot be bridged from the human side—leaving us dependent upon the mediating functions performed for us through scriptural or ecclesiastical authority. Assuming that mature spirituality ought to enliven rather than deaden the human intellect, some degree of wonder is indispensable to philosophically reasonable religious thought.

We might now turn to the connection between experiences of wonder and our third pragmatic criterion, their relationship to our moral needs. By "moral needs" James actually had in mind the whole complex of considerations necessary to ensure the largest possible satisfaction of needs over time and through community. We might, however, narrow this consideration to the question how a highly subjective experience influences our overall ethical sensibilities. Wonder, like joy and interest, is

42. Taylor and Carlson, "Children's Fantasy Behavior."

characterized by its rare ability to elicit prolonged engagement with life. Experiences of wonder succeed in motivating creative and constructive approaches to life by imbuing the surrounding world with an alluring luster. They enable us to view the world as it exists independently of our own immediate needs, and they thereby foster empathy and compassion. It is true that wonder, *per se*, is likely to issue in contemplation rather than immediate action. Yet this is not to suggest that wonder leads to passivity or an evasion of moral responsibility. As Martha Nussbaum alerted us, wonder responds to the pull of the surrounding world. It induces modes of cognition in which "the subject is maximally aware of the object, and only minimally aware, if at all, of its relationship to her own plans."[43]

A concluding observation about experiences of wonder is that they are principal sources of what historians variously call nature religion or aesthetic spirituality. They repeatedly give rise to an enduring sensibility for the sacredness of nature—a sensibility that is mystical, and inculcates a feeling for the universe which is almost pantheistic. What is more, when assessed for its overall functional value in human existence, this wonder-driven sensibility seems to comport well with pragmatic criteria for healthy and responsible living. Insofar as all cognition is guided by one or another emotional response toward life, it would seem that wonder would be among the principal elements of any normatively conceived philosophical outlook.

43. Nussbaum, *Upheavals*, 54.

Bibliography

Atran, Scott. *In Gods We Trust: The Evolutionary Landscape of Religion*. New York: Oxford University Press, 2002.

Ben-Ze'ev, Aaron. *The Subtlety of Emotions*. Cambridge: MIT Press, 2000.

Charlesworth, William. "The Role of Surprise in Cognitive Development." In *Studies in Cognitive Development*, edited by David Elkind and John Flavell, 257–314. New York: Oxford University Press, 1969.

Clark, Candace. "Emotions and the Micropolitics of Everyday Life." In *Research Agendas in the Sociology of Emotions*, edited by Theodore D. Kemper, 305–34. Albany: State University of New York Press, 1990.

Cosmides, Leda, and John Tooby. "Evolutionary Psychology and the Emotions." In *Handbook of Emotions*, edited by Michael Lewis and Jeannette Haviland-Jones, 91–115. 2nd ed. New York: Guilford, 2000.

Davidson, Richard, et al., editors. *Handbook of Affective Sciences*. New York: Oxford University Press, 2003.

Dawkins, Richard. *Unweaving the Rainbow: Science, Delusion and the Appetite for Wonder*. New York: Houghton Mifflin, 1998.

Elkind, David, and John Flavell, editors. *Studies in Cognitive Development: Essays in Honor of Jean Piaget*. New York: Oxford University Press, 1969.

Evans, Richard. *Jean Piaget: The Man and His Ideas*. New York: Dutton, 1973.

Fredrickson, Barbara. "What Good Are Positive Emotions?" *Review of General Psychology* 2 (1998) 300–19.

Fromm, Erich. *Psychoanalysis and Religion*. New Haven: Yale University Press, 1950.

Fuller, Robert. *Spirituality in the Flesh: Bodily Sources of Religious Experience*. New York: Oxford University Press, 2008.

———. *Wonder: From Emotion to Spirituality*. Chapel Hill: University of North Carolina Press, 2006.

Gardner, Howard. *Intelligence Reframed*. New York: Basic Books, 1999.

Haidt, Jonathan. "The Moral Emotions." In *Handbook of Affective Sciences*, edited by Richard Davidson, 852–70. New York: Oxford University Press, 2003.

Harris, Paul. "On Not Falling Down to Earth: Children's Metaphysical Thinking." In *Imagining the Impossible: Magical, Scientific, and Religious Thinking in Children*, edited by Karl Rosengren, et al., 157–78. Cambridge: Cambridge University Press, 2000.

Izard, Carroll. *Human Emotions*. New York: Plenum, 1977.

Izard, Carroll, and Brian Ackerman. "Motivational, Organizational, and Regulatory Functions of Discrete Emotions." In *Handbook of Emotions*, edited by Michael Lewis and Jeannette Haviland-Ellis, 253–64. 2nd ed. New York: Guilford, 2000.

James, William. "Remarks on Spencer's Definition of Mind as Correspondence." In *Collected Essays and Reviews*, edited by Ralph Barton Perry, 41–64. New York: Longmans, Green, 1911.

———. *The Varieties of Religious Experience*. Cambridge: Harvard University Press, 1985.

Johnson, Carl. "Putting Different Things Together: The Development of Metaphysical Thinking." In *Imagining the Impossible: Magical, Scientific, and Religious Thinking in Children*, edited by Karl Rosengren et al., 179–211. Cambridge: Cambridge University Press, 2000.

Kegan, Robert. "There the Dance Is: Religious Dimensions of a Developmental Framework." In *Toward Moral and Religious Maturity*, edited by James W. Fowler et al., 403–40. Morristown, NJ: Silver Burdett, 1980.

Keltner, Dacher, and Jonathan Haidt. "Approaching Awe, a Moral, Spiritual, and Aesthetic Emotion." *Cognition and Emotion* 17 (2003) 297–314.

———. "Social Functions of Emotions at Four Levels of Analysis." *Cognition and Emotion* 13 (1999) 505–21.

Lahn, B., et al. "Accelerated Evolution of Nervous System Genes in the Origin of Homo Sapiens." *Cell* 119 (2004) 1027–40.

Lazarus, Richard, and Bernice Lazarus. *Passion and Reason: Making Sense of Emotions*. New York: Oxford University Press, 1994.

LeDoux, Joseph. *The Emotional Brain: The Mysterious Underpinning of Emotional Life*. New York: Simon & Schuster, 1996.

Lewis, Michael, and Jeannette Haviland-Jones, editors. *Handbook of Emotions*. 2nd ed. New York: Guilford, 2000.

Maier, Henry. *Three Theories of Child Development*. New York: Harper & Row, 1969.

Nemeroff, Carol, and Paul Rozin. "The Makings of the Magical Mind: The Nature and Function of Sympathetic Magical Thinking." In *Imagining the Impossible: Magical, Scientific, and Religious Thinking in Children*, edited by Karl Rosengren et al., 1–34. Cambridge: Cambridge University Press, 2000.

Nussbaum, Martha. *Upheavals of Thought: The Intelligence of Emotions*. Cambridge: Cambridge University Press, 2001.

Piaget, Jean. *The Psychology of Intelligence*. London: Routledge & Kegan Paul, 1950.

Plutchik, Robert. "The Circumplex as a General Model of the Structures of Emotion and Personality." In *Circumplex Models of Personality and Emotions*, edited by Robert Plutchik and Hope Conte, 17–46. Washington, DC: American Psychological Association, 1997.

———. *Emotions and Life: Perspectives from Psychology, Biology, and Evolution*. Washington, DC: American Psychological Association, 2003.

Rosengren, Karl, and Anne Hickling. "Metamorphosis and Magic: The Development of Children's Thinking about Possible Events and Plausible Mechanisms." In *Imagining the Impossible: Magical, Scientific, and Religious Thinking in Children*, edited by Karl Rosengren et al., 75–98. Cambridge: Cambridge University Press, 2000.

Schachtel, Ernest. *Metamorphosis: On the Development of Affect, Perception, Attention, and Memory*. New York: Basic Books, 1959.

Shiota, Michelle, et al. "The Nature of Awe: Elicitors, Appraisals, and Effects on Self-Concept." *Cognition and Emotion* 21 (2007) 944–63.

Slingerland, Edward. *What Science Offers the Humanities: Integrating Body and Culture*. New York: Cambridge University Press, 2008.

Smith, John E. *Experience and God*. New York: Oxford University Press, 1998.

Taylor, Marjorie, and Stephanie Carlson. "The Influence of Religious Beliefs on Parental Attitudes about Children's Fantasy Behavior." In *Imagining the Impossible: Magical, Scientific, and Religious Thinking in Children*, edited by Karl Rosengren et al., 247–68. Cambridge: Cambridge University Press, 2000.

Tremlin, Todd. *Minds and Gods: The Cognitive Foundations of Religion*. New York: Oxford University Press, 2006.

Vidal, Fernando. *Piaget Before Piaget*. Cambridge: Harvard University Press, 1994.

3

Wonder and the Beginning of Philosophy in Plato

SYLVANA CHRYSAKOPOULOU

> So the seer declared, untroubled as he bore his shield all of bronze.
> No device was on its round, however;
> his wish is not the appearance of prowess but its reality,
> for he crops the deep furrow from which good counsel grows.[1]

---

1. Aeschylus, *Seven against Thebes*, 590–94 (trans. Collard). In these verses, the opposition between *phainesthai* (appearance) and *einai* (true being) that permeates Plato's reformulation of the notion of *thauma* echoes to a certain extent the account of being expounded by the goddess in the Parmenidean poem. On the possibility of a Parmenidean influence on Aeschylus in those verses, see Rösler, *Reflexe vorsokratischen Denkens*, 16–21. See also Zeitlin, *Sign of the Shield*, 114: "The most important semiotic fact about the sixth shield is that it is blank, that it bears no message but the profound meanings of its silence." I owe the comparison of those verses to my reading of the *Theaetetus* 155c–d to Dr. Agis Marinis, who read the present chapter several times and generously offered me his judicious counsel, practical help, and encouragement throughout the process of its composition. I also owe special thanks to the editor, without whose moral support, intellectual openness, meticulous care, and immense patience, this chapter would have never seen the light. Last but not least, I thank Professor James Lesher for his last-minute illuminating observations and comparisons, which completed the picture of the present chapter. Professor Thomas Szlezák was the last reader of this chapter: I thank him deeply for the "wonderful" conversation, the insightful remarks and parallels he established with my text. All misreadings and mistakes are entirely my own.

Sylvana Chrysakopoulou—*Wonder and the Beginning of Philosophy in Plato*

No wonder that Socrates in the *Theaetetus* begins the genealogy of philosophy with "wonder"—a highly ecstatic yet profoundly disorientating state of consciousness arising when experiencing the unfamiliar as strangely familiar and vice versa, or when unexpected attraction for the unknown triggers memories of a life one has never lived. It could not have escaped Freud's attention either: the founder of psychoanalysis would much later explain the "Unheimliche"[2] along similar lines, while linking it to the "Wissenstrieb," the drive to knowledge, and the "Wissbegierde,"[3] the desire to know—regardless of how confusing and frightening the experience of self-knowledge may appear at first sight. Tracing the way from "trauma" back to *thauma* in its original Platonic sense could open up a new path not only to psychoanalysis but also to all disciplines pertaining to what we may still call the human soul. In the present chapter, we will endeavor to analyze the Platonic notion of wonder (*thauma*) following its traces throughout the Platonic dialogues, while also taking into account its pre-Platonic instances.

In the *Theaetetus*, the "aporetic" dialogue concerned with the question of knowledge, Plato sets forth the experience of *thauma* (wonder) by setting up the following scene (155c): suddenly young Theaetetus falls in a state of perplexity (*thaumazô*), his head spinning (*skotodiniô*) as a result of the realization of his profound ignorance when looking into the unresolved epistemological riddles Socrates presents him with. In fact, Theaetetus appears on the verge of mental collapse as he is confronted with the startling paradoxes inherent in the epistemological questions with which Socrates ceaselessly challenges him. Although Socrates addresses Theaetetus as "an experienced fellow in such matters," the youth admits to his profound ignorance with a sense of bewilderment: *Thaumazô* . . .

Before proceeding further, it is worth going back to the first use of the term *thauma* in the *Theaetetus*: in fact, this term is used twice within

---

2. Freud, *Das Unheimliche*.

3. Cf. Aristotle's *Metaphysics* (982b), where Aristotle clearly associates wonder with the desire for knowledge. "It is through wonder that men originally began, and still begin, to philosophize, wondering at first about obvious perplexities, and then . . . experiencing perplexity about greater matters . . . Now the man who is perplexed and wonders thinks himself ignorant . . . therefore, if it was to escape ignorance that men practiced philosophy, it is clear that they pursued knowledge for the sake of knowing, and not for the sake of anything useful . . ." (trans. Nightingale, "On Wandering and Wondering," 43). Although he seems to follow Plato verbatim in this respect, to the extent that he also considers wonder as the beginning of philosophizing, he in fact proceeds by demystifying the Platonic sense of wonder that we intend to bring out in this chapter.

the same context, marking the beginning and end of the description of Theaetetus by Theodorus. In the opening of the dialogue, the geometer Theodorus describes his student Theaetetus to Socrates as an ugly fellow; he does not hesitate to compare him with Socrates himself in this respect (143e): *proseoike de soi tên te simotêta kai to exô tôn ommatôn*. However, the resemblance with Socrates extends to his intellectual capacities as well: Theaetetus is described as "wonderfully bright" (*thaumastôs eu pephukota*) (144a)[4] and, as if in fulfillment of this "wonderful" nature ascribed to him earlier in the dialogue, the overwhelming feeling later defined (155d) as "wonder" raises Theaetetus above the natural human condition (*huperphuôs*). This is precisely the moment where Theaetetus himself uses for the first time the verb "to wonder" (*thaumazô*): "I wonder: By the gods, Socrates, what on earth are those things? When I sometimes really look into them (*kai eniote hôs alêthôs blepôn eis auta*), I lose my sight and I become vertiginous (*skotodiniô*)" (155c).

The opposition between light and darkness, beauty and ugliness, outer appearance and inner nature foreshadows the notion of *thauma* from the very beginning of the dialogue. Intrinsically connected to the sight of supernatural beauty well attested in the common expression *thauma idesthai*[5] ("a wonder to behold"), the notion of *thauma* in its original sense seems to be in contrast with the semantic reformulation of it that Plato introduces in the *Theaetetus* behind the curtains. Nonetheless, it is precisely this link between *thauma* and divine beauty that Plato emphasizes in his dialogues as will be further shown, though this is attended by a deliberate displacement of the sense of visual perception and visuality in general.

Nightingale, in her recent article on the philosophical significance of *thauma*, directs our attention to the first instance of wonder related to vision and more specifically to the sight of supernatural beauty. She traces this kind of wonder to "the famous scene near the end of the *Iliad*, where the aged Priam visits his enemy Achilles[6] to offer gifts for the ransoming of his dead son Hector. When Priam first arrives, Achilles and his companions 'look with wonder' at him and, though they know who he is, pronounce him to be 'godlike' (*theoeidea*).

---

4. See also 142c: *kai syggenomenos te kai dialechtheis panu agasthênai autou tên phusin*.

5. Very appropriately chosen by Prier as the title of his book dealing with the vocabulary relating to wonder in archaic literature (see bibliography).

6. Herrero, in "Priam's Catabasis," attempts to establish that Priam's journey to Achilles' quarters is depicted as a journey to Hades. This reading is compatible with the analysis of the homologous scene in the *Theaetetus* developed in this paper.

'And Dardanian Priam looked with wonder (*thaumaz'*) at Achilles / for he was like the gods to behold face-to-face. /And Achilles looked with wonder (*thaumazen*) at Dardanian Priam / as he gazed upon his visage. (24.629–32)'"[7]

What is more, Nightingale remarks that in the sight of this "godlike" (*theoeidea*) beauty, they both recognize a strange kinship between each other, which makes them feel as father to son, though they are in fact the worst of enemies: Achilles has just killed Priam's son, Hector. This sense of kinship, closely entangled with its opposite, namely a sense of strangeness, is one of the most recurrent features of *thauma* as will be further shown: similarly to Priam and Achilles, Socrates and Theaetetus resemble each other in appearance as father to son. Yet, as opposed to the godlike Homeric heroes who are immediately stunned[8] (*thaumazein*) by the divine beauty they recognize in each other, both Socrates and Theaetetus are described by a third person, Theodorus—not without a sense of reticence—as resembling each other in ugliness: "Now Socrates don't be angry with me, but he is like you in his snub nose and protruding eyes" (143e–144a). Yet, in contrast to their comic description, the same person provides an account of Theaetetus' genius, his hidden nature, so to speak, which is described as "wonderful" (*thaumastôs eu pephukota*).

The intellectual kinship between Socrates and Theaetetus is, thus, insinuated by their common looks. The expression "wonderfully bright" ascribed to Theaetetus, transposes physical beauty—conventionally associated with wonder—from the visual to the intellectual realm. Moreover, this "wonderful nature" applies not merely to his intelligence, but to his character as a whole, which is depicted in heroic terms. It is scarcely by chance that Theodorus calls Theaetetus *andreion* (144a), an epithet directly derivative from the epic-heroic tradition and yet very suitable for Theaetetus. In the first opening of the dialogue, where Euclides reports to Terpsion that Theaetetus was being transported from the camp at Corinth and had been almost killed in battle, the verb *thaumazô*, put in Euclides'

---

7. See Nightingale, "On Wandering and Wondering," 45. Cf. *Od.* 8.459: *thaumazen d' Odyssêa en ophthalmoisin horôsa* (when Nausicaa beholds Odysseus for the last time). Prier, in his attempt to provide an answer to the question, "what is the sense of the formulaic *thauma idesthai*, this abstraction of overpowering experience?" remarks that "the marvel in the presence of immortals extends to recognition in an act of direct, instinctual communication" (see *Thauma idesthai*, 86).

8. Prier, op. cit. 88: "*Thambein*: The verb *thambein* is used similarly to *theêsthai* and *thaumazein* and tends to mean something on the order of 'to express a stupefied wonder.'"

mouth occurs in the dialogue for the very first time: Euclides "wonders at Socrates'" prophetic gift, in what he said about him (Theaetetus). "He said he would surely become a notable man (*ellogimon*) if he lived" (142d).

The portrait of Theaetetus as depicted in the dialogue is erected like a funerary stele in honor of a brave man, an *andreios* of Socrates' time. The dialogue itself bearing Theaetetus' name is presented as a philosophical kudos, an *egkômion* to a young philosopher marching bravely towards death. The prophetic gift that allowed Socrates to foresee Theaetetus' death, reserves to Socrates himself the same destiny. Theaetetus is expected to act as an *andreios* and to throw himself in battle, knowing that death awaits him. "It would have been much more remarkable (*thaumastoteron*) if he had not so conducted himself," Terpsion replies to Euclides. Not only does Theaetetus look like Socrates, but he also thinks and acts likewise. Euclides goes so far as to characterize Theaetetus as *kalon te kai agathon*, though he is later described by Theodorus as being far from beautiful: "I heard some people praising him highly for his conduct in the battle" (142b). In the Platonic context, the epithet *andreios* no longer describes the Homeric hero who is literally *kalos kagathos*, but virtue pure and simple associated with braveness in all respects, in battle and in the mind, a marvelously brilliant nature.[9] The true resemblance between Socrates and Theaetetus is hidden under the ugly mask of a comic figure, signaling the same tragic destiny for both heroes-protagonists of the new drama that Plato composes: philosophical dialogue.

Indeed, in the *Theaetetus* Plato systematically employs dramatic elements that allow him to move from an apparent level of description to a hidden one, perceivable by the soul rather than the eye. When "unmasking" Theaetetus from his disappointing appearance, which nevertheless arouses our sympathy—being described like a mask of ancient comedy[10]—he transposes our attention to the utmost brightness of the latter's

---

9. Cf. *Symposium* 220c–221c, where Alcibiades gives a detailed account of Socrates' unparalleled courage and stamina in the battlefield. The use of the word *thauma* that marks the end of this account twice is accompanied by the claim that Socrates resembles no man of past or present. He is a most remarkable human being, a *thauma* in the Platonic sense.

10. Cf. *Symposium* 215a–215c, where Socrates is compared by Alcibiades to Marsyas the Satyre and is said to be even more wonderful (*thaumasiôteros*) than the latter, to the extent that he exerts an irresistible influence on his interlocutors. More importantly, prior to this comparison, Alcibiades compares Socrates to the busts of ugly Silenus, also pertaining to the comic tradition. Nevertheless, those ugly statues of Silenus reveal beautiful images of gods when opened in the middle. Alcibiades comes back to the same comparison a bit later in his praise for Socrates (216e7–217a2): there

quicksilver spirit, which goes hand in hand with a calm temper, a real wonder to behold with the eye of the soul. Theodorus gives a detailed account of Theaetetus' wonderful mix by emphasizing a further antithesis, which is no longer based on the opposition between his brilliant mind and his disappointing appearance, but on the marvelous combination of an acute intelligence with a placid character:

> *Theo.* He is quick to learn, beyond almost anyone else, yet exceptionally gentle, and moreover brave beyond any other; I should not have supposed such a combination existed and I do not see it elsewhere. On the contrary, those who, like him, have quick sharp minds and quick memories, have also quick tempers; they dart off and are swept away like ships without ballast; they are (by nature) excitable, rather than courageous (*manikôteroi ê andreioteroi phuontai*) . . . But this boy advances towards learning and investigation smoothly and surely and successfully with perfect gentleness like a stream of oil that flows without a sound, so that one marvels (*thaumasai*) how he accomplishes all this at his age!— *Soc.* You bring good news! (*Eu aggelleis!*) (144a–b)

Key elements of ancient drama are at play in the setting Plato creates at the beginning of the dialogue: Theodorus' description of Theaetetus to Socrates as similar to the latter in appearance and character prepares for the scene of their mutual recognition, not to mention that Theodorus himself is likened by Plato to the messenger bringing good news to Socrates. The use of the word *thauma* at the beginning and at the end of Theaetetus' description announces the scene of the latter's recognition by Socrates. When *thauma* (wonder) actually occurs in Theaetetus' soul, this is no wonder to Socrates, the receiver of the good news: the expression *eu aggelleis* indeed announces the coming of Iris, the divine messenger *par excellence*, Thaumas' daughter, according to the mythological account Plato uses within the same context. Theaetetus' portrait as drawn by Theodorus, thus, prefigures the experience of *thauma* step by step. Theaetetus' accomplishments, as presented by Theodorus, have invested the term *andreios* with a totally new sense, applying not merely to the battlefield, but to any endeavor requiring heroic courage. Indeed, Theaetetus' "marvelous" nature is fit enough to sustain the overwhelming drama of the soul

---

the adjectives *thaumaston* and *thaumasion* occur three times within the same context, describing the surprising, overwhelming effect Socrates had on the youth. Socrates never ceased to amaze Alcibiades and to take him by surprise, precisely because of the antithesis between his comic appearance and his inner godlike beauty. (I thank professor Lesher for bringing the last passage to my attention.)

Practices of Wonder

entailed by *thauma*. Theaetetus possesses not only the brightness, but also the firm character such an existential shock requires. Although the experience of wonder is described as painful to the eyes to the point of causing dizziness, it bears the spark of genius and the promise of learning, three elements which are prefigured in the description of Theaetetus' character.

As opposed to the delightful sight of stunning divine beauty described in the *Iliad*, as quoted above, the Platonic version of philosophical *thauma* is described by Theaetetus in terms of loss of sight while in a state of vertigo. At this very moment of apparent mental confusion and helplessness, described as a gradual black-out of consciousness, as a fall from above, Socrates comes to Theaetetus' rescue, because he has recognized in precisely this state the first distinctive mark of their kinship, their common "passion," namely philosophy, which begins and ends in *thauma*, as will be further explored: "For this feeling (*pathos*) of wonder (*thaumazein*) shows that you are a philosopher, since wonder is the only beginning of philosophy (*ouk allê archê philosophias*)[11] and he who said that Iris was the child of Thaumas[12] made a good genealogy"[13] (155d).

To Socrates, wonder is a "passion," a *state* to which the soul is subjected—in accordance with the meaning of *pathos* in ancient Greek.[14] Although *thauma* is described as a malady, a kind of malaise that captures the soul all of a sudden, wonder is not only welcome, but also necessary in order to begin philosophizing. Theaetetus experiences it as an overpowering, agonizing experience, which makes him feel vertiginous when looking, as it were, "from above" (*huperphuôs*)[15] into things he fails to recognize as such. In this ecstatic mental state, as if magnetized by the

---

11. See also Edwards (*De l'émerveillement*, 14–15), who introduces his study of the "marvelous" with a discussion of the *Theaetetus*.

12. Hes. *Theog.* 780.

13. Trans. Fowler.

14. Compare Heidegger's remarks in *What Is Philosophy?* "Astonishment (*Das Erstaunen*), as *pathos* is the *archê* (the beginning) of philosophy. We must understand the Greek word *archê* (beginning) in its fullest sense. It names that from which something proceeds (*Es nennt dasjenige, von woher etwas ausgeht*). But this 'from there' is not left behind in the process of going out, but the beginning rather becomes that which the verb *archein* expresses, that which governs. The pathos of astonishment thus does not simply stand at the beginning of philosophy, as, for example, the washing of his hands precedes the surgeon's operation. Astonishment carries and pervades philosophy (*Das Erstaunen trägt und durchherrscht die Philosophie*)" (81).

15. The translation of *huperphuôs* given earlier as "above the natural human condition" becomes more literal in this context, pointing to coexisting and complementary levels of meaning.

depths of ignorance, the soul feels as if it is falling into things it fails to grasp. Paradoxically, this vertiginous feeling of losing focus and ground is the only possible first ground of philosophizing, its only beginning: *ouk allê archê philosophias*. The wisdom-seeking of philo-sophy starts with an experience of *thauma* unveiling the complete ignorance of the person who seeks knowledge. Indeed, *thauma* is a starting point that is totally disorientating, so hard to sustain and to define that it causes temporary loss of one's sight. Nevertheless, the illumination that follows thanks to *thauma* is announced in the Platonic dialogue by the advent of the bearer of light *par excellence*: she is known as the first messenger of the Olympian gods and her name is synonymous with the marvelous sight of the rainbow. Iris, appearing like an *iridescent* vision through the dark mists of the soul's ignorance, is the arc, the *archê* (beginning, principle) bridging over philosophy in the quest for wisdom.

Plato thus presents the beginning of philosophizing as a divine phenomenon, a sort of epiphany, related to the sight of divine beauty, and Iris is its representative *par excellence*. Precisely for this reason the question of *archê* as the origin of philosophy is first answered by Plato in a theogonical context. In his attempt to construct the genealogy of philosophy, Socrates goes back to the first genealogical model, the one promoted by Hesiod in the *Theogony*. In this context, the birth of philosophy acquires a religious sense, which introduces the reformulation of the traditional Homeric-Hesiodic religion in a gradual manner, while *prima facie* adhering to it. If Thaumas is the father of philosophy, because his name echoes the word *thauma*, he is very conveniently mentioned by Hesiod as the father of Iris, the first messenger of the Olympian Gods.[16] According to the *Theogony*, Thaumas is the son of the first gods, the primordial Gaia and Pontus, Pontus himself having been born from Gaia by parthenogenesis. One cannot avoid the comparison between Thaumas and his brother Proteus: widely utilized by Plato as a symbol of sophistic artfulness, constantly changing colors and shapes to avoid being captured,[17] Proteus is opposed to Thau-

---

16. According to later sources (Ptolemy Hephaestion, *New History* 6 apud Photius, *Bibliotheca*, 190) Thaumas was also the father of Arke, the messenger of the Titans, whose name sounds like *archê*, the beginning. Plato in the *Theaetetus* may have been aware of this genealogical version, when etymologizing Thaumas' name as the beginning of philosophy.

17. Cf. Plato, *Euthydemus* 288b-c: "I repeat to you what I said to Cleinias just now, that you do not perceive the wonderful nature of our visitors' skill. Only they are unwilling to give us a display of it in real earnest, but treat us to jugglers' tricks in the style of Proteus the Egyptian adept. So let us take our cue from Menelaus, and not leave hold of these gentlemen till they give us a sight of their own serious business"

Practices of Wonder

mas who captures the soul of the philosopher through sudden and frontal bewilderment. Although in the *Odyssey* Proteus is the old man of the sea who symbolizes truth,[18] in the *Theaetetus* it is Thaumas who becomes the mythical father of the search for truth, not only because of the apparent etymologizing of his name, but also because Hesiod made him the father of Iris, the first divine messenger of the Olympian gods.

Iris is a recurrent figure in Platonic mythology. In the *Cratylus* (408b) she is associated with Hermes—her male counterpart[19]—through the verb *eirein*, according to which Plato etymologizes both divine names, the term *logos* revealing their essential attribute as the gods' messengers. In the myth of Er in the *Republic*, Iris is identified with the bright column (616b)[20] holding together the earth and the heavens, appearing as a marvelous vision at the end of the trip of the souls to the roots of the cosmos. Furthermore, Plato in the *Republic* makes Iris the symbol of the unfathomable visions of beauty (*theas amêchanous to kallos*) which the soul beholds before its incarnation, and which is one of the key elements that may unlock the meaning of *thauma* in the Platonic context according to the following analysis. Last but not least, Patrizia Pinotti in her relevant article[21] reads in *Eros thaumastos* of the *Symposium* (178a) another mythological version transmitted by Plato, which makes Iris the mother of Eros and which survives much later in Plutarch (*Amat.* 765f.).[22] This reading is

---

(trans. Jowett). On this passage, see McCabe, "Protean Socrates," 109–12. Cf. *Euthyphro* 15d–e (on which, see Fineberg, "Myth of Proteus," 65–70); also Plato, *Ion* 541e: "... but you are only deceiving me, and so far from displaying the subjects of your skill, you decline even to tell me what they are, for all my entreaties. You are a perfect Proteus in the way you take on every kind of shape, twisting about this way and that ..." (trans. Lamb).

18. *Odyssey* 4.384–5: *gerôn halios nêmertês, athanatos Prôteus* ...

19. While in the *Iliad* she is the only divine messenger, in the *Odyssey*, Hermes replaces her.

20. Cf. 21B32 DK (=Diels and Kranz, *Die Fragmente der Vorsokratiker*) where Xenophanes presents Iris as a purple cloud in his endeavor to demystify Homeric theology. According to Lesher (*Xenophanes*, 143–144), *thauma* was an important word for Xenophanes *not* to employ in relation to Iris, the "thauma idesthai" *par excellence* in the epic tradition.

21. Pinotti, "La meraviglia del filosofo," 44.

22. Ibid., note 15: "Dell'immagine dell'arcobaleno Plutarco ha avvertito la forte suggestione. Nel suo archivio di memoria letteraria e filosofica, l'arcobaleno visualizza mitologemi, *topoi* poetici e nuclei argomentativi. . . L'elemento della *poikilia* da un lato e il carattere enigmatico e fascinatorio dall'altro sono tratti comuni alla Sfinge e ad Iride, alla Sfinge e ad Eros, in *De amore*, fr. 176. Su questi aspetti insiste anche il passo del'*Amatorio* citato, nel quale la sapienza egizia e la guida platonica conducono, nel dialogo, al *mythos* di Eros figlio di Iride e da questo, per transizione metonimica,

compatible with the ensuing analysis which aspires to bring together the *Theaetetus*, the *Symposium* and the *Phaedrus* under the notion of *thauma*.

As the mother of Eros in the *Symposium* and the daughter of Thaumas in the *Theaetetus*, one may say that Iris becomes the symbol of philosophical Annunciation: visited by the winged daughter of Thaumas, the soul of the philosopher becomes pregnant with the divine message Iris carries in her wings. In his effort to see things from above, he feels vertiginous, as in a state of nausea. At this point, Socrates comes to his rescue in his capacity as the philosopher's midwife. Indeed, Socrates' claim in the *Theaetetus* regarding the wondrous origins of philosophy is preceded by the so-called digression of midwifery as the model *par excellence* of his method in search of wisdom.[23] In other words, if *thauma* signals the birth of philosophy, Socrates has recognized in young Theaetetus' first use of the verb *thaumazô*, further described by the verb *skotodiniô*, the first sign of philosophical childbearing:

> Soc. Yes, you are suffering the pangs of labour (*ôdineis gar*) Theaetetus, because you are not empty, but pregnant. — The. I do not know Socrates; I merely tell you what I feel (*ouk oida ô Socrates; ho mentoi pepontha legô*). (148e)

Socrates indeed uses Theaetetus' words to describe *thauma* as a *pathos*, an affect. Furthermore, the verb *skotodiniô* describes no ordinary pain, but the pangs of childbirth. To Socrates, this state of vertigo, of

---

all'arcobaleno-metafora e alla sua funzione, erotica, mnestica e riflettente, di guidare lo sguardo dalle apparenze al bello divino e meraviglioso (*thaumasion*)."

23. In this chapter my intention is not to defend the traditional interpretation, according to which Socratic midwifery is to be associated with recollection in the *Meno*. Although, according to my interpretation, the midwifery digression pertains to the recollection of divine beauty in the *Symposium* and the *Phaedrus*, this does not entail a recollection of the Platonic ideas in the metaphysical or epistemological sense of the term. On this question, see Brisson, "Socrates the Midwife," note 1. According to the traditional interpretation, Socratic midwifery has to do with recollection as described in the *Meno*, the *Phaedo* and the *Symposium*. This interpretation was questioned by M. F. Burnyeat, "Socratic Midwifery, Platonic Inspiration," 53–65. David Sedley has listed five modern interpretations in his *Midwife of Platonism*, 1–6. See also ibid, 30, in the context of a distinction between levels of discourse, and speaking of the "dramatic" level: "This Socrates—far more reminiscent of the *Apology* than of the *Phaedo*—certainly has no theory that all learning is recollection, let alone recollection of transcendent Forms. But it seems to me equally clear that, from a Platonic perspective, we are meant to recognize that this primitive Socrates is practicing a method by which he extracts, from the interlocutor's inner resources, beliefs which are already present there, if only in embryo, and some of which will when tested turn out to be true." On the same question see also Szlezák, "Socrates' voraussetzungslose maieutische Kunst."

losing one's head and one's sight, previously described in the context of midwifery as a feeling of pain (*ôdina*) is more than welcome, for it signals the beginning of childbirth in the philosophical context: Socrates gives a full description of the mental state of his associates (*emoi suggignomenôi*), their suffering (*paschousi*), being in pain (*ôdinousi*) night and day and full of troubles (*aporias*), like women in childbirth (*tauton tais tiktousais*). However, Socrates presents himself not only as the healer, but also—and this is most noteworthy—as the instigator of this suffering which leads to childbirth: "My art can arouse this pain and cause it to cease" (151a). This is precisely what Socrates does in Theaetetus' case: in full demonstration of his art, he inflicts mental pain on the youth through his battering questioning, leading to the latter's complete surrender to his masterful expertise.

"I am the son of a noble (*gennaias*) and burly midwife, Phaenarete," Socrates reveals to Theaetetus in his attempt to reassure him, when the latter first complains about his being in pain—"Phaen-aretê" aptly denoting the one who brings virtue to light (149a). In the detailed comparison between his art and the actual midwifery, Socrates introduces a fundamental difference that goes hand in hand with his lineage stemming from his mother (150b): "But my art differs in being practiced on men, not women, and in tending their souls in labor, not their bodies." This particular passage echoes verbatim the *Symposium*, where Diotima makes the same distinction between men who become pregnant in their souls, as opposed to men who are inclined to begetting children in women's bodies:

> Those who are pregnant in the body only, betake themselves to women and beget children—this is the character of their love; their offspring, as they hope, will preserve their memory and give them the blessedness and immortality which they desire in the future. But souls which are pregnant—for there certainly are men who are more creative in their souls than in their bodies—conceive that which is proper for the soul to conceive or contain. And what are these conceptions?—wisdom and virtue in general. And such creators are poets and all artists who are deserving of the name inventor. (208e–209b)

Moreover, in Pausanias' speech in the *Symposium*, Plato operates the same distinction regarding the two kinds of Eros: the one who accompanies Urania, that is to say heavenly Aphrodite, the motherless daughter of the first god, Uranus (180d), "who does not partake of female, only of male" (181b); and the common Eros, who accompanies Aphrodite

Pandêmos, that is, "common." "Common Aphrodite" is the daughter of Zeus and his female counterpart, Dione, as revealed by the etymology of her name, which derives from the genitive theme of *Zeus*, namely *Dios*:

> The Love who is the offspring of the common Aphrodite is essentially common and has no discrimination, being such as the meaner sort of men feel, and is apt to be of women as well as of youths, and is of the body rather than of the soul. Those who partake of Eros Pandêmos desire more the bodies of women to the souls . . . But the offspring of the heavenly Aphrodite is derived from a mother in whose birth the female has no part, she is from the male only; this is that love which is of youths, and the goddess being older, there is nothing of wantonness in her. Those who are inspired by this love turn to the male, and delight in him who is the more valiant and intelligent nature; any one may recognize the pure enthusiasts in the very character of their attachments. For they love not boys, but intelligent beings whose reason is beginning to be developed, much about the time at which their beards begin to grow. (181b–d)

Theaetetus is precisely of that very age in the homonymous dialogue and this is one of the primary reasons that make him so exceptional: ". . . one marvels (*thaumasai*) how he accomplishes all this at his age" (144b). Socrates, on the other hand, is old enough and wise in matters of Eros and hence able to present himself as a true adept of Heavenly Aphrodite. He exercises his maieutic art on the souls of his students, because he is in love with the conceptions they bear: "wisdom and virtue in general," as priestess Diotima puts it in the *Symposium* (209b). In spite of the fact that the process of producing knowledge, as described by Socrates, requires cooperation between the youth and himself, the relationship between them is asymmetrical. They are both seekers of wisdom, the one—Theaetetus—in his own soul and the other—Socrates—in other persons' souls. In other words, they cannot make a match after the model of sexual reproduction under the protection of Common Aphrodite, for the youth is fertile, while Socrates is sterile.

Being excluded from the process of childbearing, Socrates shares a common feature with midwives, namely sterility[24] (150c): ". . . for I have

---

24. For discussion of the meaning of Socrates's barrenness, see Sedley, *The Midwife of Platonism*, 30–35, where we find a list of what Socrates seems to know and does not seem to know. A similar list is already (2004) to be found in the *Theaetetus* chapter by Szlezák, in *Das Bild des Dialektikers*. On the same subject, see also Dorion, *Socrate*, 43–55 and Mintz, "*Chalepa ta kala*: Fine things are difficult."

Practices of Wonder

this in common with the midwives . . . I am sterile in point of wisdom." Nevertheless, this is precisely the reason why Socrates presents the midwives as the best match-makers: "They are wise in knowing what union of man and woman will produce the best possible children" (149d)—as if their wisdom compensated for their supposed sterility. They are not in a position to bear children any longer and yet thanks to their past experience they are in a position to know the best matches that will ensure the best births. In other words, they hold an impartial position, that of a wise intermediary. A reminder of his supposed sterility in the knowledge-bearing process occurs later, when Theaetetus grants Socrates the knowledge he denies possessing (157c–d):

> You forget, my friend, that I myself know nothing about such things, and claim none of them to be mine, but am incapable of bearing them and am merely acting as a midwife to you, and for that reason am uttering incantations and giving you a taste of each of the philosophical theories, until I may help to bring your own opinion to light. And when it is brought to light, I will examine it and see whether it is a mere wind-egg or a real offspring. So be brave (*tharsei*) and patient and in good and manly fashion (*andreiôs*) tell me what you think of my questions . . .

This is, indeed, a focal point in the dialogue, for it is not only indicative of Socrates' position in the teaching procedure,[25] but it is also explicative of his maieutic method, which ultimately leads to the birth of knowledge in the youth's soul. The youth cannot expect from Socrates to present him with the offspring of his knowledge in full flesh, because of his supposed sterility in this regard. Thus, Socrates cannot be personally involved in the procedure of begetting: he is neither the bearer of the fruit of knowledge, nor is he the one who will go through the labor of childbearing. This part is allocated to the youth who is pregnant with the seed of knowledge, which is nevertheless produced by Socrates' questioning. Yet Socrates pretends (Socratic irony) that he is only there to help deliver the knowledge he does not possess as the philosophical midwife.

By describing wonder (*thaumazein*) as a *pathos*, a suffering of the soul, Socrates draws a clear parallel between wonder and labor in the preceding midwifery digression. The use of the same vocabulary in both cases is demonstrative of the intrinsic connection between the two. That is to say that the reason why he welcomes this suffering with enthusiasm is his

---

25. Comparable to the position of a psychoanalyst: see Lacan, "La position de l'inconscient."

knowledge that it will ultimately lead to birth in the soul of the sufferer: "Yes, you are suffering the pangs of labor, Theaetetus, because you are not empty but pregnant" (148e). This birth cannot be guaranteed without Socrates' intervention, the intervention of someone sterile in wisdom, yet experienced in delivering it. The genealogy of philosophy that Socrates invokes emphasizes this very point, but also its purpose, namely the wondrous birth of wisdom: *Thaumas*, according to Hesiod, is the father of winged Iris, the first messenger of the Olympian gods. Like Socrates, who helps his associates achieve the birth of wisdom in their souls, yet without claiming paternity over it, Iris is the goddess who carries and delivers the gods' messages, but not the one answerable for them.

Exactly like winged Eros in the *Symposium*, the son of Poros on the one hand and Penia on the other, who is synonymous with Aporia, yet through its highlighting of the absence of Poros,[26] Iris is the divine messenger, an intermediate between (*metaxu*) gods and men, wisdom and ignorance (*sophias te kai amathias en mesôi estin*, *Symposium* 203e). Similarly to Iris and to Socrates himself in the *Theaetetus*, Eros in the *Symposium* is not a divinity in full possession of wisdom, while similarly to Thaumas, Iris' father, Eros is a passion, inspiring love for wisdom: "because wisdom is among the most beautiful of beings and love is love of beauty"—*Esti gar dê tôn kallistôn hê sophia, erôs d'estin erôs peri to kalon* (204b). Thus, Eros becomes the emblematic philosopher, the seeker of wisdom, standing between wisdom and ignorance. Once again in the *Symposium* (204b), Plato gives a mythological explanation of Eros' philosophical nature following the Hesiodic genealogical model, as is the case with *thauma* in the *Theaetetus*: "For Love (Eros) is by necessity a philosopher, and being a philosopher he is between wise and unwise, the reason being that he is born from a father who is wise and resourceful (*Poros*) and from a mother who is unwise and without resources (*Penia*)."

Hence, Eros is neither wise nor beautiful. He is rather a *lover* of beauty and wisdom, a *philo-sophos* in the primary sense of the word. He is neither a god nor a human, but an intermediary between them, a demon[27] who brings together men and women with a view to reproduction. In this respect, he resembles Socrates in his role as midwife, for "the true midwife is the only proper match-maker" (150a). What is more, Eros and Socrates

---

26. *Aporia* in the sense of bewilderment and puzzlement is synonymous with the term *thaumazein*: cf. *Symposium* 208b, where the verb *thaumazein* is used in the sense of *aporia*.

27 See Detienne, *La notion de daimon*.

have the same purpose: reproduction with a view to immortality.[28] Reproduction is thus considered to be divine, for it is the only way mortals can escape mortality. Moreover, since reproduction is divine, it is necessarily beautiful, and this is the reason why Eros is a lover of beauty, for "no birth can occur outside beauty."[29] Eros is thus the demon between mortals and immortals, inspiring the desire to men and women to give birth in beauty: *tokos en tôi kalôi* (206b), because "love is love of beauty."

Similarly to *thauma*, which is intrinsically connected to the sight of divine beauty, Eros is presented as the seeker of divine beauty *par excellence*. Yet it is noteworthy that Plato in both cases effects a switch from an exterior to an interior viewpoint, divine beauty being related to wisdom rather than physical appearance, hence the *Eros-philosophos* as the seeker of wisdom, as we just heard (204b). On the other hand, both *thauma* and *Eros* lead to reproduction either in the body or in the soul. More specifically, the *uranian* kind of Eros as opposed to the *bodily* Eros—the "common" Eros, so to speak—ultimately leads to the birth of wisdom in the soul of the one seized by it, as is the case with *thauma* in the *Theaetetus*. Thus, *thauma* can be identified with this latter kind of *Eros*, especially since both *thauma* and *Eros* are clearly described by Plato as passions of the soul related to sudden desire, pain, and loss of one's senses, literally and metaphorically, leading to a certain kind of madness (*mania*), a possession of the soul due to divine intervention.

At this point, it is worth going back to Stesichorus' recantation in the *Phaedrus* (241d–243e), which explains Eros along similar lines, namely, as a sort of madness due to divine inspiration. Once again Eros' divine origin is accounted for through its relation to the vision of divine beauty encountered by the soul. Moreover, what is notable in Stesichorus' account is that this vision comes as a revelation during the mysteries that the soul attends in its pre-incarnate state. Likewise, in the *Theaetetus*, the

---

28. Lear, "Permanent Beauty," 118: "To repeat, my suggestion is that in the *Symposium* Socrates presents and makes use of a connection between beauty and immortality. Beauty appears godlike in its relationship to time and change. In fact, its manifestation of its atemporal imperviousness to change is exactly what strikes the lover as being so wonderful about beauty."

29. Ibid., 112–14: "It is heartening to notice that every example Diotima mentions of giving birth in beauty is a case in which the lover is actually attracted by his beloved's beauty. This suggests that Socrates thinks of giving birth in beauty as a special case of the universal pursuit of happiness. And that, in turn, suggests that beauty is required not to facilitate the lover's pursuit of good, but to facilitate his *unusual* means of pursuing the good [emphasis added] . . . In any case, the emphasis in Diotima's speech is overwhelmingly on the ethical effect of beauty . . ."

experience of *thauma* precedes the youth's initiation by Socrates to the mysteries of the *kompsoteroi*[30] (the more sophisticated) as opposed to the *amousoi* (devoid of Muse): *mellô soi ta mustêria legein* (156a). Thus, what *prima facie* entails both *Eros* and *thauma* in Plato is an awakening of the soul to its pre-incarnate state of existence through a sudden remembrance of the divine vision of truth witnessed in its first initiation. Similarly to the lover seized by Eros, Theaetetus "in wonder" bears the mark of the initiate to the mysteries of the soul. Socrates, on the other hand, plays the role of the divine intermediary who will lead him back to the remembrance of those mysteries and to the rebirth of wisdom in his soul through proper initiation (*Phaedrus* 244a–d):

> Soc. Know then, fair youth, that the former discourse was the word of Phaedrus . . . And this which I am about to utter is the recantation of Stesichorus . . . and is to the following effect: 'I told a lie when I said that the beloved ought to accept the non-lover when he might have the lover, because the one is sane, and the other mad. It might be so if madness were simply an evil; but *there is also a madness which is a divine gift, and the source of the chiefest blessings granted to men . . . as the ancients testify, is madness superior to a sane mind* (sôphrosunê) *for the one is only of human, but the other of divine origin* . . .

It is striking to note the way in which Plato passes from the delightful praise of the inspired madness provoked by Eros to a rigid argumentation on the question of the soul's immortality as a proof for Eros' divine origin (245b–c): "And we, on our part, will prove . . . that the madness of love is the greatest of heaven's blessings . . . But first of all, let us view the affections and actions of the soul divine and human . . . The beginning of our proof is as follows: The soul through all her being is immortal, for that which is ever in motion is immortal; but that which moves another and is moved by another, in ceasing to move ceases also to live. Only the self-moving, never leaving self, never ceases to move, and is the fountain and beginning of motion to all that moves besides."

Plato's account of the immortality of the soul echoes to a large extent the account on "being" revealed by the goddess to Parmenides of Elea in his poem *On Nature*.[31] In this didactic poem written in epic verse, Parmenides

---

30. Cf. *Sophist* 246a–e.

31. Plato's intellectual debt to Parmenides is recognized not only in the homonymous dialogue, but also pointedly in the *Sophist*, where the Eleatic Stranger presents himself as a descendant of the Eleatic tribe (*ethnos*) beginning with Xenophanes and followed by the "father" Parmenides (242d).

employs the first person to introduce himself as the *kouros*—that is, the initiate according to mystery language[32]—who surpasses mortal barriers. Seized by his *thumos*, a Homeric term prefiguring the Platonic *thauma* to the extent that it entails an overwhelming desire which captures the mind and stretches it to its limits (28B1,1 DK: "as far as desire goes"), Parmenides begins his journey over the world. Similarly to the Platonic *thauma* which is associated with courage, *thumos* in the epic context is considered to be responsible for heroic deeds.[33] Driven by his mind's overpowering impetus, Parmenides rides the chariot led by the Sun maidens to the premises of the goddess, who reveals to him the truth about being. Likewise, Plato in the *Phaedrus* makes use of the chariot imagery to present the soul itself or rather its divine component—"the pilot of the soul," as Plato calls divine Intelligence—as the winged charioteer transporting it to the heavens, where it attends the mysteries of true being. Similarly, Parmenides is led to the premises of a goddess who resides beyond mortal access and who reveals to him the truth about being. There have been several attempts at identifying the anonymous[34] goddess with traditional Greek deities and more particularly with Persephone, the goddess of the Underworld, who welcomes the souls of the dead, hence presenting Parmenides' journey as a *katabasis* (a descent to the underworld). Such a reading would also be compatible with the myth of Er at the end of the *Republic*, where the journey of the souls is presented in a similar fashion except for the chariot imagery. On the other hand, a number of scholars consider Parmenides' journey as an ascension to the heavens rather than a descent to Hades.[35] In any case, what matters in our analysis is that, similarly to Parmenides, the souls in the *Phaedrus* perform their celestial journey in winged chariots to a *locus incertus*, situated beyond mortal access, where they are initiated to the truth of being. What is more, Plato follows the pattern of the account of being revealed to Parmenides by the goddess, in order to present his own account on the immortality of the soul as a proof for Eros' divine origin. At this point, it is worth recalling that Parmenides' praise of Eros in the *Symposium* (178a-b) plays a decisive role to the extent that it corrects

32. Burkert, "Das Proömium des Parmenides."

33. Lesher, "The Significance of "kata pant' <astê]>," 1–20.

34. Chrysakopoulou, "L'anonymité de la déesse." Professor Szlezák brought to my attention the fact that already in the *Odyssey* L, the trip to Hades by Odysseus is described as a horizontal journey, so to speak, which involves neither an ascent to the heavens, nor a descent to Hades.

35. Fraenkel, "Studies in Parmenides," 1–47; Frère, "Aurore, Eros et Ananké," 459–70.

the Hesiodic *Theogony*, by presenting Eros as the first and the oldest of all gods, abolishing thus the idea of genesis,[36] which is incompatible with the Parmenidean axiom of the exemption of being from generation and corruption (28B8, 1–3, 20–21 DK): "One path only is left for us to speak of, namely, that It is. In it are very many tokens that what is, is uncreated and indestructible . . . If it came into being, it is not; nor is it if it is going to be in the future. Thus is becoming extinguished and passing away not to be heard of."[37]

In a similar argumentative fashion, Plato ascribes to the soul most of the attributes the Parmenidean goddess confers on being (*Phaedrus* 245d): "Now, the beginning is unbegotten, for that which is begotten has a beginning; but the beginning is begotten of nothing, for if it were begotten of something, then the begotten would not come from a beginning. But if unbegotten, it must also be indestructible; for if beginning were destroyed, there could be no beginning out of anything, nor anything out of a beginning."

In conclusion, Plato makes use of the Parmenidean formulation in order to prove the soul "unbegotten" and "indestructible" and thus exempt from generation and corruption. Furthermore, similarly to Parmenides, he presents the strict rational arguments on the immortality of the soul as a revelation to the initiate. Indeed, the vivid imagery of the *kouros'* heavenly journey to the goddess's premises in Parmenides is succeeded by a strictly rational account, meant to be heard and understood by the *kouros* through his *logos*. In other words, this revelation does not entail a vision, but the teaching of a *logos*, as is the case in the *Phaedrus*, where the vision that the divine Intelligence beholds in its pre-incarnate state is not to be grasped by sight, but by *logos*. Accompanied by all other immortals, the "pilot of the soul" beholds the heaven which is above heavens (*Phaedrus* 247c–d):

> But of the heaven which is above the heavens, what earthly poet ever did or ever will sing worthily? It is such as I will describe; for I must dare to speak the truth, when truth is my theme. There abides the very *being* with which *true knowledge* is concerned; the colorless, formless, intangible essence, *visible only to mind*, the pilot of the soul. The divine intelligence . . . rejoices at beholding reality, and once more gazing upon truth, is replenished and made glad, until the revolution of the worlds

36. See Strauss and Bernardete, *The Being of the Beautiful*, 47.
37. Trans. Burnet.

> brings her round again to the same place. In the revolution she beholds ... *knowledge absolute, not in the form of generation or of relation, which men call existence, but knowledge absolute in existence absolute* ...

Likewise, the goddess in the Parmenidean poem receives the initiate, after he has completed his celestial journey, in her premises which are located above the heavens, and she addresses him in the name of truth, as is precisely the case with the account of divine intelligence in the *Phaedrus*. Similarly to the Platonic vision which the divine intelligence beholds, the account of being conferred by the Parmenidean goddess can only be perceived by the divine Intellect (*Nous*) and judged by Logos, as opposed to the human senses (28B7,2–6 DK): "... and do thou restrain thy thought from this way of inquiry. Nor let habit force thee to cast a wandering eye upon this devious track, or to turn thither thy resounding ear or thy tongue; but do thou judge the subtle refutation of their discourse (*logos*) uttered by me ..."

Put differently, "the way of truth" the Parmenidean goddess opens in the Parmenidean poem is similar in inspiration to the vision of truth that the divine intelligence beholds in the *Phaedrus*. Parmenides differentiates between the way of truth and the way of opinion (*doxa*) to which his cosmology pertains: truth does not primarily bear on the cosmos—"the heavens," in Platonic terms—but on being *per se*, which may only be perceived by the mind, not by the senses. Likewise, Plato grants divine intelligence with the vision of "heavens above heavens ... which is colourless, formless, intangible essence, visible only to mind." Such a vision "what earthly poet ever did or ever will sing worthily," unless a philosopher, as it was admittedly the case with Parmenides,[38] praised by Plato in the *Symposium* and the *Sophist*, exactly because his monistic account is opposed to the poetic chimeras of the epic poets.[39]

Indeed, according to the Stesichorus account, not all souls are philosophical. The only soul resembling that of the philosopher is the soul of the lover, for he is also a seeker of the divine beauty he beheld in the mysteries before entering his body: "...the soul which has seen most of truth shall come to the birth as a philosopher, or artist, or some

---

38. Nevertheless, the close affinity between Parmenides' and Empedocles' poems and the account of the soul in the *Phaedrus* projects them as emblematic philosopher-poets capable of relating the account of truth presented in the Stesichorus-recantation, Stesichorus also being a well-known poet who "converted" to philosophy, as proved by the end of his recantation.

39. Chrysakopoulou, "Heraclitus and Xenophanes," 75–80.

musical and loving nature; . . . only the soul of a philosopher, guileless and true, or the soul of a lover, who is not devoid of philosophy, may acquire wings; . . . And he who employs aright these memories is ever being initiated into perfect mysteries and alone becomes truly perfect" (*Phaedrus* 248c–249d). Only such souls grow wings, the wings of Eros, or Iris, which transport them back to the heavenly realm. For this reason, the lover and the philosopher seem mad to "the vulgar," as Plato calls the "uninitiated" (*Theaetetus* 155e), who are also devoid of Muse (156a), unable to remember the mysteries of being.

In the closing of his recantation, Stesichorus passes once again from the philosophical madness to the lover's madness, which corresponds to the opening theme of his praise of *Eros*. So far, the close resemblance between the two kinds of madness proves to be a recurrent topic in Plato, to the extent that both the philosopher and the lover are possessed by their sudden desire for the divine beauty they encountered in the pre-incarnate state of their soul. They both rejoice within their souls in the memory of true being as witnessed in the beatific vision of the mysteries attended before incarnation. They both suffer the same insomnias, pains and "pangs" when they are away from the source and clinging to this memory. Indeed, both in the *Theaetetus* and the *Phaedrus*, Plato employs the same terms to describe the suffering of the philosophers before the delivery of wisdom in their souls and of lovers when they find themselves in the absence of their beloved. Within the same line of thought, he describes both *thauma* and *Eros* as passions by divine instigation having similar effects on the souls of their sufferers. The healing of this suffering comes through contact with the beloved in the case of the lover and with the midwife of wisdom in the case of the philosopher. Such then is the task of the philosophers' midwife, namely to reawaken the beatific vision of true being in the soul of the beholder, a vision witnessed in its prenatal existence, in order to bring it from the painful state of obscurity into light.[40] Triggered by Eros for wisdom, the philosophical soul recovers from its amnesia of the vision of truth, rejoices in its memory, is nourished by it and gives birth to truth.

This element of pleasure and suffering, related to the passion for beauty aroused by irresistible *Eros*, which Plato emphasizes in his dialogues, is totally lacking in the Parmenidean poem, as well as in most pre-Platonic thinkers. The soul of the philosopher in Plato takes immense pleasure in beholding the beauty of truth, just as it is tortured, in its absence, by the pain of ignorance. In the *Theaetetus* and the *Phaedrus*, Eros and Socrates

---

40. On the pangs of childbirth, cf. *Phdr.* 251e–252a.

are described both as instigators and as healers of this suffering. Seduction in the name of truth and virtue[41] is the Socratic undertaking leading to pleasure in the soul of its seeker when encountering it and to suffering when losing sight of it. Like the lover who is cured at the sight of divine beauty in the visage of his lover, philosophers are cured when bringing to light the offspring of wisdom hidden in their souls, for "no birth can occur devoid of beauty" and Beauty (*Kallonê*) is the true name of the Fate present in every birth, according to Diotima's account in the *Symposium* (206b–d).[42] Likewise, in the *Phaedrus* itself, love is described in a similar fashion to *thauma* in the *Theaetetus*, namely as a sort of *mania* (madness) provoked by the recollection of divine beauty. To this effect, the recantation of Stesichorus closes as follows (249d–252b):

> Thus far I have been speaking of the fourth and last kind of madness, which is imputed to him who, when he sees the beauty of earth, is transported with the recollection of the true beauty; . . . he who loves the beautiful is called a lover because he partakes of it . . . There was a time when . . . we philosophers . . . beheld the beatific vision and were initiated into a mystery which may be truly called most blessed . . . Now he who is not newly initiated or who has become corrupted, does not easily rise out of this world to the sight of true beauty in the other; he looks only at her earthly namesake, and instead of being awed at the sight of her, he is given over to pleasure, and like a brutish beast he rushes on to enjoy and beget . . . But he whose initiation

---

41. Cf. Alcibiades' praise for Socrates in the *Symposium*, where the latter makes Alcibiades "think that his present life is not worth living (*biôton*) since there is so much of importance that he lacks (215d7–216a5) . . . So, to sum up, the experience of beauty—both the Beautiful itself and its images—is the feeling of being shaken from one's way of living, so that one feels that it is better to live in association with this beautiful thing and to alter one's whole life accordingly" (Lear, "Permanent Beauty," 114). It is also notable that in Diotima's account in the *Symposium*, the union with Beauty itself leads to the only *bios* (way of life) which is worth living (211b).

42. Trans. Bernadete, *The Being of the Beautiful*, 37, where *Kallonê* is described as a cult name for Artemis-Hecate: "This thing, pregnancy and bringing to birth, is divine, and it is immortal in the animal that is mortal. It is impossible for this to happen in the unfitting; and the ugly is unfitting with everything divine, but the beautiful is fitting. So *Kallonê* is the Moira and Eileithyia for birth" (206d). Also see Lear, "Permanent Beauty," 118: "If the interpretation I have suggested is correct, we are in a position to understand why beauty is the goddess of erotic creativity. The point is not, as Price worried, that beauty and immortality both happen to be divine attributes. The divine is beautiful because it manifests its immortal possession of the good. This is why Diotima says that beauty in all things harmonizes with the divine and is the midwife of creativity."

is recent, and who has been the spectator of many glories in the other world, is amazed when he sees anyone having a godlike face or form, which is the expression of divine beauty; . . . and the soul is oppressed at the strangeness of her condition, and is in a great strait and excitement, and in her madness can neither sleep by night nor abide in her place by day. And wherever she thinks that she will behold the beautiful one, thither in her desire she runs. And when she has seen him, and bathed herself in the waters of beauty . . . has no more pangs and pains; and this is the sweetest of all pleasures at the time . . . and is the object of his worship, and the physician who can alone assuage the greatness of his pain. And this state, my dear imaginary youth to whom I am talking, is by men called love . . .

At the end of Stesichorus' recantation, the hymn to *Eros* converges into a promise to the god of love of devotion to philosophical discourse, as if philosophy might be the only remedy for *Eros* or as if the "madness" aroused by the god could only be appeased by philosophy.[43] It is also noteworthy that, as is the case with *thauma* in the *Theaetetus*, *Eros*' *mania* is related to deprivation of sight. Stesichorus indeed concludes his incantation to the god by pleading with him not to take his sight away. He also prays to him to make him look better in the eyes of the fair, by giving him the right insight, one might say, into philosophical discourse. So far, the intrinsic relationship between *thauma* and Platonic *eros* is explained through their relation to the sight of divine beauty. This is precisely the reason why Plato chooses *thauma* in order to describe the experience of the emergence of wisdom in the soul of its seeker.

Andrea Wilson Nightingale, in her seminal article on the notion of wonder,[44] emphasizes this very point of the relationship between wonder and the sight of divinity leading to philosophical *theôria* both in Plato and in Aristotle: "wandering" related to pilgrimage and to witnessing foreign rituals in the religious sense of the term *theôria* leads to "wonder" in its philosophical sense. Although in the wake of Nightingale's thorough analysis, one cannot doubt the close connection between wonder and *theôria*, which is also the central topic of her exhaustive book on the matter,[45] our

43. Cf. Theocritus, *Idyll* 11 (*Cyclops*) 1–4: "There's no drug, Nicias, to cure desire: no/ Hot compress, powder, ointment, or suspension/ Except for song: a sweet alleviation,/ But not so easy, sometimes. You should know./ You're a doctor; and, what's more, the nine/ Muses love you, better than they love most" (trans. Svarlien).

44. Nightingale, "On Wandering and Wondering."

45. Ibid., 44: "This Aristotelian path from wonder to certainty, from *aporia* to *theôria* is, I think, clear enough. Let me turn now to a different conception of wonder,

intention in this chapter is to emphasize another crucial aspect of *thauma*: its relation to the invisible rather than to the visible in a religious context. In this respect, divine beauty becomes a metaphor for the Invisible that is seen with the eyes of the soul during initiation. Yet again, Nightingale is right to emphasize the relation between *thauma* and vision leading to *theôria* in the philosophical sense of the word and to champion Plato as the first thinker who gave a priority to vision as opposed to hearing, predominant in the pre-Platonic thinkers.[46] Nonetheless, what has been argued and will be argued further, in the closing of this chapter, is that the beauty involved in this vision is not to be grasped by sight, but solely by in-sight, in other words by *Nous*. In this respect, seeing and hearing converge in understanding, which is then again another way of rendering the notion of "hearing" in archaic literature.[47] What is more, in the language of initiation this understanding is akin to the *logos* revealed by the goddess in the Parmenidean poem as well as by Heraclitus in his *logos* and by the *Muse* in Empedocles. It is a *logos* that is heard and delivered but cannot be seen. In this respect, Plato uses the language of the mysteries, which entails, according to the etymology of the term, shutting the eyes (*mueô*) of the body—in order to open the eyes of the soul.

Thus, Socrates becomes the philosopher-seer who lost his sight, in order to gain the insight to being and bring it to light again through his "fellows" in the quest for truth. Indeed, in the midwifery digression, Socrates has already explained to the youth that he is forbidden by god[48] to produce the knowledge he brings forth (150c). It is striking to note

---

'Platonic wonder,' which occurs at the end, rather than the beginning, of the philosophic quest. This kind of wonder has its roots in the very earliest Greek texts . . ."

46. Ibid., 29: "In pre-Platonic thinkers, truth is something that is heard or spoken, not something to be seen. The philosophers who developed the 'spectator theory of knowledge' in the fourth century were thus engaging in a novel enterprise, which needed to be defined and defended. In the effort to both conceptualize and legitimize this new intellectual practice, these philosophers invoked a specific civic institution that the ancients called *theôria*. *Theôria* is generally defined as a journey or pilgrimage to a destination away from one's own city undertaken for the purpose of seeing as an eye-witness." On religious *theôria*, see also Rutherford, "Theôria and Darsan," and Elsner and Rutherford, *Pilgrimage*.

47. Note also the use of *akouein* in Heraclitus' proem (22B1 DK), where the Logos in whose name Heraclitus speaks is destined to be *heard* in the first sense of the verb, but it is not *understood*, in the second sense of it.

48. See Friedlaender, "Daimon and Eros," 33–58. The *daimonion* in Socrates has a similar function: it warns him against people or things and thus plays a foreboding role rather than an inspiring one (151a).

the way in which Plato presents Socrates as a philosophical Teiresias,[49] the blind seer who was deprived of his sight by Apollo, but could share the god's prophetic gift, for he could "see" the past, the present and the future. Furthermore, it is far from accidental that Teiresias was known as the only male figure in Greek mythology who was turned into a woman for seven years, giving birth to Manto,[50] whose name echoes the mantic art. Similarly to Teiresias, Socrates likens himself to a woman, exercising the maieutic art, which recalls the "mantic" art of Teiresias associated with Apollo, particularly since in the beginning of the dialogue the first mention of Socrates underlines his prophetic gift (142c).

Indeed, Socrates likens himself to his mother, the midwife, at the time when she could no longer be a mother (149b–c): "No one of them attends other women while she is still capable of conceiving and bearing, but only those who have become too old to bear . . . They say the cause of this is Artemis, because she, a childless goddess, has had childbirth allotted to her as her special province." Artemis is thus the protector of the maieutic art *"timôsa tên autês homoiotêta,"* similarly to her brother Apollo, who is the protector of the mantic art. Like Teiresias, who is deprived by god of his sight but who can see the truth,[51] Socrates claims that "the god compels me to act as midwife, but he never allowed me to bring forth. I am then, not at all a wise person myself, nor have I any wise invention, the offspring born of my own soul; but those who associate with me, although at first they seem very ignorant, yet, as our acquaintance advances, all of them to whom god is gracious make wonderful (*thaumaston*) progress . . . but the delivery is due to the god and me (*tês mentoi maieias o theos te kai egô aitios*)" (150c–d).

Like blind Teiresias, barren Socrates presents himself as the god's instrument, while likening himself to a woman, leading to the birth of wisdom in his students' souls, which begins with the experience of intellectual pregnancy, the experience of *thauma*. By calling Theaetetus *thaumasie* (151c)[52] in a rather playful tone, Socrates anticipates the *thauma* of the birth of wisdom in his soul. However, Socrates does not associate with any youth who pretends to bear the seed of wisdom. Socrates' *daimonion*,

---

49. See *Eustath. Schol.* κ 494, p. 1665, v. 40: *para to eirein etumologeitai* . . .: it is notable that this explication of Teiresias' name echoes Plato's etymologizing of Iris' name in the *Cratylus* (408b).

50. On the story of Teiresias, see Loraux, *Les expériénces de Tiresias*.

51. Cf. Zeitlin, *Sign of the Shield*, 115: "The sightless surface of Amphiaraos' shield is itself a sign of the seer, the mantic emblem of blindness and insight."

52. See also 164d.

if not identical to god, plays a similar role to the latter, when it comes to preventing Socrates from associating with students who have abandoned the painful procedure of childbearing before delivering. Although Socrates claims that he does not possess the knowledge he foresees in the other person's soul, his aid is indispensable, in order for knowledge to see the light: ". . . when such men come back and beg me as they do, with wonderful eagerness (*thaumasta drôntes*), the daimonion that comes to me, forbids me to associate with some of them, but allows me to converse with others, and these again make progress" (151a).

Indeed, Socrates in the *Theaetetus* describes *thauma* as an affect of the soul, which comes unexpectedly and marks the beginning of the "initiation" to the "mystery" of the birth of true knowledge[53] or the abortion of false perceptions (161d). This initiation (*muêsis*) echoes *maieusis*. The process of initiation itself could be paralleled to the one led by Diotima, the female priestess in the *Symposium* (201d) introduced by Socrates as his teacher in matters of Eros.[54] It is notable that in this case Socrates presents himself as the naive student, while Diotima is presented as the wise and skillful teacher who teaches Socrates the mysteries of Eros. It is noteworthy that Diotima in her speech establishes a relationship between Eros and procreation[55] which could serve as a model for Socratic maieutics in the *Theaetetus*. What is more, Socrates refers to Diotima as the priestess who taught the Atheneans how to perform sacrifices against the plague. This information, independently of its historicity,[56] could prove an important clue in the analysis to follow, to the extent that Plato in the *Theaetetus* uses the exact terminology employed by Empedocles in the beginning of his *Purifications*, where he initiates Pausanias to his teaching, not to mention that the term *katharmoi* (purifications) itself denotes the same kind of practices ascribed to priestess Diotima by Socrates.

Indeed, the *thauma* overtaking the soul of the homonymous youth provides Socrates with the occasion to begin the former's initiation to

---

53. See Lesher, "Gnôsis and Epistêmê." Maeutics in its negative sense leads to the abortion of what is not sustainable by reason. See also Sedley, *Midwife of Platonism*, 34: "*Refutation*. The requirement that a midwife should be able to recognize a false or unviable offspring (150b9–c3) makes Socrates an expert at exposing falsehood in argument, thus (210b11–c5) disabusing people of the belief that they know what in fact they do not know. *This is actually the most important of his maieutic skills* (105b9–c3)" (emphasis added).

54 See Halperin, "Why Diotima Is a Woman," 257–308.

55. On the question of procreation as a model for Eros within the frame of Dionysian religion see Acker, "Dioniso, Diotima, Socrates," 37–39.

56. On this question, see Waithe, "Diotima of Mantinea," 101–9.

Sylvana Chrysakopoulou—Wonder and the Beginning of Philosophy in Plato

the "hidden truths of famous men" (155e, 156c). It is far from accidental that the first verb Plato uses to call upon the youth's attention is exactly the same Empedocles employs when addressing young Pausanias (31B3,9 DK): *Athrei!* ("Look!") In the beginning of his poem destined to Pausanias, Empedocles promises to reveal to him what is unfathomable for common human beings who believe only in what they themselves encounter in their poor lives through their meager senses before they perish like smoke (31B2, 1–5 DK): They do not see, they do not listen, they do not understand what Empedocles will reveal to Pausanias, who is already far away from them (31B2,7-8 DK). Through the imperative form of the verb *athreô* Empedocles prompts young Pausanias to use all his senses, in order to understand (*noei*) how everything manifests itself. It is notable that Socrates uses the same sensorial vocabulary to attract Theaetetus' attention. Through the same verb, he incites the youth to "look around" (*athrei periskopôn*) and to make the observation that none of the uninitiated is listening (*epakouei*)—the term *epakouein* also meaning understanding. The "uninitiated," as Socrates calls the latter, are described similarly to the common mortals in Empedocles: "They think nothing is, except what they can grasp firmly with their hands and they deny the existence of actions and generation and all that is invisible (*aoraton*)" (155e). He also describes them as the *amousoi* (devoid of Muse), another element that is reminiscent of the Empedoclean Muse, to whom Empedocles prays in order to reach human wisdom to its fullest extent without offending the sense of sacredness (31B3,1-6 DK).

Both Empedocles and Socrates enshroud their teaching with the religious cloak of initiation. What is more, before starting their students' initiation, they first recognize in them the intellectual courage that differentiates them from most mortals: Empedocles addresses Pausanias as the son of *daiphrôn* Agchites (B1 DK), as if he were a Homeric hero, while Socrates recognizes in Theaetetus a brave man in the heroic sense of the word, not to mention that the state of *thauma* itself is the mark of the initiate.[57] Parmenides, who comes before Empedocles in the same tradition of didactic poetry, is the first to present his poem as a revelation addressed by the goddess to the youth (*kouros* being another word for the initiate[58]), who surpasses human measures and visits her in her premises, which are

---

57. The element of the selection (*eklogê*) of the initiated is also present in the *Republic* 534–540. I thank Professor Szlezák for drawing this parallel. On the Tübingen School analysis of the relationship between the language in the mysteries of Eleusis and the Platonic doctrine see Szlezák, *Platon und die Schriftlichkeit der Philosophie*.

58. Burkert, "Das Proömium des Parmenides."

Practices of Wonder

out of reach (*ektos patou*) for mortals, beyond the dominion of day and night. In other words, all three students chosen to be initiated have shown a similar trait: a heroic intellectual disposition, one might say: *hoson t' epi thumos hikanoi* ("as far as your mind takes you") of Parmenides, offspring of a *daiphrôn* (courageous in battle) of Pausanias, *andreios* of Theaetetus. After recognizing the mark of heroism in their initiates, their mentors proceed to the initiation itself by demanding their pupils' full attention: all three ask them to employ their senses in a manner distinct from that of the multitude, who neither really see nor listen, despite having eyes and ears.[59] Common mortals on the other hand are described in all three texts in a similar manner. They only believe in what they grasp (*toin cheroin labesthai*) in the *Theaetetus*[60] and (*hotôi prosekursen hekastos* 31 B2,5 DK) in Empedocles, whereas the initiates use their senses in order to perceive the invisible. The verb *mueô* (close one's eyes), from which the noun "mystery" derives, is aptly used in the *Theaetetus* (164a), being highly reminiscent of the following precept by Parmenides: "Look that what is absent is firmly present in the mind" (28B4,1 DK). Likewise, Empedocles asks Pausanias to "Shelter his teachings in the soundless[61] mind" (31B5 DK). Last but not least, in all cases, the initiates are taught to use their *logos* (*logô krinai*), rather than their senses, in order to gain a good understanding of the teaching. It is the *logos* that reveals the *thauma* to them (*Theaetetus* 157d): *thaumasiôs phainetai hôs echein logon*. This is even more striking in the case of the "thaumaturge" of antiquity par excellence, Empedocles, who at the end of his poem promises Pausanias that thanks to his teaching, which is nevertheless within the human capacities of *logos*, he will be able to change the weather conditions and to resurrect the dead.

This notion of an understanding that comes through *logos*, rather than the senses, is a recurrent theme in the *Theaetetus* and in the *Symposium*, where the priestess Diotima reveals to Socrates the mysteries of initiation to love, similarly to Stesichorus in the *Phaedrus*. Indeed Diotima presents Socrates with a vision of truth very similar to the one the goddess reveals to the youth in the Parmenidean poem,[62] a vision one does not behold with the eyes, but with the mind. The philosophical initiation

---

59. Cf. Heraclitus 22B34 DK: *axunetoi akousantes kôphoisin eoikasi* . . . Also cf. 22B107 DK: *kakoi martures anthrôpoisi ophthalmoi kai ôta barbarous psychas echontôn*.

60. Cf. the description of the materialists in the *Sophist* as opposed to the lovers of Forms (246a–e).

61. Plato in the *Phaedrus* (275e–276a) uses similar vocabulary for the silence that ought to be kept by the initiates with regard to the non-initiated.

62. Waithe, "Diotima of Mantinea," 85.

to the invisible world that wonder imports seems to have a long tradition before Plato as it is echoed in the *Theaetetus*. Nonetheless, what Plato effects in both dialogues is the establishment of a relationship between invisible beauty and the idea of bringing forth. In the *Theaetetus*, wonder, in the sense of vertigo caused by the soul's pangs of labor, ultimately leads to another kind of wonder, described as a vision of the invisible that only the eye of the soul can recognize. What is ultimately at stake in the *Theaetetus* and the *Symposium* is the process of initiation to the invisible realities which begin and end in wonder, as Nightingale expresses it correctly.[63] As is the case in the *Theaetetus*, in the *Symposium*, the theme of the reminiscence of the wondrous beauty seen with the eye of the mind is associated with bringing forth and nourishing the offspring of true virtue, which leads to immortality (210e–211e):

> "He who has been instructed thus far in the things of love, and who has learned to see the beautiful in due order and succession, when he comes toward the end will suddenly perceive a nature of wondrous beauty (*exaiphnês katopsetai ti thaumaston têi phusin kalon*)[64] (and this, Socrates, is the final cause of all our former toils)—a nature which in the first place is everlasting, not growing and decaying, or waxing and waning; . . . but beauty absolute, separate, simple, and everlasting, which without diminution and without increase, or any change, is imparted to the ever-growing and perishing beauties of all other things. He who from these ascending under the influence of true love, begins to perceive that beauty, is not far from the end. . . . This, my dear Socrates," said the stranger of Mantineia, "is that life above all others which man should live, in the contemplation of beauty absolute . . . Remember how in that communion only, beholding beauty with the eye of the mind, he will be enabled to bring forth, not images of beauty, but realities (for he has hold not of an image but of a reality), and bringing forth and nourishing true virtue to become the friend of God and be immortal, if mortal man may. Would that be an ignoble life?

The relation between the life of the soul, physical death, and rebirth through metempsychosis is also to be found in the *Republic* associated with the vision of invisible Beauty. Indeed, Plato closes his *Republic* with

---

63. Nightingale, "On Wandering and Wondering," 44.

64. See also Lear, "Permanent Beauty," 114: "Interestingly, Alcibiades describes his own encounter with the beauty of Socrates in exactly the same terms, Socrates always appears to him 'all of a sudden' (*exaiphnês*, 213c1) . . . "

Practices of Wonder

the so-called myth of Er, who came back from Hades, the realm of the invisible, where the souls linger before choosing their next incarnation. Similarly to Theaetetus, Er is characterized as a brave man, *alkimos*[65] being the heroic epithet Plato employs in his case (614b). Like Theaetetus, Er was also supposed to have been slain in battle: Theaetetus' dying body was transported from the battle of Corinth to Piraeus in the opening scene of the homonymous dialogue, while Er's body was taken from the battlefield, where he was lying unconscious for ten days: "On the twelfth day, as he was lying on the funeral pile, he returned to life and related what he had seen in the other world . . ." He was told by the judges seated in between the two worlds at a *locus incertus* (*topos daimonios*)[66] "that he was to be the messenger who would carry the report of the other world to men, and they bade him hear and see all that was to be heard and seen in that place (*aggelon anthrôpois genesthai tôn ekei*)" (614d). As is the case in Parmenides, Empedocles, the *Theaetetus* and the *Symposium*, the "initiate" is prompted to use his senses—sight and hearing—and to become the messenger of what is imperceptible to all other mortals in this world. What is more, in the myth of Er, the latter is supposed to become the witness *par excellence* of the other world. Yet again, it is in the realm of the invisible that Er is said to have witnessed sights of unfathomable beauty (*theas amêchanous to kallos*, 615a). In other words, once again Plato construes the invisible realm as the stage of a beauty beyond perception. More importantly, the adjective *amêchanos* for beauty is practically synonymous to *thaumasios* in this context, not merely because of the association of both with beauty, but also because of the sense of bewilderment inherent in *amêchanos*. On the other hand, these marvelous sights pertaining to the mechanism of the Universe reflect the manner in which Parmenides presents his cosmology in the second part of his poem, which is ascribed to *Doxa* (seeming), as opposed to the first part, the account of being that is ascribed to Truth. Nonetheless, it is thanks to Plato's outlook that the sight of the Universe as a whole becomes, for the first time in the history of ideas, the stage of

---

65. In a rather significant *jeu de mots*, Plato juxtaposes the Homeric "Alcinoos account" to the myth of Er, by attributing the heroic epithet *alkimos* to the latter, in his intent to reform the heroic-epic ideal and to replace the Homeric mythology with a new type of theology. On this question see Chrysakopoulou, "La critique xénophanienne contre l'anthropomorphisme des dieux chez les poétes épiques à la lumière de la théorie de la *mimêsis* platonicienne," in *Théologie versus Physique*, 43–68.

66. This place is very similar in description to the premises of the Parmenidean goddess in the Proemium: note the use of the expression *chasm' achanes* in 28B1,18 DK. On the question of the resemblances between the Parmenidean Poem and the Myth of Er, see Morisson, "Parmenides and Er," 59–68.

wonder: a true object of *theôria*, in contrast to the manner in which it is related to Parmenides by the goddess, that is, as the realm of *doxa*. On the other hand, the sight of the marvel of the cosmos in Plato ultimately leads to the marvel of the perception of being in itself without any reference to this world, a stance that in fact reflects Parmenides' attitude towards the cosmos. Plato introduces a shift of focus from the notion of invisible truth, which is a central one in Parmenides, to the notion of beauty in itself, a beauty beyond any shape or form one may encounter in this world.

It is precisely on this sense of beauty that the notion of wonder in the *Theaetetus* is founded, preparing for a return of the soul to its pre-natal state, a rebirth effected through the initiation into the mysteries it attended before coming to this world. In those mysteries there is no place for generation, corruption, increase, decrease or any kind of change. This rebirth, beginning with wonder, leads to a new perception of life, a life of beauty, imperceptible to the majority of mortals. Therefore, such a concept of rebirth also serves as a consolation, in view of Theaetetus' death in the battlefield, which is announced at the beginning of the dialogue, an event prefiguring Socrates' own death as well—a connection based on their kinship, the fact that they "miraculously" resemble each other as father to son. Already within the scene of their mutual recognition, the heroic ideal of *kalos kagathos*, ascribed to both Theaetetus and Socrates, acquires a new sense in the Platonic context, pertaining to invisible rather than visible beauty and to quality of moral character rather than physical strength. It is, indeed, no coincidence that the Platonic ideas of *kalon* and *agathon* become the underlying principles of Plato's endeavour, which involves an attempt to replace the Homeric heroic ideal by philosophy as a way of life. Hence, philosophical experience beginning in wonder (*archê*) also serves as an end, a *telos*, attained by the initiated (*teleios*) in the *teletê* (ceremony of initiation) of the rebirth of wisdom in the soul: a preparation for the advent of the death of the body, the moment that the soul will be separated from it again, in order to rejoin the other immortals and rejoice in the vision of the unfathomable beauty of truth.

Bibliography

Primary Texts

Aeschylus. *Persians and Other Plays*. Translated by C. Collard. Oxford: Oxford University Press, 2008.

Diels, Hermann, and Walter Kranz. *Die Fragmente der Vorsokratiker*. 3 vols. 1903. Reprint. Berlin: Weidmann, 1974.

Plato. *Euthyphro*. Translated by W. R. M. Lamb. Cambridge: Harvard University Press, 1967.

———. *Phaedrus*. Translated by Benjamin Jowett. Oxford: Oxford University Press, 1892.

———. *Symposium*. Translated by Seth Benardete. Chicago: University of Chicago Press, 2001.

———. *Theaetetus*. Translated by H. N. Fowler. 1928. Reprint. Cambridge: Harvard University Press, 2002.

Theocritus. *Idyll 11 (Cyclops)*. Translated by Diane Arnson Svarlien. *Arion* 5 (1997) 161–63.

Secondary Literature

Acker, Clara Britto da Rocha. "Dioniso, Diotima, Sócrates e a Erosofia." *AISTHE* 2 (2008) 27–43.

Benardete, Seth. "Plato's *Theaetetus*: On the Way of the Logos." *The Review of Metaphysics* 51 (1997) 25–53.

———, translator. *The Being of the Beautiful: Plato's* Theaetetus, Sophist, *and* Statesman. Chicago: University of Chicago Press, 1984.

Brisson, Luc. "Socrates the Midwife." In *Plato's Theaetetus: Proceedings of the Sixth Symposium Platonicum Pragense*, edited by Aleš Havlíček and Filip Karfík, 30–54. Prague: Oikoumeni, 2008.

Burkert, Walter. "Das Proömium des Parmenides und die Katabasis des Pythagoras." *Phronesis* 14 (1969) 1–30 [= *Kleine Schriften* VIII, edited by Thomas A. Szlezák and Karl-Heinz Stanzel, 1–27. Göttingen: Vandenhoeck and Ruprecht, 2008].

Burnet, John. *Early Greek Philosophy*. 4th ed. London: A. & C. Black, 1930.

Burnyeat, Myles. F. "Plato and Self-Refutation in Plato's *Theaetetus*." *Philosophical Review* 85 (1976) 172–95.

———. "Socratic Midwifery, Platonic Inspiration." *Bulletin of the Institute of Classical Studies* 24 (1977) 7–16.

Chrysakopoulou, Sylvana. "Théologie versus Physique dans la Poésie Presocratique." PhD diss., Université de la Sorbonne (Paris IV), 2003.

———. "Heraclitus and Xenophanes in Plato's *Sophist*." *Ariadne* 16 (2010) 75–98.

———. "L'anonymité de la déesse dans le Poème de Parmenide." *Platon* (forthcoming 2012).

Cooper, John M. "Plato on Sense Perception and Knowledge: *Theaetetus* 184–86." *Phronesis* 15 (1970) 123–46.

Detienne, Marcel. *La notion de daimon dans le pythagorisme ancien de la pensée religieuse à la pensée philosophique*. Paris: Les belles lettres, 1963.

Dorion, Louis-André. *Socrate*. Paris: Presses Universitaires de France, 2004.
Edwards, Michael. *De l'émerveillement*. Paris: Fayard, 2008.
Elsner, Jas, and Ian Rutherford. *Pilgrimage in Graeco-Roman and Early Christian Antiquity: Seeing the Gods*. Oxford: Oxford University Press, 2005.
Fineberg, Stephen. "Plato's Euthyphro and the Myth of Proteus." *Transactions of the American Philological Association* 112 (1982) 65–70.
Ford, Andrew. "Protagoras' Head: Interpreting Philosophic Fragments in *Theaetetus*." *American Journal of Philology* 115 (1994) 199–218.
Fraenkel, Hermann. "Studies in Parmenides." In *Studies in Presocratic Philosophy*, vol. 2, *The Eleatics and Pluralists*, edited by R. E. Allen and D. J. Furley, 1–47. London: Routledge & Kegan Paul, 1975 [= *Wege und Formen frühgriechischen Denkens*, 157–97. 2nd ed. Munich: Beck, 1960 = "Parmenidesstudien," *Nachrichten der Gesellschaft der Wissenschaften in Göttingen* 2 (1930) 153–92.]
Frère, Jean. "Aurore, Éros et Ananké. Autour des dieux parménidiens." *Les Études philosophiques* (1985) 459–70.
Freud, Sigmund. "Das Unheimliche." In *Studienausgabe*, vol. 4, *Psychologische Schriften*, edited by Alexander Mitscherlich et al., 241–74. Frankfurt am Main: Fischer, 1982 [1919].
Friedlander, Paul. "Daimon and Eros." In *Plato*, 1:33–58. New York: Random House, 1958.
Halperin, David M. "Why Diotima Is a Woman: Platonic Eros and the Figuration of Gender." In *Before Sexuality: The Construction of Erotic Experience in the Ancient Greek World*, edited by David M. Halperin et al., 257–308. Princeton: Princeton University Press, 1990.
Haring, E. S. "Socratic Duplicity: *Theaetetus* 154b1–156a3." *The Review of Metaphysics* 45 (1992) 525–42.
Heidegger, Martin. "Vom Wesen der Wahrheit: zu Platons Höhlengleichnis und Theätet." In *Gesamtausgabe*, vol. 34. 2nd ed. Frankfurt am Main: Klostermann, 1997.

———. *Was ist das—die Philosophie?* 10th ed. Pfullingen: Günther Neske, 1992 [= in *Gesamtausgabe*, vol. 11, *Identität und Differenz*. Frankfurt am Main: Klostermann, 2006.]

———. *What Is Philosophy?* Translated by William Kluback and Jean T. Wilde. London: Vision Press, 1968.
Herrero, Miguel. "Priam's Catabasis: Traces of the Epic Journey to Hades in *Iliad* 24." *Transactions of the American Philological Association* 141 (2011) 37–68.
Kofman, Sarah. "Beyond Aporia?" Translated by David Macey. In *Post-Structuralist Classics*, edited by Andrew Benjamin, 7–44. London: Routledge, 1988.
Lacan, Jacques. "La position de l'inconscient." In *Écrits*, 829–50. Paris: Seuil, 1966.
Lear, Gabriel Richardson. "Permanent Beauty and Becoming Happy in Plato's Symposium." In *Plato's Symposium: Issues in Interpretation and Reception*, edited by James H. Lesher et al., 96–123. Cambridge: Harvard University Press, 2006.
Lesher, James Hunter. "Gnôsis and Epistêmê in Socrates' Dream in the *Theaetetus*." *Journal of Hellenic Studies* 89 (1969) 72–78.

———. "The Significance of *kata pant' a<s>tê* in Parmenides Fr. 1.3." *Ancient Philosophy* 14 (1994) 1–20.

———, translator. *Xenophanes of Colophon—Fragments*. 2nd ed. Toronto: University of Toronto Press, 2002.

Loraux, Nicole. *Les experiénces de Tiresias: le feminin et l'homme grec*. Paris: Gallimard, 1989.
McCabe, Mary M. "Protean Socrates: Mythical Figures in the *Euthydemus*." In *Ancient Philosophy of the Self*, edited by P. Remes and J. Sihvola, 109–23. New Synthese Historical Library 64. Heidelberg: Springer, 2008.
Mintz, Avi I. "*Chalepa ta kala*: Fine Things Are Difficult: Socrates' Insights into the Psychology of Teaching and Learning." *Studies in Philosophy and Education* 29 (2010) 287–99.
Modrak, Deborah K. "Perception and Judgement in the *Theaetetus*." *Phronesis* 26 (1981) 35–54.
Morisson, J. S. "Parmenides and Er." *Journal of Hellenic Studies* 75 (1955) 59–68.
Nightingale, Andrea Wilson. "On Wandering and Wondering: 'Theôria' in Greek Philosophy and Culture." *Arion* 9 (2001) 23–58.
———. *Spectacles of Truth in Classical Greek Philosophy*: Theôria *in Its Cultural Context*. Cambridge: Cambridge University Press, 2004.
Pinotti, Patrizia. "Aristotele, Platone e la meraviglia del filosofo." In *Il meraviglioso e il verosimile tra antichità e medioevo*, edited by Diego Lanza and Oddone Longo, 29–55. Florence: L. S. Olschki, 1989.
Prier, Raymond Adolph. *Thauma idesthai: The Phenomenology of Sight and Appearance in Archaic Greek*. Tallahassee: Florida State University Press, 1989.
Rösler, Walter. *Reflexe vorsokratischen Denkens bei Aischylos*. Meisenheim am Glan: Anton Hain, 1970.
Rowe, Christopher. *Plato and the Art of Philosophical Writing*. Cambridge: Cambridge University Press, 2007.
Rutherford, Ian. "*Theôria* and *Darsan*: Pilgrimage and Vision in Greece and India." *Classical Quarterly* 50 (2000) 133–46.
Sedley, David. *Midwife of Platonism: Text and Subject in Plato's Theaetetus*. Oxford: Oxford University Press, 2004.
Strauss, Leo, and Seth Benardete. *On Plato's Symposium*. Chicago: University of Chicago Press, 2001.
Szlezák, Thomas. *Das Bild des Dialektikers in Platons späten Dialogen. Platon und die Schiftlichkeit der Philosophie*. Berlin: de Gruyter 2004.
———. *Platon und die Schriftlichkeit der Philosophie. Interpretationen zu den frühen und mittleren Dialogen*. Berlin: de Gruyter, 1985.
———. "Socrates' voraussetzungslose maieutische Kunst." In *Plato's Theaetetus: Proceedings of the Sixth Symposium Platonicum Pragense*, edited by Aleš Havlíček and Filip Karfík, 11–29. Prague: Oikoumeni, 2008.
Waithe, Mary Ellen. "Diotima of Mantinea." In *A History of Women Philosophers, 600 B.C.–500 A.D.*, edited by Mary Ellen Waithe, 83–116. Dordrecht: Martinus Nijhoff, 1987.
Zeitlin, Froma I. *Under the Sign of the Shield: Semiotics and Aeschylus' Seven against Thebes*. Rome: Edizioni dell'Ateneo, 1982.

4

Wonder, Perplexity, Sublimity
Philosophy as the Self-Overcoming of Self-Exile in Heidegger and Wittgenstein

STEPHEN MULHALL

FOR BOTH HEIDEGGER AND Wittgenstein, philosophy begins not so much in wonder as in bewilderment, or rather in a mode of wonder that is inflected rather more towards bewilderment than towards, say, amazement or awe or admiration. Heidegger begins *Being and Time* by identifying himself with those "who used to think we understood [the expression '*being*,' but] have now become perplexed";[1] and Wittgenstein tells us that "a philosophical problem has the form: 'I don't know my way about.'"[2] This much seems uncontroversial.[3] What I want to examine in this essay is the

1. Heidegger, *Being and Time*, 19; hereafter cited as *BT*.
2. Wittgenstein, *Philosophical Investigations*, § 123; hereafter cited as *PI*. I have occasionally modified the translation.
3. I believe that this starting point with respect to Heidegger is also essentially consistent with Mary-Jane Rubenstein's contribution to this volume, since her fascinating argument almost entirely concerns much later Heideggerian texts. She does claim in passing that the author of *Being and Time* explicitly mentions *thaumazein*, glossed as the contemplation that wonders at being, only once (in order to distinguish it from inauthentic curiosity); I suppose that my claim might then be reformulated as the suggestion that this same philosophical wonder is also explicitly invoked at the book's outset by means of a pivotal Platonic dramatization of it as perplexity, and is thereafter implicitly at work throughout.

question of whether such bewilderment is an initial condition that both philosophers aspire to transcend, so that philosophical progress is a matter of our recovering from this perplexity and disorientation altogether, with the aim of establishing an untroubled re-inhabitation of the everyday, even if only until our next loss of bearings; or whether both rather see it as part of their task to maintain themselves (and so their readers) in bewildered wonder, so that what one might call a continuous perception of the perplexing extraordinariness of the ordinary, a continually recovered sense of amazement at the sublimity of the world and of our inhabitation of it, is internal to our recovery of orientation within that world.

1. Heidegger's Perplexity

Being and Time insists on presenting itself as finding its own origin in the Platonic origins of the subject—more specifically, as a response to a specific moment in Plato's dialogue the *Sophist*, a pivotal exchange in the Eleatic Stranger's imagined dialogue between himself and a group he calls tellers of myths about Being. For the book's introduction is itself prefaced by a quotation from that dialogue, which is itself followed by a sequence of rhetorical questions and answers whose style is simultaneously reminiscent of numerous exchanges between Socrates and his interlocutors:

> "For manifestly you have long been aware of what you mean when you use the expression '*being*.' We, however, who used to think we understood it, have now become perplexed."
>
> Do we in our time have an answer to the question of what we really mean by the word "being"? Not at all. So it is fitting that we should raise anew *the question of the meaning of Being*. But are we nowadays even perplexed at our inability to understand the expression "Being"? Not at all. So first of all we must reawaken an understanding of the meaning of this question. Our aim in the following treatise is to work out the question of the meaning of *Being*, and to do so concretely.[4]

In this highly condensed opening, Heidegger invites his readers to recognize themselves as presently standing in the position of those addressed by the Eleatic Stranger, but as needing to take up his position instead. In other words, he wants us to recognize that we not only do not have an answer to the question of the meaning of Being, but that we do not really understand the question; so his primary task is to engender a mood of

---

4. Heidegger, *BT*, 19.

perplexity in his readers about that question, and thereby get us to see that there is a difficult question to ask here. In other words, what he needs to do first of all is to bewilder or disorient us—leave us at a loss.

But this mood of perplexity is not one that the reader of *Being and Time* is in a position to leave behind by the end of the book. For even though the most that its author aspires to do with respect to the question of the meaning of Being is to work it out concretely—that is, not to answer the question but to get us in the position of being able to ask it in a way that is sufficiently clear or intelligible for us to be able to seek an answer—he all but declares on the final page of his book that it has failed to achieve even this apparently minimal aspiration: "And can we even *seek* the answer as long as the *question* of the meaning of Being remains unformulated and unclarified?"[5] In effect, then, the mood of bewilderment that Heidegger aims to create is one that never dissipates; it is rather the mood in which the book as a whole maintains its readers at every point. So unless we are willing to imagine that its author regards *Being and Time* as neither embodying nor enacting any genuinely philosophical work, seeing it simply as engaging in endless preparatory, pre-philosophical maneuvers, the implication seems to be that genuine philosophizing requires that mode of attunement throughout its labors, that the sign of the authentic philosopher is his ability to live within perplexity from first to last. But why and how can philosophizing find its way by maintaining itself in a state of disorientation? What makes bewilderment or perplexity essential if the philosopher is to be properly attuned to his subject matter?

Etymologically speaking, perplexity is not just a condition in which human beings might find themselves, it is also a condition that objects and situations might manifest. Someone can be perplexed; but if so, that is because something or someone is perplexing them—confusing, bewildering, or tormenting them; and in at least some cases, they will be having that effect precisely because they are themselves entangled, involved or complicated. The Latin term *perplexus* derives from the verb *plectere*, which means plait, interweave or involve. In sixteenth-century English, one could talk of a perplexed object—one whose parts were intricately intertwined.

Textually speaking, Heidegger's invocation of the *Sophist* points us towards the Eleatic Stranger's famously perplexing conception of Being and non-Being as intricately interwoven—his solution to the problem of saying of that which is not that it is not. And this invocation of the *Sophist*

---

5. Ibid., 83. 487.

prepares the ground for Heidegger's own initial characterization, in his first introductory chapter, of what the term *Being* might mean—a characterization without which his inquiry could not possibly begin, and which presents Being as something plaited or interwoven in a rather different (although not unrelated) sense. For that characterization is further oriented by an apparently passing reference to Aristotle's idea that the universality of Being is transcendental—that is, that it consists in a unity of analogy, in what Heidegger calls the "categorial interconnectedness" holding between the various ways in which beings can be grasped as existing and as manifesting a particular kind of existence. The idea is more fully and explicitly developed in his analysis of what he calls the ontological priority of the question of Being.

He begins by pointing out that our pretheoretical comprehension of the phenomena of everyday life is never absolutely final or complete, but rather always capable of being further refined or developed, even of being radically revised or reconceived; in this sense, our everyday grasp of things is inherently open to question. We might accordingly think of disciplinary practices such as biology, zoology and anthropology (Heidegger calls them ontic sciences) as what results from making an issue of this everyday understanding; we rigorously thematize it with a view to systematically interrogating it, and develop thereby a body of knowledge which may surpass or even subvert our initial understanding, but which is made possible by it and which is no less open to further questioning.

After all, what we learn reveals what we don't yet know; it orients our attempts to acquire that further knowledge; and it may also lead us to question the assumptions that governed our initial theorizing. Moreover, everything we come to know in this manner takes for granted certain basic ways in which this ontic science demarcates and structures its own area of study—conceptual and methodological resources that can themselves be thematized and interrogated (when, for example, biology was revolutionized by Darwinian theories of natural selection, or physics by relativity theory—or when a philosopher of science inquires into the validity of inductive reasoning). Such inquiries concern the conditions for the possibility of such scientific theorizing, what Heidegger calls the ontological presuppositions of ontic inquiry; and whether one inquires into them as a practitioner of the discipline or as a philosopher, the subject matter could not be within the purview of a purely intradisciplinary inquiry (which would necessarily presuppose what is here being put in question). It is, in short, the business of philosophy.

The object of investigation here is thus a regional ontology; every domain of ontic knowledge presupposes one, and thus invites this kind of philosophical questioning. And the results of that questioning themselves provoke further inquiry: given that each ontic region discloses an ontology, the relations between the various regional ontologies inevitably become a matter for philosophical inquiry. For on the one hand, each ontology will differ from others, as each ontic region has its own distinctive nature. But on the other, each region may open up onto cognate regions (as chemistry might shed light on biology and zoology, or as Heidegger thinks theology has deformed anthropology, psychology and biology[6]), thus revealing that its ontology bears upon those others; and of course each regional ontology is an ontology—each performs the same determinative function with respect to its region (determines the Being of a certain range or domain of beings), even if differently in each case. How, then, is this synthesis—this plaiting or interweaving—of categorial diversity and categorial unity to be understood? What is it for beings to be? This is the question of fundamental ontology.

The universality of Being is thus manifest in a threefold categorial interconnectedness. First, there is the internal articulation of philosophy, or ontological inquiry. To engage properly in any regional ontology, one must acknowledge not only that region's distinctiveness, but also its context—the way in which its ontology is located amongst and hence related to others, as well as the way in which the diversity-in-unity of regional ontology invites the question of fundamental ontology (since to thematize that diversity-in-unity just *is* to ask the question of fundamental ontology). Hence, any authentically penetrating exercise of philosophy in any of its regions must also bear in mind its place in, and hence its bearing upon, the broader articulated unity of philosophical inquiry as such. In short, there can be no properly rigorous philosophy of science or philosophy of literature in the absence of a properly rigorous inquiry into the question of the meaning of Being; and to inquire into that question necessarily involves reflecting upon the diversity-in-unity of philosophy.

The second level concerns the ontic sciences upon whose existence and nature distinctively philosophical inquiry is focused. Philosophy is thus parasitic upon the existence of ontic sciences; hence, insofar as regional ontological inquiries hang together with one another in the articulated unity of philosophy (qua intellectual discipline or tradition), then so must the ontic sciences from which those inquiries take their bearing

6. Ibid., 10.

and motivation. Philosophy makes sense (can be seen to hang together as an intelligible, interwoven but singular field) only insofar as regional ontologies do so; and for regional ontologies to hang together just is for individual ontic sciences to do so. Their results hang together internally (making it possible to form coherent bodies of knowledge, as opposed to accumulations of purely local data) and externally (insofar as the understanding they systematize has a bearing upon other such forms of understanding—whether by complementing, qualifying, challenging or otherwise putting it in question).

The third level of Heidegger's picture concerns the domain from which both ontic knowledge and ontological inquiry emerge, the domain embodying those pretheoretical modes of questioning comprehension whose reflexive radicalization generates the systematic forms of human understanding of the world—everyday human existence. For, of course, the construction and pursuit of ontic and ontological knowledge is itself an achievement of human beings, hence an aspect of their comprehending, questioning mode of existence. And whilst such modes of comprehension might embody radical revisions and subversions of our pretheoretical grasp of things, they must also be essentially continuous with that understanding: they must be made possible by it and the resources it makes available; and the ways in which the various aspects of this understanding implicitly hang together must be such that their rigorous thematization is possible in an articulated and unified way. In short, if philosophy makes sense only if ontic science makes sense, then both make sense only insofar as the everyday ways in which Dasein grasps and interrogates its world make sense.

The human way of being is thus not just the origin and condition for the possibility of all forms of discursive understanding; its articulated unity as a being (its Being), the articulated unity of the discursive fields of our culture, and hence the particular articulated unity of philosophy, stand or fall together. They are simply different ways of disclosing the same phenomenon, the categorial interconnectedness of Being. And Heidegger sees this diversity-in-unity on the model of a conversation or a dialogue, of the kind exemplified in the Platonic origins of the subject and recapitulated in Heidegger's immediate, opening dialogic response to that exemplar. In other words, he is implicitly conceiving not just of Being, and of philosophy, but of the Being of Dasein itself, as comprehensible only in those terms—quite as if Dasein's distinctive way of being is to converse (with its world, with other Dasein, and with itself).

But if the mode of attunement Heidegger implicitly recommends as appropriate for any proper acknowledgement of the categorial interconnectedness of Being is perplexity, then he is not only inviting us to be impressed by the overwhelming intricacy of these dialogical interweavings, but also to apprehend them as convoluted, tormenting and disorienting. If perplexity is the appropriate mood, then the plaiting of these structures of Being must be constitutively bewildering—say, riddling or enigmatic. And one way of seeing how Heidegger's initial sketch of the field of Being accommodates this essential feature is to ask how that sketch invites us to think of the place of philosophy in the conversation of human culture.

On the one hand, philosophy is one more field of discourse—hence one more domain or region of intelligibility, one potential conversation partner in the ramifying dialogical interrelations of the human form of life. But on the other hand, philosophy's subject matter is the possibility of discourse as such—that is, the sheer possibility of human discursive understanding of reality; and so it necessarily aspires to take in or survey the whole field of possible discursive interchange, including presumably its own place in that field, as specified by its own distinctive capacities for questioning and being questioned by other discursive enterprises (science, literature, history, and so on). But can the place from which any such survey might conceivably be made also be a place within that which is being surveyed? Can the possibility of intelligibility as such ever be properly encompassed by one concrete instance of intelligible discourse, however self-aware and self-questioning? Does philosophy's defining aspiration therefore place it within the field of culture, or must any such suggested placement inevitably undermine itself, so that philosophy no sooner finds itself (somewhere in particular) than it is obliged to displace itself—as if endlessly fated to lose any specific orientation it manages to acquire? What exactly is the place of philosophy in the conversation of humanity?

One might say: its place is to torment itself about its own, inevitable but ultimately bewildering, entanglement within the phenomenon it aspires to acknowledge as a whole, to enact its self-subverting drive to place itself beyond the discursive field of culture, as if at once yearning to inhabit what it thinks of as a wilderness (essentially beyond cultivation) and reluctantly recognizing that each such self-displacement—being itself more discourse—simply amounts to the further extension of the field of discourse that culture is (as if demonstrating that there is no wilderness for it to inhabit, since if its inhabitation is even conceivable, then it is within the reach of culture). Then one might say that the perplexing involutions of Being are crystallized in the perplexing unlocatability of philosophy in relation to those involutions; for if philosophy cannot be placed either wholly within or wholly without the categorial interconnectedness of discourse, then the simple fact of philosophical discourse—the sheer existence of philosophy as a cultural enterprise—indicates that the field of human discourse as such is inherently, enigmatically self-transcending and so fated to place itself beyond its own grasp, since the position from which alone it might be comprehended, and so the possibility of such comprehension, cannot itself be comprehended. Little wonder, then, that the authentic philosopher will find himself undergoing the self-inflicted torment of disorientation and bewilderment; for only that mood bears genuine witness at once to the nature of his subject matter and the nature of his own enterprise.

In this respect, however, the condition of philosophy (and so of the philosopher) reflects or manifests something about the human condition more generally (as one might expect given Heidegger's assumption that our access to the question of Being can only run through our capacity to disclose the Being of Dasein, distinctively human being, which he thinks of as Being-in-the-world). For this vision of philosophy's grounding impulse all but declares that it is internal to the nature of finite comprehending beings to be subject to the mysterious, unsatisfiable desire to transcend their own finitude. Our unending struggle with the question of whether it makes sense even to try making sense of the many and varied ways in which reality does (and does not) make sense to us is, on Heidegger's view, the most fundamental way in which human beings manifest the essentially enigmatic finitude of their being.

This internal human relation to mystery—to that which resists comprehension—is equally evident when Heidegger analyses the issue from the point of view of the individual human being rather than that of the culture or one of its central disciplines. For it is central to his account of authentic human existence that it involve an acknowledgement of mortality; and for Heidegger, death amounts to a crisis of intelligibility (both for individual Dasein and for phenomenological philosophy) through which the conversion or metanoia required for authenticity can alone be engendered.

The central truism from which Heidegger begins is the fact that our death amounts to the annihilation of our existence as such—our complete and utter non-being. This is not simply a matter of our having a finite as opposed to an infinite lifespan; it is rather that every moment of our existence might be our last—hence that each is equally intimately related in its being to the possibility of our utter non-being; so that what is at issue for us at each moment of our existence is our (possibly not) Being-in-the-world as such. Acquiring a proper awareness of this will necessarily involve our attempting to grasp our individual existence as a limited whole—not just insofar as all that we are is, in principle, at stake in each and every moment of it, but also insofar as the sheer contingency of each such moment (in both content and reality) contributes to the sheer contingency of a whole life, bounded by birth and death, and lacking external grounding or necessitation at every point.

For Heidegger, that perception of ourselves is what makes possible the transition from inauthenticity to authenticity, from a lower to a higher state of the self. But if being mortal is a matter of every moment of our lives being internally related to utter nullity or annihilation, that amounts to their being internally related to that which is beyond our comprehension. For recall, death is our utter nonexistence: so death is not an event in life, not even the last. But the human capacity to comprehend anything is (on Heidegger's account) a matter of allowing it to manifest itself to us as it is in itself; so if our death is not something we encounter, it is something that we cannot possibly comprehend. Or perhaps it would be better to say that it manifests itself to us precisely as something incomprehensible—in the fact that every moment of our existence is shadowed by the incomprehensible but ineluctable prospect of our utter non-being. Death raises the question of the meaningfulness of our lives precisely because every moment of our mortal life, with whatever freight of meaning it carries, is internally related to something of which we can make no sense. And any account of that mortality which fails to acknowledge the tormenting, perplexing, traumatic nature of its refusal of intelligibility—which regards its resistance to sense as attributable to our failure to make sense of it, and so as overcomeable—will count as an avoidance of its reality.

This is why Heidegger's phenomenology of death is not a matter of his adding an account of death (as, say, a peculiar existential possibility) to his account of Being-in-the-world; it is a matter of recounting his analysis of Being-in-the-world in such a way as to display the internal relation between every element of that analysis and some version or inflection of the concept of nothingness, nullity or negation (e.g., guilt, conscience, temporality). So, in *Being and Time*, Dasein displays itself as a limited whole only against an ungraspable background; and this shows that to comprehend ourselves as authentic individuals is not so much to comprehend our incomprehensibility—it is to comprehend that the kind of sense our existence makes is the kind that emerges from and returns to, hence is internally related to, non-sense. It means that "in any [mode of human] Being towards entities as entities there lies *a priori* an enigma."[7] Against that background, Heidegger's vision of the practice of philosophy as grounded in an unavoidable but unfulfillable commitment to taking in the field of human discourse as a limited whole should seem utterly unsurprising; for if philosophy did not share in the enigmatic perplexity of distinctively human conditionedness, it simply would not be what it has to be if it is to be anything at all—namely, the singular cultural place in which the internal relation between human sense-making and non-sense, at both the collective and the individual level, can find acknowledgment (or fail to).

2. Wittgenstein's Sublimity

I noted at the outset that Wittgenstein famously characterizes the moment of philosophy, or of philosophy's awakening, as one of disorientation, loss of bearings, bewilderment; he further claims that philosophy is "a struggle against the bewitchment of our understanding by means of language."[8] Whether or not one reads that remark as identifying language as both the cause of our bewitchment and the means of its overcoming, the implication certainly appears to be that this bewitchment is to be overcome—that reorientation is the goal. And other remarks appear to reinforce that impression: "When philosophers use a word ... and try to grasp the essence of the thing, one must always ask oneself: is the word ever actually used in this way in the language in which it is at home?—What *we* do is to bring words back from their metaphysical to their everyday use."[9] Here, the everyday appears as the domain in which our words, and so we ourselves, are at home, and that restoring us to this *Heimat* from which the bewitchments of metaphysics have removed us is the goal of his philosophical practice.

On the other hand, this formulation also implies that our words are always to be brought back to home, hence that philosophy essentially encounters them as always already away from home or not at home, and so that it encounters the everyday as at once having-been-lost and

---

7. Ibid., 1.23.
8. Wittgenstein, *PI*, § 109.
9. Ibid., § 116.

to-be-recovered. The everyday of this philosophical practice is thus the kind of *Heimat* from which it appears that its inhabitants repeatedly exile themselves; the homeliness of the ordinary is revealed only in one's return to it, a revelation that necessarily incorporates a disclosure of itself as essentially capable of casting us out, hence of ourselves as inveterate self-exilers. And here we need to recall that what Wittgenstein means by the "metaphysical uses" of words to which we endlessly find ourselves attracted is not really a specific kind of word use, but rather a condition in which we find ourselves meaning nothing by those words, despite being possessed by the conviction that what we have it at heart to say is of fundamental importance. So what we find ourselves exiled to is a mode of meaninglessness or nonsense; and we thereby discover that our everyday life with words harbors within it a certain uncanny possibility of undisclosed or self-concealing senselessness. Once again, then, the everyday meaningfulness of our existence appears as endlessly emerging from and returning to non-sense. There is plainly the potential for some perplexity here.

In the immediate context within which these methodological remarks find their home in the *Investigations*, however, Wittgenstein invites us to further interpret our capacity to perplex ourselves in terms of a concept that is often employed in conjunction with, or as a further interpretation of, the concept of wonder—that of the sublime. In fact, having earlier characterized our metaphysical impulses as expressive of "a tendency to sublime the logic of our language,"[10] he introduces these methodological remarks as a whole by asking: "In what way is logic something sublime?"[11] Taken by itself, the earlier remark would appear to associate perceptions of (the logic of) language as sublime exclusively with modes of self-exile, instances of self-concealing senselessness; but the later remark at least holds open the possibility that there is a sense in which the logic of our language really is sublime, and so a sense in which one might legitimately wonder at its sublimity without thereby indulging in a metaphysical subliming of it. What, however, does Wittgenstein mean by this subliming tendency?

I have pointed out elsewhere that Wittgenstein's highly figurative deployment of the term appears to have three interrelated dimensions of significance. The first derives from a perception of the depth to which logical or grammatical investigation takes us: "logical investigation . . . seeks to see to the bottom of things . . . It takes its rise from an urge to understand the

10. Ibid., § 38.
11. Ibid., § 89.

basis, or essence, of everything empirical,"[12] which is accordingly pictured as "something that lies within, which we see when we look into the thing, and which an analysis digs out"; consequently, we perceive "*the essence [a]s hidden from us.*"[13] We might think of this as the sublime understood as the subliminal—as that which lies below the threshold of ordinary awareness or surface appearance.

But the Wittgensteinian "sublime" also contains the idea of sublimation or refinement—the process of extracting a substance from a solution, separating it out in solid form by (for example) heating the solution beyond a certain threshold. He tries to hit off this idea by talking of our trying "to purify, to sublimate the signs" of our language;[14] and by saying that "no empirical cloudiness or uncertainty can be allowed to affect [logic]—It must rather be of the purest crystal."[15] Here, the priority of logic to the empirical realm which it nevertheless informs is pictured as the pollution or dilution of logic by the world of everyday experience; we must distil its crystalline forms from the impurities in which it is suspended.

But the idea of the sublime as sublimation also invokes a notion of sublimity in the Kantian or more generally the Romantic sense—a notion of exaltation or excellence, of being elevated to or beyond a certain threshold, as if standing at the very limits of human experience, being made of aware of the finitude of human understanding and thereby (surely?) of that which passes beyond it. This connotation is activated when Wittgenstein tells us that "the ideal, as we think of it, is unshakeable. You can never get outside it; you must always turn back. There is no outside; outside you cannot breathe."[16] The semi-colon of that last sentence marks a critical metaphorical and metaphysical shift, the point at which our idea of the ideal as an uttermost limit transmutes into an idea of the ideal as a limitation, as fencing us off from something—even if only a void inimical to human life and its bodily conditions. Is there no outside, or just no outside for us (living, breathing creatures)? This sense of the sublimity of logic takes us "on to slippery ice where there is no friction and so in a certain sense the conditions are ideal, but also, just because of that, we are unable to walk."[17] The purity and emptiness of the void makes it humanly

12. Ibid.
13. Ibid. § 92.
14. Ibid., § 94.
15. Ibid., § 97.
16. Ibid., § 103.
17. Ibid., § 107.

uninhabitable; but ice is, after all, not nothing, not a void—it merely refuses human locomotion; so this way of picturing the limits of human experience in fact transmutes them into limitations.

Throughout this third strand of images, the sublime appears as antithetical to the human, threatening suffocation, muteness, paralysis; but its threshold also appears as a barrier or constraint (as if the limits of logic locked us up fast in a room).[18] It is as if the very inhumanity of the sublime seduces us, as if transcending the human condition amounted to an infinitely desirable purification or refinement of ourselves. That image of imprisonment is also implicit in the two other dimensions of the concept of the sublime: the sublime understood as the subliminal, and the sublime understood as sublimation, both ask us to think of logic as hidden or imprisoned in the empirical or the ordinary, as needing to be dug or crystallized out of the circumstances of ordinary human life. But if we think of logic as imprisoned in the ordinary, and ourselves as imprisoned by logic, then we must be thinking of ourselves too as imprisoned in the ordinary; so attempting to dig logic out from the everyday will at once symbolize and realize our attempts to enact our own desired freedom from ordinariness.

The threefold connotations of the sublime given figurative release in Wittgenstein's methodological remarks turn out to be implicit in that concept's single earlier appearance in the *Investigations*, at work in the book's first concrete example of how metaphysical subliming operates. Having asked himself "What is the relation between name and thing named?" in section 37, thereby recommencing the investigation of words, names and ostensive definitions that has been underway since the opening section of the book, Wittgenstein goes on in section 38 to point out that "strange to say, the word 'this' has been called the only *genuine* name; so that anything else we call a name was one only in an inexact, approximate sense." This conception of demonstratives as the only true names—which Wittgenstein later associates with the name of Russell—thus activates, and so depends upon, a contrast between genuine or authentic names, names properly so called, and those words that are ordinarily called "names," but that only approximate to that status, and hence are not properly speaking names at all. Some words are names in name alone—their claim to that title is purely nominal; and the only words that do really merit it are typically not awarded it—their genuinely nominative essence is unacknowledged, hidden beneath another label altogether (for example, "demonstrative").

18. Ibid., § 99.

Here, the ideas of the sublime as the subliminal and as sublimation intersect: the true or authentic or pure essence of naming is hidden within or beneath the ordinary, and must be crystallized out of the empirical impurities that occlude it. The Russellian conception thus presupposes a view of names as evaluable in terms of authenticity or inauthenticity, propriety or impropriety, legitimacy or illegitimacy; so that even proper names (those paradigms of everyday namehood, the names of particular persons, animals, objects, countries and so on) might turn out to be not, properly or purely speaking, worthy bearers of the name "name" at all.

Wittgenstein is quick to tell us that this conception is queer, and that it springs from a tendency to sublime the logic of our language. But when he begins to explore its underlying motives more closely, in section 39, he deploys a striking example in order to do so.

> But why does it occur to one to want to make precisely this word into a name, when it evidently is *not* a name?—That is just the reason. For one is tempted to make an objection against what is ordinarily called a name. It can be put like this: *a name ought really to signify a simple*. And for this one might perhaps give the following reasons: The word "Nothung," say, is a proper name in the ordinary sense. The sword Nothung consists of parts combined in a particular way. If they are combined differently Nothung does not exist. But it is clear that the sentence "Nothung has a sharp blade" makes *sense* whether Nothung is still whole or is broken up. But if "Nothung" is the name of an object, this object no longer exists when Nothung is broken in pieces; and as no object would then correspond to the name it would have no meaning. But then the sentence "Nothung has a sharp blade" would contain a word that had no meaning, and hence the sentence would be nonsense. But it does make sense; so there must always be something corresponding to the words of which it consists. So the word "Nothung" must disappear when the sense is analyzed and its place be taken by words which name simples. It will be reasonable to call these words the real names.[19]

By citing the sword whose vicissitudes hold together the tangled plot of Wagner's *Ring* cycle, Wittgenstein implicitly but immediately moves his diagnosis of this instance of metaphysical subliming into a mythical or mythological register; and he continues more explicitly within that register when, in section 46, he asks: what lies behind this idea that names ought to signify simples?—or otherwise translated: what's the story behind it? For

19. Ibid., § 39.

the specific story he then offers is taken from Socrates in the *Theaetetus*, where he reports other unnamed people as subscribing to the existence of what the English translation of a German translation of Plato's Greek calls "the primary elements out of which we and everything else are composed"—elements that exist in their own right, *an und für sich*, of which no account could be given, for each of which nothing is possible but a bare name; its name is all it has. What Socrates is recounting here is thus a mythology of the world as composed of essentially unchanging and indestructible Ur-elements—call them simples.

The key point of Wittgenstein's ensuing critical discussion of the *Theaetetus* myth of simples is that "it makes no sense at all to speak absolutely of the 'simple parts of a chair.'" The term "simple" simply means "non-composite"; and there is no single, compulsory, absolute or context-independent way of identifying the parts of which any given thing might be said to be composed.

> If I tell someone without any further explanation: "What I see before me now is composite," he will legitimately ask; "What do you mean by 'composite'? For there are all sorts of things it may mean!"—The question "Is what you see composite?" makes good sense if it is already established what kind of compositeness—that is, which particular use of this word—is in question. If it had been laid down that the visual image of a tree was to be called "composite" if one saw not just a trunk, but also branches, then the question "Is the visual image of this tree simple or composite?" and the question "What are its simple constituent parts?" would have a clear sense—a clear use. And of course the answer to the second question is not "The branches" (that would be an answer to the *grammatical* question: "What are here *called* 'simple constituent parts'?") but rather a description of the individual branches.[20]

The force of Wittgenstein's tree example is clear: there is no single, absolute pre-given articulation of things into simple elements from which all other things must be composed; there is rather a variety of ways in which language users can articulate things into simple and complex, component and whole, in terms of which they can then go on to describe whatever they encounter. The moral of his critique is thus not solely that this mythological intuition about the absolutely simple, hence immortal, foundations of the world is a displaced recognition of the need for what one might call

---

20. Ibid., § 47.

grammatical elements (for example, simples) if certain language-games are to be played ("What looks as if it *had* to exist is part of the language"[21]); it is also that no particular language-game, with its given elements, needs to be played—that there is a variety of such forms of language, and that that variety is limited only by the limits of one's creative imagination as that plays itself out in the domain of grammar and the world. In other words, the *Theaetetus* myth imposes a kind of absolute or unconditioned fixity on the world and its inhabitants: each element of its substance is unchanging, hence essentially unconditioned by the material contingencies of spatio-temporal embodiment. Such a mythology of the world is plainly continuous with the icy void, lacking air and friction, which Wittgenstein later invokes to hit off the third connotation of metaphysical sublimity—its deep attraction to that which transcends human finitude.

By staying within this mythological register of the text, however, we can learn more about how Wittgenstein appears to imagine an alternative to such metaphysical subliming. For his initial invocation of the sword from Wagner's *Ring* in the context of a concern with its composition or decomposition refers us to one of that cycle's primal scenes—the moment when Siegfried and his foster father Mime employ very different approaches to the task of reforging Nothung, which Siegfried had inherited from his father Siegmund, but only as shattered into fragments by Wotan's spear. Mime relies upon solder: that is, he conceives of the task of remaking Nothung as a matter of taking each splinter and shard of the sword and reconnecting it to its fellows, as if it were a broken vase or a jigsaw puzzle. Of course, the general idea that a sword is a complex object made of parts is perfectly intuitive; but that is because we share a sense of the identity of those parts (the handle, the hilt, the blade)—a sense that is determined by our prior grasp of the identity of the whole of which they are parts (our sense of what it is for a sword, like a tree, to fulfill its function). But Mime is treating the fragments into which Nothung has been shattered as if they were parts of Nothung in just the sense in which its handle, its hilt and its blade are its parts. Nothung was not made by making or taking those shards and splinters and combining them in a particular way, as if each shard were to perform a particular function within the sword as a whole: it was rather unmade by breaking its natural or normal parts (particularly, of course, its blade) into mere fragments—bare pieces rather than parts. Not just any way of breaking up an object reduces it to its constituent parts;

---

21. Ibid., § 50.

sheer destruction is not a mode of disarticulation or dismembering, any more than anarchy is a specific breakdown of order, a mode of disorder.

Siegfried's reforging strategy is very different. He fixes Nothung's fragments one by one into a vice, and then files each to shreds; he then transfers the filings to a crucible, melts them down, pours that molten metal into a mould, and then works the resulting blade on the anvil into a sword strong enough to split that anvil with a single stroke. In other words, he gives the actual fragments into which Nothung was shattered no particular significance as parts. Rather than have their arbitrary geometry dictate his labors, he reduces them in turn to equally meaningless fragments, then to a molten fluid to which the very idea of a fragment, let alone a constituent part, has no application; and from that formless stuff he reconstitutes the sword in terms of the parts which its identity as a sword dictates. Nothung's recreation thus passes through a moment of utter decreation—a formless fluidity upon which the conception of a structured whole, or indeed structural complexity of any kind, can find no purchase; but what emerges from that fiery substance is indeed Nothung itself, resurrected, awoken to new life after death.

What Wagner is here tapping into is a characteristically mythological understanding of identity as fluid or metamorphic—its blazing, brilliant plasticity capable of undergoing the most extreme transformations without losing integrity, of suffering endless reshapings without loss of continuity. And as with the object, so with their possessors: it is as if Siegmund and Siegfried are momentary concrete particulars molded from that underlying substance, each a distinct realization of one and the same stuff, hence each identical to and distinct from the other. And just as Siegfried's identity is not graspable except as a reincarnation of his father, so it is not graspable as essentially distinct from his sister Sieglinde, or his father's father, or from Brünnhilde—any more than he experiences it as separable from that of his (father's, and so of course his father's father's) sword, which partakes of the identity of the tree from which it was drawn, itself both a particular tree integrated into a particular house, and also an avatar of the world-tree or tree of life, from which Wotan first tore the spear that will twice confront itself in the form of a sword. Such chains of equivalence, of simultaneous identity and non-identity, constitute the world of the *Ring*, making it such fertile soil for psychoanalytic interpretation in all its varieties, through which each apparently individual person and object is read as internally related to every other as part of the structure of the human psyche as such. The molten fluid that is Nothung thus embodies the flux from which the Wagnerian universe of gods, dwarves, giants and heroes is forged.

How does this mythic tale of the world compare with that recounted in the *Theaetetus*? Taken one way, it would not be unnatural to regard the world of the *Ring* as having primary or primal elements out of which it has been composed—a sword, a ring, a helmet; gods, giants, dwarves; the tree of life, and the genealogical roots, trunk and branches of the Volsungs. In Wagnerian rather than Socratic myth, however, the nature and hence the mode of composition of those elements differs quite significantly. More precisely, it is not so much a matter of composition—of combining or soldering parts—as one of blending, mixing, inflecting or infusing types or archetypes. If, in the terms of the *Theaetetus* myth, people are thought of on the model of objects (as constituted out of pre-given parts), in the terms of the *Ring* myth, objects are thought of on the model of people (as playing a part, occupying pre-given roles and confronting a fate that both makes them the object they are and weaves them into the repeating pattern of an endlessly unfolding metaphysical fabric).

Taken another way, however, the myth of the *Ring* might rather be thought of as entirely rejecting the compositional model invoked by that of the *Theaetetus*. For what Siegfried's reforging of that sword appears to adumbrate is a world in which questions of existence and identity cannot ultimately be approached in terms of parts and wholes at all; they are simply not conceivable as a matter of which elements in which combination comprise the given thing. Such a compositional vision is inflexible and shut-ended; it makes creation a fundamentally mechanical process that can only result in a finite number of possibilities that are fundamentally predictable from an acquaintance with the basic, indestructible and unalterable pieces of which reality consists—elements whose possibilities of combination are predetermined, written into their nature. In the myth of the *Ring*, creation is a matter of molding and remolding white-hot fluid— an essentially plastic substance which no sooner coalesces into a concrete particular than it dissolves, only to realize itself in another concrete particular. The possible range of such realizations is neither predetermined nor wholly unconstrained; identity is essentially malleable, its metamorphoses allowing for creativity whilst always presupposing continuity at a fundamental level.

Accordingly, if one wanted a mythological counter to the sublimely mechanical fixity of the *Theaetetus* myth of reality and its inherent structure or articulation, one could hardly do better than the sublime operatic fluidity of the *Ring*; for its pivotal image of Siegfried's reforging of Nothung precisely embodies an understanding of human beings as not needing to allow the given articulations and disarticulations of the world to dictate their modes of response to it, but rather as capable of reforging reality in such a way as to reconstitute its modes of being without ever being able to recreate it *ex nihilo*. The thought that there is no one way in which the world is always already arrayed, and the thought that even the most imaginative reforging of the world must acknowledge its resistances (which might be the result of prior modes of its articulation), meet and merge under the creative blows of Siegfried's hammer. If we reconceive the logic of our language in this way, we will at once overcome any sense of that logic as imprisoned in the ordinary, and thereby overcome any sense of ourselves as imprisoned in the everyday. But we would not thereby have altogether overcome a sense of those limits as sublime; we would rather have reoriented our sense of wherein their sublimity resides—namely in the human capacity to meet, acknowledge and respond to the ways in which those limits condition, and so make possible, genuinely creative responses to the world.

If, however, Wittgenstein's philosophical practices are to maintain their fundamental sensitivity to the sublime creativity of language, then they must not themselves succumb to unduly mechanical or rigid modes of application. Take, for example, the methodological principle stated in *PI*, § 116—that of overcoming metaphysical subliming by bringing words back to the language in which they are at home. Many Wittgensteinians take that to mean locating the language-game in which the relevant word is ordinarily used, and they take that in turn to require that we identify the grammatical norms or rules that govern the use of the word in those ordinary contexts. But there may be words whose everyday use is such that it is obscured rather than laid open to view by those who seek to present it in the form of a grammatically ordered language-game.

Cora Diamond has drawn our attention to one such linguistic context—that in which religious believers talk of God as speaking to them—when, in her essay "Wittgenstein and Religious Belief: The Gulfs between Us,"[22] she offers an innovative interpretation of Wittgenstein's obscure remarks about the indispensability of a picture or pictures in the life of a religious believer. She begins by linking the centrality of the belief that God has a name in a certain tradition of Judeo-Christian thought to the particular significance we attach to the individuality of those human

---

22. Diamond, "Wittgenstein and Religious Belief."

beings we love or care for, our sense that their significance is unique and irreplaceable, and so not capturable in any general terms (say, by reference to their distinguishing characteristics). This conception, she points out, might include acknowledgment of the ways in which an encounter with a particular person might transform our concepts—as George Eliot, that magnificently ugly woman, gave a totally transformed meaning to the term "beauty" for Henry James. Eliot shows the concept up, moving James to use it almost as a new word, certainly as a renewed one. And Diamond suggests that part of the importance of the idea of God as having a name lies in the sense that His self-revelation similarly reorients our concept of "divinity."

The Judeo-Christian God is viewed as having revealed Himself, in deed and word (those of His prophets and, in the Christian case, those of Christ himself), and as having thereby made it possible for His hearers to speak and act in response to this unprecedented self-revelation; it is only in the terms made newly available through God's actions in history that the hearer can understand the kind of conduct truly expected of her. God himself has thereby given a transformed content to the word "God": Diamond, following Rosenzweig, calls this the conversion of our concepts through God's self-revelation. Think of this as a picture of God as speaking to His people. In what circumstances would it be natural to say that this picture is indispensable to the religious believer concerned?

Imagine a Wittgensteinian philosopher who wants accurately to characterize this aspect of our believer's life with words. He will note that she describes her language-game as one in which God speaks and is responded to; but he will naturally want to ask what, in her game, counts as God's having spoken—what, one might say, the grammatical criteria are that she and her fellow believers employ in playing this language-game. From the believer's point of view, however, the very form of that question implies that we—in our ways of speaking—are the ones who ultimately determine what counts as God's speaking; whereas it is essential to her understanding of the God of whom she speaks that her ways with religious words have a kind of openness to God's actions, an openness which means that it is not for her (or anyone other than God himself) to lay down rules for what counts as God's speaking. To do otherwise would mean arrogating to ourselves the authority to determine the limits of God's capacity to reveal Himself, rather than remaining open to the ineliminable possibility that His self-revelation might show up our current ways of talking about Him as utterly shallow or misconceived.

The picture of God's speaking thus lies at the basis of all this person's religious thought, because it is central not only to the religious language-games that she plays but also to the way she regards or relates to those language-games—namely, not as practices in which what counts as God's speaking is ultimately subject to determination by our rules. She will therefore resist any philosophical description of her religious language that makes its deployment ultimately a matter of our modes of speaking rather than God's. As a result, any Wittgensteinian commitment to eliciting the grammatical criteria for her ways of speaking, where those criteria are taken to be hers or her tradition's to determine and employ, will precisely misrepresent that way of speaking: this signature Wittgensteinian concept will here prevent us from simply acknowledging the reality of what lies before us, unless one radically recasts an aspect of its normal grammar that one might hitherto have taken to be both essential to it and uncontroversial in its implications.

This particular way of using words religiously might be seen as offering us a way of regarding the limits of our language as sublime limitations, but without conjuring up visions of the metaphysical sublime, or otherwise subliming those limits. For whilst such believers aspire to leave themselves open to the discovery that everything they have hitherto said about God is utterly misconceived, they conceive of any such discovery as a matter of having our religious concepts suffer conversion—that is, of their undergoing a radical reorientation through which we acquire the ability to speak about God more authentically. Accordingly, such conversions do not themselves amount to a transcendence of the limits of language (they are rather a refashioning of them, the acquisition of a new way of speaking possessed of a new logic), and neither do they require the positing of an absolutely transcendental source (for that source is specifically conceived of as speaking to us, hence as capable of revealing Himself in the forms of our life with words). Such a conversion of our concepts is thus a genuinely sublime instance of the creativity of language in its flexible marriage with reality (call it their meet and happy conversation, their open-ended and mutually disclosive intercourse), rather than a registration of God's nature as metaphysically sublime, as if inhabiting a domain from which our finitude definitively and damagingly excludes us.

But Diamond's way of using this example is also designed to teach us a salutary lesson about Wittgensteinian philosophical practice—namely, the possibility that even the methods of those most extensively committed to the plain registration of our forms of life with words can take on a rigidity that works against that commitment. Even the signature Wittgensteinian concept of a language-game can be employed in such a way that what appears to be an utterly indisputable feature of anything worth calling a use of language (e.g., that the meanings of our words are ours to determine) may turn out to be not only an imposition upon a given use of language, but one that precisely occludes its human point or purpose. In this way, Wittgenstein's philosophical practices might be said to have become themselves an object of wonder—but here, one of perplexity or bewilderment rather than awe or amazement; for there is surely something painfully enigmatic about the fact that conceptual tools designed above all to avoid the metaphysical sublime can themselves be subject to metaphysical subliming (projected as necessarily present in all linguistic phenomena, hence as sometimes needing to be sublimated from their context, and as fixed or rigid in their essence). To be more precise (and thereby more Heideggerian) about it: since a Wittgensteinian philosopher is also a human being, and since his practices of perspicuous presentation of language envision human beings as perversely inclined to exile themselves from their everyday *Heimat* with words, he may be shocked but he should not be surprised to find that he is just as perversely capable of exiling himself from his philosophical *Heimat*—as if it is no sooner located than lost, or at least essentially losable, because necessarily lacking immunity to the very metaphysical subliming its inhabitants seek to counter in the fields of discourse they aspire perspicuously to represent. Should we therefore conclude that the truly perplexing sublimity of humankind resides in this inescapable subjection to perversity?

Bibliography

Diamond, Cora. "Wittgenstein and Religious Belief: The Gulfs between Us." In *Religion and Wittgenstein's Legacy*, edited by D. Z. Phillips and M. von der Ruhr, 99–138. London: Ashgate, 2005.

Heidegger, Martin. *Being and Time*. Translated by J. Macquarrie and E. Robinson. Oxford: Blackwell, 1962.

Wittgenstein, Ludwig. *Philosophical Investigations*. Translated by G. E. M. Anscombe, P. M. S. Hacker, and J. Schulte. 4th ed. Oxford: Blackwell, 2009.

5

Heidegger's Caves
On Dwelling in Wonder[1]

MARY-JANE RUBENSTEIN

It happens every time I teach Heidegger. While working through an essay like "The Onto-Theological Constitution of Metaphysics," my students will be holding on as best they can, writing furiously as I try to take them through Heidegger's elusive prose. We will make our way through metaphysics' occlusion of being, through the way that representational thinking reduces beings to objects of human consumption, and might just gain some ground on Heidegger's shift from unconcealment (*alêtheia*) to the unconcealment of concealment (*Ereignis*)—when all of a sudden there will be two heads inclined toward one another, some whispering, and a few dropped jaws at the back of the room. "Everything okay?" I will ask. "Sorry," a student will respond. "I hadn't known Heidegger was a Nazi . . ." "*Heidegger was a Nazi*?" someone will chirp from the front. And this will bring all my talk of re-vealing and re-veiling to an abrupt halt. Somewhat reluctantly, I will lead them on a detour through what has become a great stumbling block for continental philosophy and critical theory, a question asked too much by some and too little by others; in short, what

---

1. Adapted from *Strange Wonder: The Closure of Metaphysics and the Opening of Awe* by Mary-Jane Rubenstein. Copyright © 2009 Columbia University Press. Used by arrangement with the publisher.

Mary-Jane Rubenstein—*Heidegger's Caves*

was Heidegger thinking? Which is to say, *was* Heidegger, the thinker who called thinking back to thinking, thinking at all? When he took up the Rectorship of a nazified Freiburg University in 1933, an act that he may or may not have come to call the greatest stupidity of his life, was he thinking the way he has taught us to think? Or was this commitment something more like a refusal to think; a failure to heed what called for thinking, a foreclosure of his own task of thinking?

One of the most provocative accounts of Heidegger's great stupidity can be found in a piece Hannah Arendt wrote to commemorate his 80th birthday. In this essay, Arendt ranks Heidegger with the greatest philosophical giants of all time, even likening him to Plato.[2] She goes on to say that those of us who would like to follow such powerful thinkers encounter a formidable obstacle when we realize that philosophers often make disastrous political decisions. Heidegger's commitment in 1933 was akin, she says, to Plato's attempt to teach philosophy to Dionysus the tyrant of Syracuse in 362 BCE. Both of them were blinded to concrete political reality, and Arendt attributes Heidegger's blindness to his being stuck—of all things—in wonder. She compares Heidegger to the ancient philosopher Thales, who was so fixated on the stars above him that he fell into a well below him. Eyes set on some metaphysical revolution, Heidegger failed to notice the yellow stars in front of him, the deportations next door, the burning of temples and storefronts. In short, Heidegger embodies the figure of the typical philosopher who, having climbed out of the cave into the brilliance of the sun, returns to his subterranean home to find he can no longer see in the darkness.

It may seem puzzling that Arendt associates wonder with a *failure* to think, considering that wonder is traditionally said to be the origin of thinking itself. In Plato's *Theaetetus*, for example, Socrates tells his wonderstruck interlocutor, "this is an experience which is characteristic of a philosopher, this wondering (*thaumazein*). This is where philosophy begins, and nowhere else."[3] In the *Metaphysics*, Aristotle reaffirms that "it is owing to their wonder (*thaumazein*) that men both now begin and at first began to philosophize."[4] And Descartes locates wonder (*l'admiration*) as the first of all the passions, from which all subsequent thinking emerges.[5] So there is a broad consensus that Western philosophy cannot function

---

2. Arendt, "Martin Heidegger at Eighty," 293–303.
3. Plato, *Theaetetus*, 155d.
4. Aristotle, "Metaphysics," 982b.
5. Descartes, *Passions of the Soul*, article 53.

without wonder. Where many post-Socratic thinkers differ from one another is in the extent to which they believe philosophy ought to *stay* in wonder. Once wonder gets philosophy going, should it be sustained or eclipsed? Deepened or overcome? Along with Aristotle and Descartes, Arendt would choose the latter option. As far as she is concerned, genuine "Platonic" wonder is meant simply to be a "leaping spark"—an initial and momentary disorientation before the philosopher goes on to form concrete theories and opinions.[6] So there is nothing wrong with wonder, as long as one doesn't have too much of it. Heidegger's mistake, therefore, was not his capacity for wonder *tout court*; rather, it was his "taking up and accepting this faculty of wondering as [his] abode."[7]

While I have contested elsewhere the accuracy of Arendt's account of wonder,[8] I would nevertheless maintain that her having attributed Heidegger's Nazism to it opens a critical ethical question, namely, is wonder a "good" place for thinking to be located in the first place? Does wondering at the extraordinary, or the ideal, blind us to the ordinary world of material "shadows"? Surely the answer depends on what wonder means. I propose therefore to explore the problem of Heidegger's great stupidity, and that of philosophy's ethical engagement more broadly, through Heidegger's own work on wonder, and his two readings of Plato's allegory of the cave.

Heidegger's Wonders

While Heidegger's work shifts in focus, tone, and terminology as it matures, the corpus remains unflinching in its conviction that metaphysics cannot think its own condition of possibility. Being (or later, "beyng") sets philosophy in motion, but for that very reason remains inaccessible to philosophy. Heidegger therefore spends his career looking for a way to deliver thinking back into its "ground," which he later calls its "first beginning." And since this first beginning has never actually been thought, working back to it would amount to propelling thinking forward into "another beginning." With all of this attention to the origins of philosophy, it is perhaps unsurprising that *thaumazein* makes numerous appearances along Heidegger's paths back to the beginning.

In *Being and Time* (1927) Heidegger mentions wonder briefly, distinguishing it from the curiosity (*Neugier*) that drives

6. Arendt, "Philosophy and Politics," 97.
7. Arendt, "Martin Heidegger at Eighty," 299.
8. Rubenstein, *Strange Wonder*, 20–23.

calculative-representational thinking: "curiosity has nothing to do with the contemplation that wonders at being, *thaumazein*, it has no interest in wondering to the point of not understanding. Rather, it makes sure of knowing, but just in order to have known."[9] While curiosity seeks to amass knowledge, wonder withstands uncertainty; while curiosity flits from being to being, wonder stops and "wonders at being." Insofar as it gets back behind objectified beings to being-itself, wonder seems to be the capacity central to Heidegger's entire project. But following this brief, stunning attribution, Heidegger does not mention the mood again, concentrating instead on the ontological attunement of *Angst*.

It is not until his Freiburg lecture series in 1937–38 that Heidegger addresses the question of wonder at greater length, affirming *thaumazein* as the "basic disposition" proper to philosophy's "first beginning." Heidegger suggests that if Socrates had named "curiosity" as the origin of philosophy, then thinking might be justified in its persistent effort to explain (away) the whole world. However, "the reference to *thaumazein* as the origin of philosophy indicates precisely the inexplicability of philosophy, inexplicability in the sense that here in general to explain and the will to explain are mistakes."[10] At this point the distinction between curiosity and wonder is crucial for Heidegger, because again, finding another beginning for thinking depends on thinking through the first one. Curiosity, he insists, can only lodge us more deeply within the calculative confines of metaphysics, whereas wonder remains with the inexplicable. For this reason, it could well be the disposition that "transports [thinking] into the beginning of genuine thinking."[11] For this reason, Heidegger spends a good deal of time in these lectures trying to get wonder right.

Reserving the term *Erstaunen* to translate *thaumazein*, Heidegger sets it apart from four other moods with which it might be confused: *Verwunderung, Bewunderung, Staunen,* and *Bestaunen*. Similar to curiosity, *Verwunderung* craves, marvels at, and collects novelties, leaping from one fascinating phenomenon to another like children in a natural history museum. It does not ultimately dwell anywhere, but rather is perpetually "carried away by something particular and unusual and hence is an abandonment of what in its own sphere is particular and usual."[12] *Bewunderung* also occupies itself with that which is unusual, but, unlike *Verwunderung*,

---

9. Heidegger, *Being and Time*, 161.
10. Heidegger, *Basic Questions*, 136.
11. Ibid.
12. Ibid., 142.

it always maintains a certain distance from the object of its admiration. It is perhaps helpful here to note that, in the second *Critique*, Kant confesses that the two things that fill him with *Bewunderung* are "the starry sky above me and the moral law within me."[13] In the third *Critique*, Kant commends such *Bewunderung*, "an amazement that does not cease once the novelty is gone," over against *Verwunderung*, which fades as soon as it understands the unusual object before it.[14] Against Kant, Heidegger suggests that even *Bewunderung* falls short of *thaumazein* because it remains grounded in the known as it gazes upon the unknown, whereas genuine wonder makes the known itself unknown. *Bewunderung*, Heidegger says, is ultimately marked by measurement, comprehension, and *self*-affirmation, and therefore has very little to do with the *thaumazein*'s "wondering to the point of not understanding." Finally, *Staunen* and *Bestaunen*, while prisoners neither to *Verwunderung*'s flightiness nor to *Bewunderung*'s myth of self-mastery, lose themselves completely in a sort of stupefied amazement, abandoning the ordinary in favor of one extraordinary thing.

As it turns out, each of these moods amounts to an inadequate interpretation of *thaumazein* because of its failed relationship to the everyday. Whether forgetting it in favor of the newest craze or standing firmly in it to examine the attainments of rocket science, each of these forms of intrigue takes for granted what is most usual of all, holding the great unknown against the drab (and therefore uninterrogated) background of the known. In *Erstaunen*, on the other hand, the source of wonder is the everyday itself: "precisely the most usual whose usualness goes so far that it is not even known or noticed in its usualness—this *most usual itself* becomes *in* and *for* wonder what is most unusual."[15] We might think here of Socrates's student Theaetetus, who finds himself lost in wonder when he realizes he has no idea what knowledge is. It is here that Socrates calls this wondering the "origin of all of philosophy," saying "this is where philosophy begins, and nowhere else." Wonder wonders at the inscrutability of the ordinary—at our inability to know something as ordinary as what it is to know. Considering that not much is more "ordinary" than being itself, one might leap ahead to ask whether *Erstaunen* might perhaps be the mood most appropriate to Heidegger's "way back into the ground of metaphysics." Yet Heidegger does not make this ascription; in fact, he spends the rest of the lectures reigning in its force.

13. Kant, *Critique of Practical Reason*, 203.
14. Kant, *Critique of Judgment*, 133.
15. Heidegger, *Basic Questions*, 144.

Almost immediately after naming wonder in the 1937–38 lecture series as the mark of philosophy's fundamental "inexplicability," Heidegger launches into a detailed explication of wonder. In thirteen bullet points, he lists wonder's various attributes, eventually abandoning it as an unregenerately "ontic" attunement. *Erstaunen*, we learn, is attuned to the "what" of beings, but not to the "that" of being.[16] Evidence of this failure can be seen practically everywhere in the modern world. How else could we understand the whole earth's having been made into a stockpile for humanity's global domination? It was a refusal to wonder at being's "that" that reduced all beings to calculable objects in the first place. And now that all beings have been tagged and packaged as objects of consumption, we *cannot* wonder at being. "For centuries," Heidegger writes, "the *being of beings*, which was for the Greeks the most wondrous, has passed as the most obvious of everything obvious and is for us the most common: what everybody knows. For who is supposed not to know what he means when he says the stone *is*, the sky *is* overcast? . . . On account of its obviousness, being is something forgotten."[17] Because "we" are unable to be amazed by beings in their being, the mood of our thinking can no longer be one of genuine wonder. Wondering only at whatness, *Erstaunen* can deliver thinking back to its first beginning, but it cannot deliver us into a new one.

The 1937–38 lectures come to an end almost immediately after this discussion of *Erstaunen*: the fundamental mood of philosophy that turns out not quite fundamental enough. Just before he falls silent, however, Heidegger makes an oblique reference to a "still veiled basic disposition," which, now that wonder is impossible, might push thought "into another necessity of another original questioning and beginning."[18] Heidegger had named this "other" basic disposition only once during the lecture series, and he does not do his audience the service of repeating or elaborating upon it at the end. At the beginning of his first lecture, Heidegger invokes what he calls the "basic disposition of the relation to beyng," one that would remain "open to the uniquely uncanny fact: that there *are* beings, rather than not."[19] In other words, this disposition would be attuned to the thatness that metaphysics (and *Erstaunen*) misses. For the few minutes during which it is addressed, this disposition finds a provisional name: *Verhaltenheit*, which is usually translated as "restraint" or "reservedness."

16. Ibid.
17. Ibid., 159.
18. Heidegger, *Basic Questions*, 160.
19. Ibid., 3.

Inherent in this disposition are two equiprimordial comportments, kept in perpetual tension. The first is "terror (*Erschrecken*) in the face of what is closest and most obtrusive, namely that beings are," and the second is "awe (*Scheu*) in the face of what is remotest, namely that in beings, and before each being, being holds sway."[20] But just as in *Being and Time*, where Heidegger calls *thaumazein* "the contemplation that wonders at being" only to stop talking about it, the Freiburg lectures call *Verhaltenheit* the disposition that wonders at thatness, only to forbid further discussion of it. Heidegger warns his audience that "only one who throws himself into the all-consuming fire of the questioning of what is most worthy of questioning has the right to say more of the basic disposition than its elusive name." Yet he goes on to say that even the one who seeks thus to immolate himself will not discuss *Verhaltenheit* at any length; rather, having "wrested for himself this right, he will not employ it, but will keep silent."[21] And this is just what Heidegger proceeds to do. Unlike *Erstaunen*, that Inexplicable explicated in thirteen bullet points, the ever veiled *Verhaltenheit* is protected from direct communication—animating, perhaps, but never suffering dissection within, Heidegger's analysis.

Well, not quite "never." At the same time that he was preparing and delivering the 1937–38 lecture series, Heidegger was also composing his *Contributions to Philosophy (from Enowning)*, a quasi-aphoristic outline intended to accomplish the crossing from metaphysics into "beyng-historical thinking." It is in this text, intentionally never published during his lifetime, that Heidegger indulges in a meditation upon the foundational mood of the "other" beginning. Aside from this, the only remaining elaborations upon *Verhaltenheit* can be found in the passages Heidegger deleted from the first draft of the Freiburg lectures he was composing at the same time.[22] Heidegger, then, does not exactly "keep silent" about this veiled disposition. Rather, one might say that he both reveals and conceals *Verhaltenheit* by performing it; that is, by restraining "restraint" to pages that would only be circulated posthumously.

Before clinging too closely to this rather generous reading, however, one would also do well to consider the historical particularities surrounding the emergence of Heidegger's newly proclaimed "beyng-historical thinking" (a thinking that, of course, rejects as "historiography" such

20. Ibid., 4.

21. Ibid.

22. These pages are appended to both the German and English volumes of these lectures. See ibid., 168–86.

petty concerns as dates and dictators and wars). Heidegger deletes the passages on *Verhaltenheit, Erschreken,* and *Scheu* from his public lectures in 1937. The Nuremburg laws had passed two years earlier, *Krystallnacht* was looming on the horizon, and Karl Jaspers had just been barred from the German universities because his wife was Jewish. Heidegger, perhaps not so unaware of these events as some might like to imagine, had renounced his position as rector of Freiburg in 1934, but had still worn a Nazi badge to his friend Karl Löwith's house in 1936: a troubling wardrobe choice, even if Löwith had been a gentile.[23] While it falls out of the scope of this project to offer psychological conjectures about the extent of Heidegger's loyalty to the Nazi party, it had doubtless become clear to him by 1937 that it was a less-than-perfect alliance. National Socialism had not catapulted Germany into the new and glorious metaphysical beginning Heidegger envisioned, his own work had come under intense scrutiny by party members and opponents alike, and he may have anticipated that any direct appeal to *Erschrecken und Scheu* might look a bit too much like Nazi propaganda—especially in light of unfortunate sound bites like "we must first call for someone capable of instilling terror into our *Dasein* again."[24] Whether compelled by literary or political necessity (or both), then, Heidegger reserves "reservedness" for later.

A signal that his concern to veil this material is not *solely* political, however, is that when it is finally treated explicitly, the mood of the "other" beginning does not find systematic explication in thirteen theses. It is, instead, illuminated in periodic flashes scattered throughout the deleted and unpublished material. Heidegger even hesitates to assign it any one name, lest a conceptual stranglehold render it powerless to deliver thinking from conceptuality: "the grounding-attunement of another beginning can hardly ever be known merely by one name—and especially in crossing to that beginning. And yet, the manifold names do not deny the onefoldness of this grounding-attunement; they only point to the ungraspable of all that is simple in the onefold."[25] Among these manifold names are "intimating" and "deep foreboding," which give wonder a certain portentous resonance. Yet Heidegger spends most time on the triumvirate, nameable only "in a distant way," of *Verhaltenheit, Erschrecken,* and *Scheu.*[26]

---

23. Safranski, *Martin Heidegger*, 320.
24. Heidegger, *Basic Concepts*, 172.
25. Heidegger, *Contributions to Philosophy*, 16.
26. Ibid., 11.

Practices of Wonder

As we have seen, Heidegger limits the wonder he calls *Erstaunen* to the first beginning when he limits its "object" to the "being of beings." Focused as it is on beings as they appear, *Erstaunen* overlooks the event of appearance itself; that is, the event of being. This seems a strange failure to attribute to wonder, inasmuch as Heidegger holds *thaumazein* to be the disposition attuned to unconcealment (*alêtheia*). If wonder wonders at unconcealment itself, then how can wonder possibly miss the truth of being? The missing link here is provided in a deleted passage from the 1937–38 lectures in which Heidegger explicitly declares even *alêtheia* to be an insufficiently primordial name for "truth." What unconcealment presupposes, and for this reason cannot see, is the *concealment* to which it is perpetually bound: "truth is not simply the unconcealedness of beings—*alêtheia*—but, more originally understood, is the clearing for the vacillating self-concealment. The name 'vacillating self-concealment' is a name for being itself."[27] In the *Contributions to Philosophy* this self-donating double movement of being is rebaptized *Ereignis*, or "the event [of being's appropriation to beings]." Insofar as *Ereignis* takes place in the constant interplay of concealment and unconcealment, it makes clear what *alêtheia* risks leaving unelaborated: that truth does not exist in some Platonic realm apart from the everyday material world. Rather, it occurs as and through the ordinary. One might think here of Heidegger's insistence in *Being and Time* that "*authentic existence is nothing which hovers over entangled everydayness, but is existentially only a modified grasp of everydayness.*"[28] If truth takes place as an occurrence rather than a location, an event rather than an object, then it completely dismantles the notion that the truth is "out there" in some world of pure unconcealment. Rather, it takes place through this world—the only world there is.

It is Heidegger's abandonment of truth as *alêtheia* that necessitates his abandonment of wonder as *Erstaunen*. As he pushes on to *Ereignis*, he announces that now he must find a new foundational mood. It is crucial to note, however, that *Ereignis* is no radical departure from *alêtheia*. It is, rather, both unconcealment *and* concealment, so that truth cannot open onto *Ereignis* without going back to truth as *alêtheia*. So it is with wonder. *Verhaltenheit*, as it turns out, is nothing more—and nothing less—than a more primordially thought *Erstaunen*, a new incarnation of *thaumazein* that holds itself between wonder and *its* opposite—a wonderstruck,

27. Heidegger, *Basic Questions*, 179.
28. Heidegger, *Being and Time*, 167.

horrified, amazed kind of fright that becomes the dispositional possibility of futural thinking itself.

The work of this futural philosophy will be to think the "beyng" that has *withdrawn* from beings, giving them over to the calculating forces of modern technology. Brought into being-abandoned, beings can only appear as objects; in other words, severed from being, beings are not themselves. And yet, beings are. This, for Heidegger, is absolutely terrifying. The disposition that might unsettle thought out of its representative manipulations, then, is not a simple wonder at the thatness of beings—for who could possibly be surprised that beings are?—but rather, shock (*Schrecken*) and/or terror (*Erschrecken*) that, strictly speaking, *beings cannot be*. What instills this terrifying shock is the sudden realization "that beings can *be* while the truth of being remains forgotten"—that, like wind-up dolls with lost keys, "beings strut as beings and yet are abandoned by beyng."[29] Yet this terror is accompanied by a kind of harrowed astonishment: "just as wonder bears in itself its own sort of terror, so does terror involve its own mode of self-composure, calm steadfastness, and new wonder."[30]

This "new wonder" is *Scheu*, a mood Heidegger describes as "awe in the face of what is remotest, namely that in beings, and before each being, beyng holds sway."[31] Awe is the second, more enduring movement of this new wonder, a response to the shock of *Er/schrecken*. So if *Erschrecken* registers that that which is, cannot possibly be, then *Scheu* sees that it nonetheless *is*. While *Erschrecken* recoils at the abandonment of being, *Scheu* marvels that being nonetheless gives itself through this withdrawal. In short, this "new wonder" marvels that beings cannot be, and yet beings are, that is to say, being *happens*. Where being cannot possibly happen.

In sum, Heidegger gives us two substantial treatments of wonder. The first is *Erstaunen* as the first disposition of philosophy, and the second is *Verhaltenheit* as the disposition that might transport thinking back to its deepest roots, and into a new beginning. In both incarnations, it is important to note that wonder wonders not at the extraordinary as such, but rather at the uncanniness of the everyday. Wonder wonders at the extraordinary in and as the ordinary. What then does this mean for the philosopher who attempts to dwell in it?

We will remember that Hannah Arendt likened Heidegger to the philosopher whose eyes are so trained on the brilliance of the Forms that

29. Ibid., 169.
30. Ibid.
31. Ibid., 4.

he can't see a thing in the ordinary world—who is so lost in wonder that he fails to find his way around once he returns to the cave. The problem of philosophy's ethico-political engagement therefore hinges on the *nature* of wonder. Is wonder the disengaged contemplation of disembodied Forms, in which case Arendt is right to discourage us from it, or does wonder prompt us to think differently about the way the philosopher ought to live in relation to the everyday world of the cave?

Heidegger's Caves

Heidegger considers Plato's allegory of the cave so provocative that he reads it twice: once in his 1931 lectures at Freiburg (followed by a series on Plato's *Theaetetus*), and again in an essay written in 1947, after the University's denazification committee had prohibited him from lecturing in public.[32] Each reading is accompanied by Heidegger's own translation of the tale—the 1931 version a Heidegger-inflected revision of the then-standard Schleiermacher translation, and the 1947 version a substantial revision of the first.

In his 1931 effort, Heidegger divides his translation and commentary into four parts. The first part of the story introduces us to the hypothetical inhabitants of a hypothetical cave underground. Held in chains from the time of their birth, the people who live there can only see a wall in front of them, onto which shadows of various objects are projected by means of a hidden fire and screen.[33] From the viewpoint of the prisoners, as Plato tells us, these shadows are not shadows but things-in-themselves. In a more Heideggerian register, these images are what is unconcealed and therefore constitute "the true" (*alêthes*) at this stage. For the cave dwellers, in other words, the shadows are beings. In the second stage (515c–515e), one man somehow loses his chains and turns to face the objects and the fire behind him. In comparison to the shadows to which he was accustomed, the things he now sees are truer, "more unconcealed" (*alêthetera*), and therefore "more *beingful* beings," although he cannot yet recognize them as such.[34] The third stage (515e–516e) follows this man as he is dragged from the cave into the blinding light of day, learning how to gaze upon objects under the sun and ultimately the sun itself, an allegory for the Good. To refer to this "truest"

---

32. The first account can be found in Heidegger, *Essence of Truth*, 1–106. The second can be found in Heidegger, "Plato's Doctrine of Truth," 155–82.

33. Plato, *Republic*, 514a–15c.

34. Heidegger, *Essence of Truth*, 26.

truth, as well as the other Forms, Heidegger borrows a term from book 6 of the *Republic* (484c): *ta alêthestata*, the "most unconcealed, the essentially unconcealed, the primordially unconcealed, because the unconcealment of beings *originates* in them."[35] Finally, the fourth part of the story (516e–517a) tracks the liberated man's return to the cave, where he is ridiculed and quite possibly killed by the cave dwellers. If he survives, Plato tells us, he will come to rule the cave as the philosopher-king.

One great insight that emerges during the course of Heidegger's analysis is that truth, here narrated as a process of liberation, does not reside statically in any one of these stages. Rather, it *takes place* in the transitions between them. Accustomed to two-dimensional projections, the prisoner initially will not understand what he sees when he turns around to face the objects and the fire behind him. In fact, simply because they are more familiar, he will probably be inclined to think the shadows are truer than what is now revealed to him.[36] Similarly, when this man is hauled out of the cave, the sunlight will seem so bright by comparison to the darkness that, at first, he will be unable to see anything. Once his eyes adjust a bit, he will be able to see the things that most resemble the projections inside the cave; that is, shadows. Gradually, he will be able to look at reflections, then objects in a dim light, objects in the sunlight, and finally the sunlight itself. Only at that point will he finally understand the shadows in the cave *to be shadows*. Liberation—that is, the *occurrence* of truth itself, and not simply its recognition—therefore depends upon the gradual adjustment of one's vision: truth happens in the transitions.[37]

Yet Heidegger argues that Plato misses the import of these transitions by locating truth statically in the Forms outside the cave. Had he emphasized the transitions rather than the stages themselves, Plato would have seen that hiddenness belongs to revelation: that there is no unconcealment without concealment, no truth without untruth. After all, what is ontologically most unconcealed (i.e., the realm of the Forms) is most *concealed* from the perspective of the cave dwellers and vice versa. Perhaps most radical of all, then, is Heidegger's recognition that the prisoner is not fully freed for the truth in the "third" stage, when he looks upon the Forms, but rather in the "fourth" stage, when he returns to the cave: "the ascent does not proceed upwards, to something higher, but *backwards*."[38]

35. Ibid., 49; translation modified.
36. Ibid., 26.
37. Ibid., 44.
38. Ibid., 58.

Practices of Wonder

Again, Plato crowns as philosopher-king the one who chooses to endure the pain of this homeward journey, but for Heidegger the re-descent is not just a matter of compassion or duty; it is a matter of the happening of truth itself. If truth is not lodged within the Forms, but in the transitions between truth and untruth, then the one who simply takes up residence outside the cave *is not actually free*. As Heidegger puts it, "whoever comes out of the cave only to lose himself in the 'appearing' of the ideas would not truly understand these . . . as wrenching beings from hiddenness and overcoming their concealment. He would regard the ideas themselves as just beings of a higher order. Deconcealment would not *occur* at all."[39] Since truth only takes place as the transition from hiddenness to unhiddenness, there *is* no truth without hiddenness. Truth's very occurrence therefore depends upon "*a return* from the sunlight."[40]

It is at this point, however, that matters begin to get complicated. When Heidegger calls the cave an allegory for the occurrence of truth, he does not mean that it tells the story of a person's learning a truth that exists somewhere. To the contrary, truth itself *happens* as the one man exits and returns to the cave. This is to say that truth depends on the liberated person it forms: "the essence of truth *qua alêtheia* is deconcealment, therefore located in man himself." Admitting that he has performed a "daring" reduction of Truth to "something human," Heidegger adds the qualification that, of course, "everything depends on what 'human' means here."[41] The truth does not come into being through everyday, cavely people (cf. "the they" of *Being and Time*), but only through the one who makes it out of and back into the cave. Effecting the truth, this man effectively *becomes* truth, becomes himself as truth. And so the formation of this "man" as unconcealment-itself makes him the unconceale*r*: the man is finally liberated when he becomes liberat*or* of the people who remain in the cave. Ultimately, then, the fourth stage in the gradual emergence of truth is decisive for Heidegger because it marks the arrival of this liberator:

> Liberation does not achieve its final goal merely by ascent to the sun. Freedom is not *just* a matter of being *un*shackled, nor just a matter of being free *for* the light. Rather, genuine freedom means *to be a liberator* from the dark. The descent back into the cave is not some subsequent diversion on the part of those who have become free, perhaps undertaken from curiosity about

---

39. Heidegger, *Essence of Truth*, 66.
40. Ibid., 63.
41. Ibid., 54, 55.

how the cave looks from above, but is the only manner through which freedom is genuinely *realized*.[42]

As we know both from Plato's account and Heidegger's gloss, however, this liberator's homecoming is not exactly celebrated with a ticker tape parade. Just as his eyes were blinded by the sun in the transition to the third stage, they are blinded again by the darkness in the transition to the fourth. Far from greeting him as their leader and following him to freedom, his compatriots begin to say of him that he went all that way to wreck his eyesight, and if he tries to help them see, they will probably try to *kill* him.[43] With this difficulty in mind, Plato goes on to discuss the gradual readjustment from light to darkness that the philosopher-king would first have to undergo before helping his cavemates to adjust their eyes from darkness to light: "Therefore each of you in turn must go down to live in the common dwelling place of the others and grow accustomed to seeing in the dark. *When you are used to it*, you'll see vastly better than the people down there."[44] Concretely, this acclamation takes shape for Plato as fifteen years of practical political training in the cave (539e–540a). The Heideggerian account, on the other hand, cuts out before all of this: "if they could somehow get their hands on him, wouldn't they kill him?" And here Heidegger's story ends.

Bound by this execution, Heidegger's account of the occurrence of truth is entirely tied up with violence. The liberator's tendency to be murdered is merely the final phase of what has been an ethically questionable process from the beginning. Heidegger writes: "liberation, in the sense of turning around towards the light of the sun, is *violent*. Attaining what is . . . unhidden involves violence, thus . . . resistance, such that the one to be freed is forced up along a rugged path. The ascent demands work and exertion, causing strain and suffering . . . a sudden ripping loose, followed by, outside the cave, a *slow adaptation*."[45] What is offensive to Heidegger about the murder of the philosopher, then, is not the introduction of force into the history of truth, but rather the use of force by the *wrong party*. Because he is attuned to truth, only the liberator may exert force over others. Because he understands beings' unconcealment, he is transformed into beings' unconceal*er*, and "only then does he gain power to the violence he

---

42. Ibid., 66.
43. Plato, *Republic*, 517a.
44. Ibid., 520c; emphasis added.
45. Heidegger, *Essence of Truth*, 32.

must employ in liberation."⁴⁶ This necessary violence takes two different forms in Heidegger's 1931 lectures. The first is that the philosopher will force others to repeat his journey, "dragging . . . the others out into the light which already fills and binds his own view."⁴⁷ It should be noted here that, inasmuch as the liberator's vision is still exclusively "bound" to the light, he has not taken any time at all—let alone Plato's fifteen years—to learn how to see in the dark before dragging others out of it. So the "slow adaptation" is for some reason limited to the space outside the cave. Inside the cave, Heidegger does not seem to hold out much hope at all for an equal and opposite readjustment to the darkness. He maintains that since the liberator's "assertions fail to correspond to what everyone down there agrees upon is correct," the liberator will not even try to see from their perspective (in the manner, one might say, of Socrates): "The philosopher will not himself challenge this all too obligatory cave-chatter," Heidegger announces, "but will leave it to itself, instead immediately seizing hold of *one* person (or a few) and pulling him out, attempting to lead him on the long journey out of the cave."⁴⁸

From what immediately follows this passage, however, we see that while the philosopher will not stoop to the level of engaging this mindless "cave-chatter," he does not just "leave it to itself," either. Rather, he openly contradicts what the cave people say by means of "assertions" the people will never understand—that is, whenever he is not leading forced marches out of the cave. "The liberated one returns to the cave with an eye for *being*," Heidegger explains.

> This means that he who has been filled with the illuminating view for the being of beings will make known to the cave-dwellers his thoughts on what *they*, down there, take for beings. He can only do this if he remains true to himself in his liberated stance. He will report what he sees in the cave from the standpoint of his view of essence. . . . On the basis of his view of essence, *he knows in advance, before he returns to the cave,* what "shadows" mean, and upon what their possibility is grounded. Only because he *already knows* this is he able, returning to the cave, to demonstrate that the unhidden now showing itself upon the wall is caused by the fire in the cave, that this unhidden is shadow.⁴⁹

46. Ibid., 60.
47. Ibid.
48. Ibid., 63.
49. Ibid., 64–65; emphasis added.

If the forced marches out of the cave constitute one form of violence, I would argue that these "assertions" inside it constitute another. There is no mention here of the slow and painful recalibration that the being-dazzled philosopher must undergo in order to see the shadows in the cave again. He knows everything he needs to know before he heads back down, and so never takes the time to learn to see what the cave folk see. This is the reason that his view will remain incompatible with theirs. His relationship with the people in the cave is thus irremediably agonistic, for all this "liberator" can do is lecture at an audience that will never understand him or *force* a few of them to understand him by tearing them away from the cave, at which point the others will want to kill him. And, in the midst of all this violence and counterviolence, Heidegger mentions incidentally that these philosophers "are to become *phulakês*, guardians. Control and organization of the state is to be undertaken by philosophers."[50] Somehow, even though the philosophers can't understand the shadows within it, fail to communicate inside it, provoke homicidal tendencies among those who live there, and spend most of their time wrestling one or two promising young boys *out* of it, the philosophers will rule the cave.

What has happened here?

Heidegger, it seems, has lost sight of his most profound insight: that truth takes place in the *transitions*, or encounters, between darkness and light, *and vice versa*. By ignoring the considerable problem of the neophyte philosopher's inability to see in the dark, by insisting that his focus is solely on being and essence and light, Heidegger not only makes a violent and useless polemicist out of the philosopher-king but also reinscribes precisely what he calls "*Plato's* doctrine of truth." For, if the liberator returns to the cave with his eyes trained only on what is *not* in the cave, then the implication is that, *before* he returns, he already has—and already *is*—the truth. If nothing in the thoughtless chatter of the cave people can teach him anything about the being and truth and essence that he knows "in advance," then *truth does not occur in the cave at all*. Surely if concealment and unconcealment happen through one another, then the descent must be seen as integral to the occurrence of truth—not just an opportunity to report on it. But by the end of this account, truth is simply located, just as it is for Heidegger's Plato, outside the cave: in a being without beings, transcendence without worldliness, and unconcealment without concealment.

Heidegger, I would argue, is partly justified and partly unjustified in reading *Plato* in this manner (but his *own* lapse into this vision remains

---

50. Heidegger, *Essence of Truth*, 73.

very puzzling indeed). On the one hand, Plato seems to authorize the notion that the return to the cave cannot teach the philosopher anything. In the illustration of the divided line, for example, Plato describes the highest form of *nous* as reaching conclusions "without making use of anything visible at all, but only of forms themselves, moving on from forms to forms, and ending in forms."[51] On the other hand, Plato has Socrates ridicule those otherworldly philosophers who live out their days on the "Isles of the Blessed," and who stubbornly refuse "to go down again to the prisoners in the cave and share their labors and honors."[52] In this notion of "sharing," Socrates preemptively repudiates Heidegger's insistence that the returned philosopher will refuse to listen to "cave chatter." Even more radical, however, is Socrates' account of the end of the cavely readjustment period that Heidegger omits. After fifteen years of political training in the cave, Socrates says, "at the age of fifty, those who've survived the tests and been successful both in practical matters and in the sciences must be led to the goal and compelled to lift up the radiant light of their souls to what itself provides light for everything. And *once they've seen the Good itself*, they must each in turn put the city, its citizens, and themselves in order, using it as their model."[53] This is nothing if not astonishing: what Socrates says quite explicitly here is that it is only *after* the philosophers have readjusted their vision to the blinding darkness that they finally see the Good itself. *In the midst of the cave.* And is this not what Heidegger has been saying all along? That the truth always and only opens in and through the untruth that conceals and reveals it? Why then does Heidegger cave in to such a facile bifurcation between the cave and the open, untruth and truth, shadows and things-in-themselves? And what would it mean to retell the story in such a way that truth might genuinely take place in their between—in the interstices of what is embodied in the "cave" and what is promised in the "open"?

Heidegger's second translation and interpretation of this allegory gets us a bit closer than the first to opening this betweenness, if ultimately by shutting it down in the opposite direction. In his 1947 essay on the cave, Heidegger stresses even more strongly the priority of the transitions over the stages themselves and, promisingly, almost always counters his references to the upward adjustment with equal and opposite rhetorical nods to the downward adjustment. In the first few pages, for example, he argues that

---

51. Plato, *Republic*, 511b–c.
52. Ibid., 519c–d.
53. Ibid., 540a–b.

"the 'allegory' recounts a series of movements rather than just reporting on the dwelling places and conditions of people inside and outside the cave. In fact, the movements that it recounts are movements of passage out of the cave into the daylight and then back out of the daylight into the cave."[54] In this version of the story, even more explicitly than in the first, the one who makes his way out of the cave is meant to make his way back *down* to free those who are still imprisoned within it. The most striking difference between the two narratives, however, is that the second presents its reader with a liberator who has very little confidence in his ability to liberate.

In 1947, what concerns Heidegger far more than it had sixteen years earlier—before the war, before the Rectorship, before the humiliating appearances in front of the denazification committee—is the problem of the philosopher's night blindness. In marked contrast to the picture of poorly received triumphalism he paints in his earlier account, Heidegger now steeps his philosopher in political impotence: "the one who has been freed is *supposed to* lead these people too away from what is unhidden for them and to bring them face to face with the most unhidden. But the *would-be* liberator no longer knows his or her way around the cave and risks the danger of succumbing to the overwhelming power of the kind of truth that is normative down there, the danger of being *overcome* by the claim of the common 'reality' to be the only reality."[55]

In this version, as in the earlier one, the philosopher is "threatened with the possibility of being put to death," and the downward descent is portrayed agonistically as a "battle waged within the cave between the liberator and the prisoners who resist all liberation." Unlike the pontificator/bodysnatcher of the first scenario, however, the philosopher in this second one is a profoundly *vulnerable* character whose grasp on his "vision for essence" once he returns to the cave is tenuous at best.[56] In marked contrast to the Liberator of 1931, who descends with a full knowledge of the truth and remains blind to his blindness, this more circumspect would-be liberator of 1947 recognizes not only that it is difficult to hold fast to the truth of the "open," but also that he "no longer knows his way around the cave."[57]

Frustratingly, this newfound circumspection does not lead Heidegger to say that the philosopher should learn how to see again. The philosopher can only readjust to the dark, Heidegger maintains, insofar as he ceases to be

---

54. Heidegger, "Plato's Doctrine of Truth," 165.
55. Ibid., 171.
56. Ibid.
57. Ibid.

what he has become, giving up his vision of the truth in order to recall "the kind of truth that is normative down there." Just as in the 1931 reading, the viewpoints of the cave and the open are exclusive of one another, and only the latter is the locus of philosophy. Even though there is no talk of violent draggings or impassioned speeches in the 1947 text, there are still two totally separate abodes: "the one inside and the one outside the cave.... The kind of astuteness that is normative down there in the cave ... is surpassed by another *sophia*. This latter strives solely and above all to glimpse the being of beings in the 'ideas.' ... Outside the cave *sophia* is *philosophia*."[58] Just like the first reading, then, the second deconstructs (or reconstructs, which in a supposedly deconstructive text, amounts to the same thing). Heidegger caves, reconsolidating truth into its "Platonic" abode in the third stage. In fact, this second collapse is even more explicit than the first, because while Heidegger had at least initially tried in 1931 to maintain the decisiveness of the re-descent in stage 4, here he argues that "real freedom is only attained in stage three," that "authentic" liberation only occurs outside the cave.[59] So while it is the philosopher's destiny to become a misunderstood politician in the first interpretation, his best option in the second would probably be to remain out in the open where his vision of "the most unconcealed" is the most unobstructed. Equally problematic positions, the liberator of 1931 reenters the world to wage war with it, while the philosopher of 1947 would be wise, in the words of David Hume, to "make [his] escape into the calm, though obscure, regions of philosophy."[60]

At the very end of this second commentary, however, Heidegger begins to point toward a path for future thinking. He writes that while thinking must return to its origins in order to begin again, this repetition must be nonidentical in order to move thinking forward. Any "recollection" of Platonic truth cannot "take over unconcealment merely in Plato's sense"; it must also attune itself to "the 'positive' in the 'privative' essence of *alêtheia*"—that is, to forgetting, hiddenness, and untruth.[61] Presumably, then, insofar as genuine attention to truth as unconcealment would always reveal an equiprimordial concealment, such thinking would maintain itself within their relentless oscillation. It would have to take its placeless place *between* hiddenness and revelation, darkness and light, beings and being, and earth and sky. While Heidegger's own read-

---

58. Heidegger, "Plato's Doctrine of Truth," 180.
59. Ibid., 169.
60. Hume, "Natural History of Religion," 185.
61. Heidegger, "Plato's Doctrine of Truth," 182.

ings never quite sustain this possibility, then, these last moments of this essay can be heard as a call for *another* rereading of the cave—one that might *stay with* the liminality and caveliness that both of Heidegger's own accounts ultimately flee.

The philosopher in this schema would neither escape the cave forever nor live among shadows without looking at them, nor lose sight of the way shadows can be deceptive. Rather, she would be the one attuned, as Plato tells us, to the Forms and the material realm, the stars and the dirt, the truth and the shadows; moreover, to push beyond Plato, to the total interrelation of these terms: to the unconcealment of the most concealed; the truth as it opens through the most untrue; or being as it occurs in even the most negligible being.

In other words, the truth that Heidegger ultimately attributes to the exit from the cave would open in and through the cave itself. This is to say, there is no spatial separation between the "cave" and the "open," no "other world" to oppose to "this one"; rather, *the space of the cave is all there is.* Just as "authenticity" for the early Heidegger is simply a "modified grasp of everydayness," "truth" would emerge by means of the cave-chatter, as a different way of hearing. The extraordinary would show itself through the everyday, as a different way of seeing. Rather than opening onto some other world, this genuinely "Heideggerian" truth would unsettle the "Platonic" effort to abandon the ordinary by seeing the extraordinary through it. And attending to the ordinary, as Heidegger has been telling us all along, is the work of wonder. As he writes in 1937, "wonder does not divert itself from the usual but on the contrary adverts to it, precisely as what is the most unusual of everything and in everything."[62]

Once More to the Cave

So where are we? In particular, where are we with respect to Hannah Arendt's charge that Heidegger's overlooking earthly atrocities was a matter of his having dwelled too long in wonder? It seems that this charge holds only if wonder takes place in the so-called third stage—in the exit from the cave. If wonder wonders at Forms and essence and light, then coming back down to reality, to people and politics, requires abandoning wonder. What we have seen from Heidegger's analysis of wonder, however, is that it does not wonder at the extraordinary as such; rather, wonder wonders at the unusuality of the most usual of all. And what we have seen from his

---

62. Heidegger, *Basic Questions*, 145.

readings of the cave is that the philosopher *ought* to find the truth opening out through the world of the shadows. Both of these lines of analysis show that a thinking that would "dwell" in wonder, if such a thing were possible, would be fiercely attuned to the ordinary. Neither lodged in unreflective everydayness (the usual as usual) nor floating in the philosophical clouds (the unusual as unusual), wonder would dwell in between them, in that strange rhythm of *Verhaltenheit*: between the shock of the ordinary, and the awe that the extraordinary happens through the ordinary as such.

So *Er/schrecken* hits us in those moments when something familiar—something we've never thought to question or even look at properly—becomes suddenly beautiful, or horrifying, or inadmissible. This shock opens onto a "new wonder," or awe (*Scheu*), which can have the sense of gratitude, or disgust, or even outrage, as we realize that that which simply cannot be, somehow is. So shock hits in those moments when a squirrel becomes suddenly majestic, or an ordinary word like "knowledge" becomes inscrutable, or an ordinary practice like driving my car becomes ethically insupportable. And awe reveals that this majesty is what a squirrel is; that unknowability is constitutive of knowledge; and irresponsibility insists itself even through responsibility. Wonder dwells in this relentless between. And in fact, it may be that even a word like "between" fails us here, because in wonder's shock and awe, the ordinary and the extraordinary, the true and the untrue, the earthly and the ideal open in and through one another, even perhaps *as* one another. The truth in the common stuff we overlook, being in the beings we brush aside, the homely "here" where Heraclitus's gods are also. We therefore need a different dimensionality entirely; neither the vertical transcendence of the cave and the open nor some undifferentiated immanence, but something fractal, perhaps, or holographic, or chaotic. This would be the place from which we'd have to go once more to the cave; here where our most familiar story has become unfamiliar, all our bearings gone, and thinking seems impossible: "this is where philosophy begins and nowhere else."

Bibliography

Arendt, Hannah. "Martin Heidegger at Eighty." In *Heidegger and Modern Philosophy*, edited by Michael Murray, 293–303. New Haven: Yale University Press, 1978.

———. "Philosophy and Politics." *Social Research* 57 (1990) 73–103.

Aristotle. "Metaphysics." In *The Complete Works of Aristotle: The Revised Oxford Translation*, edited by Jonathan Barnes. Princeton: Princeton University Press, 1971.

Descartes, René. *The Passions of the Soul*. Translated by Stephen H. Voss. Indianapolis: Hackett, 1989.

Heidegger, Martin. *Basic Concepts*. Translated by Gary E. Aylesworth. Bloomington: Indiana University Press, 1988.

———. *Basic Questions of Philosophy: Selected "Problems" of "Logic."* Translated by Richard Rojcewicz and André Schuwer. Bloomington: Indiana University Press, 1994.

———. *Being and Time*. Translated by Joan Stambaugh. Albany: State University of New York Press, 1996.

———. *Contributions to Philosophy (from Enowning)*. Translated by Parvis Emad and Kenneth Maly. Bloomington: Indiana University Press, 1995.

———. *The Essence of Truth: On Plato's Cave Allegory and Theaetetus*. Translated by Ted Sadler. London: Continuum, 2002.

———. "Plato's Doctrine of Truth." In *Pathmarks*, edited by William McNeill, 155–82. Cambridge: Cambridge University Press, 1998.

Hume, David. "The Natural History of Religion." In *Dialogues and the Natural History of Religion*, edited by J. C. A. Gaskin, 134–96. Oxford: Oxford University Press, 1998.

Kant, Immanuel. *Critique of Judgment*. Translated by Werner S. Pluhar. Indianapolis: Hackett, 1987.

———. *Critique of Practical Reason*. Translated by Werner S. Pluhar. Indianapolis: Hackett, 2002.

Plato. *Republic*. Translated by G. M. A. Grube. Edited by C. D. C. Reeve. Indianapolis: Hackett, 1992.

———. *Theaetetus*. Edited by Bernard Williams and Miles Burnyeat. Translated by M. J. Levett. Indianapolis: Hackett, 1992.

Rubenstein, Mary-Jane. *Strange Wonder: The Closure of Metaphysics and the Opening of Awe*. New York: Columbia University Press, 2009.

Safranski, Rüdiger. *Martin Heidegger: Between Good and Evil*. Translated by Ewald Osers. Cambridge: Harvard University Press, 1998.

6

Wonder and Cognition

DEREK MATRAVERS

IN HIS SEMINAL PHILOSOPHICAL essay on wonder, Ronald Hepburn raises the following issue:

> By no means all writings on wonder see it as a highly prized mode of experience, to be fostered and stabilized. It has been seen variously (a) as signalling a check in our understanding of the world ("anxious curiosity"—Adam Smith), which we seek to "get rid of" by extending our grasp. Again, (b) allowing that some people come to love wonder for its own sake, such people have been seen as hostile to the pursuit of naturalistic explanation, preferring to marvel rather than to understand. The pursuit of scientific knowledge—it is argued—would in fact provide them with objects enough for wonder. Although in each case wonder is ousted by knowledge, the procession of problems is, for us, endless. More pessimistically, (c) some other writers have seen the growth of naturalistic explanation as necessarily and generally displacing wonder, whether we like the fact or not: and these writers do not like it at all.[1]

In this paper I am going to pursue two issues. The first is the issue of the relation between wonder and understanding or, more broadly, cognition. Wonder can come in many forms, or, rather, there is a range

---

1. Hepburn, "Wonder," 132.

of related reactions that we describe with a range of terms, such as shock, surprise, awe, astonishment, or wonder. Some of these reactions are non-cognitive. That is, they are merely affective reactions that are unrelated to understanding. Is wonder different or is it also, as Hepburn fears, a state that stands apart from understanding? That is, is it hostile to understanding (his *a* and *b*), a state that will be replaced by understanding (his *c*), or something different? The second issue I will pursue is the value of wonder. As Hepburn says, "some people come to love wonder for its own sake." Does wonder merit such love, and, if so, what is the basis of such merit?

The two issues are related in that, if we can show that wonder is a form of understanding, then that would be something valuable about it. We must not assume, however, that being a form of understanding is the only way in which wonder could be valuable. It might be the case that the value of wonder lies (at least in part) simply in its being an affective reaction to the world. Simple affective reactions to the world are not a form of understanding, as the salient fact about them is that the fact that we have rational capacities is not relevant to our feeling them. This does not exclude some sense of representation: clearly, we need to be aware that the world is such and such a way in order to have an affective reaction to it. The claim is only that such awareness does not play any further role in our cognitive economy, which, for me, is enough for it not to be a form of understanding.

One might think it obvious that merely affective reactions are valuable. After all, one of the endearing things about children is that the world is a constant source of surprise to them and it is a loveable quality in adults that they are prone to episodes of jaw-dropping. The inference from this to the value of wonder would be too hasty. The propensity for merely affective reactions might be evidence for other properties that are valuable, such as a lack of cynicism or an openness to the way the world is, without that propensity being valuable itself. Even if we grant the failure of this attempt to find wonder valuable, there seems at least one other straightforward reason for thinking merely affective reactions are valuable. I have claimed that wonder, considered simply as an affective state, does not draw on our rationality. Rather, it is a state with a positive hedonic tone: that is, a form of pleasure. Of course, inasmuch as all pleasures are valuable, such a state will be valuable. Considered merely as a positive hedonic state, however, wonder will not rise above what John Stuart Mill called the "lower pleasures." If we want to argue that wonder has more value than a sensation of pleasure, that is, that wonder is something worthy of love, then we will need to look further than its "positive hedonic tone."

Where else should we look? Is there a construal of our reaction of wonder that reveals the state to be valuable? I am going to consider three ways in which we could ground the value of wonder: first, that wonder is a reflective state (that is, one in which we somehow endorse the affect); second, that wonder is a state that has distinct affective and cognitive elements, and that the burden of the value attached to it is carried by the latter; and third, that wonder is an affective state, but of a complex and valuable kind.

The first attempt locates the source of the value of wonder in its being a reflective state, that is, a second-order attitude to our first-order engagement. Consider, for example, our feeling of wonder towards the night sky. On this account, the night sky provokes a first-order non-cognitive state in us—let us call that astonishment. Kendall Walton has suggested that this might then provoke a second-order attitude: a reflection on the first. That is, we might take delight in the capacity of the night sky to provoke our first-order attitude. The ability to reflect on our experience in this way is related to our rational capacities at least to the extent that we could not have the former without the latter. However, having a second-order attitude is not exercising our rational capacities: rather, it is finding a different and more complicated source of delight in our engagement with the world. Twisting Walton's view to fit our case, wonder would be akin to admiration for an object's capacity to astonish us.[2]

This will answer the question as to the value of wonder only if it can be shown that possession of such a second-order attitude is valuable. Rather than enter this debate, I propose to grant that it is valuable, as a more enlightening problem with this account lies elsewhere. To see this, we need to be more precise about what we mean by "wonder." Above, I claimed that it was one of a range of reactions that included shock, surprise, awe and astonishment. It would be optimistic to think that all intuitions converge on wonder as a clear and unified phenomenon distinct from these others, but we can, perhaps, make some distinctions. First, and most relevant to the defense of the value of wonder that I have just tried to mount, wonder does not generally require a second-order attitude. Consider Bill Bryson's description of seeing the Grand Canyon:

> Nothing prepares you for the Grand Canyon. No matter how many times you read about it or see it pictured, it still takes your

---

2. Walton, "How Marvellous!"

breath away. Your mind, unable to deal with anything on this scale, just shuts down and for many long moments you are a human vacuum, without speech or breath, but just a deep, inexpressible awe that anything on this earth could be so vast, so beautiful, so silent . . . It is the most awesome, most silencing sight that exists on earth.[3]

This is a paradigm instance of wonder, but it also seems to be entirely first-order: Bryson focuses on the Grand Canyon itself and not on his reaction to the Grand Canyon. The second-order attitude, on which this defense of the value of wonder relies, is not present.

What can be said to pick out an attitude of wonder from among all the other attitudes we might have to an object? We could try a variation on the above account, and use the second-order attitude not as an analysis of wonder, but as a way of determining its extension. That is, all and only objects of wonder are such that we admire them for their capacity to provide first-order engagement. This might work for the night sky (it is an object of wonder and we admire its capacity to astonish us), but it will not work for a hot shower (it is not an object of wonder, although we can admire its capacity to cause us pleasure). We seem to have no option but to consider the first-order attitude directly. What can we say that is illuminating about our attitude of wonder? In particular, moving on to our second attempt to ground the value of wonder, can we identify the thought that is at the heart of the attitude and attach value to that?

We need to proceed with caution as, to reiterate the point made above, intuition does not distinguish clearly between wonder and similar states such as awe and astonishment. In related debates, where philosophers have attempted to analyze the virtues or analyze creativity, an impasse has been reached between two groups: the first take it to be constitutive of virtues or creativity that they can serve only valuable ends, the second do not. Similar uncertainty surrounds the question whether it is constitutive of wonder that its objects are taken to be valuable. Can we wonder at an event that manifests humanity at its worst—say the sack of Constantinople? Or is that merely awe? Given the uncertainty of intuitions there seems no way of settling this issue. Maintaining a certain breadth, then, let us begin with the claim that there is a conceptual link between feeling wonder towards something and the thought that the object is in some way profound, and in some way impressive with respect to ourselves (acts of great evil can be both of these things). These two properties dovetail nicely with some of

---

3. Bryson, *Lost Continent*, 205–7.

the work from the past on wonder—or, if not specifically on wonder, on states of mind of a similar sort. I shall consider each of these—an object's being in some way profound, and being in some way impressive with respect to ourselves—in turn.

Perhaps the best way of explaining what I mean by the thought that the object is "in some way profound" is by means of a contrast. There is a surprise at the end of "The Analytic of the Beautiful" in Kant's *Critique of Judgment*. Although the experience of flames would seem to accord with his account of free beauty, Kant relegates "the changing shapes of a fire in a hearth" to the realm of the agreeable; the experience is charming and nothing more.[4] On further reflection, however, the surprise should wear off. Consider a modern equivalent: a firework display. However vivid it might be, it might be misleading to categorize our attitude as one of wonder, but rather as delight at the combination of stunning visual effects with stunning aural effects. For adults at least, the delight of a firework display is that it is all surface, all effect. There is nothing more to watching flames than the appearance they display, but for Kantian free beauty and for wonder there needs to be something more: the objects need to be significant in some way. We can capture one aspect of this by saying that we should think of the object as in some way profound.

Whilst bearing in mind the warning above not to attempt false precision, the thought associated with wonder seems narrower than the mere thought that the object is significant or profound. We also seem to need to relate the object to ourselves in some way. It is not simply that the Grand Canyon is vast that silences Bill Bryson; it is its *scale*. What we wonder at is not simply the carnage of the sack of Constantinople, but that such sacrilege, destruction, and cruelty could have been done by people like us. Other cases are more difficult to fit into this claim. We wonder at the immense complexity of the double helix of a strand of DNA; that is, we marvel that such a molecule arose through the blind machinations of nature and has the instructions for reproducing ourselves written into it. How do we think of such complexity as being related to ourselves? What is the unit of comparison? Perhaps it is the thought of the blind machinations of nature producing something with the appearance of design, beyond that of which mere human design is capable.

The claim, which is vague at best, is that the thought associated with the attitude of wonder is that the object is in some way profound, and in some way impressive with respect to ourselves. At least, these

---

4. Kant, *Critique of Judgment*, 5:243.

can serve as place-holders while we consider the relations between the various components of wonder. The suggestion under consideration is that we construe wonder as a state with this as a distinct cognitive component, where the cognitive component carries the burden of value. There is, however, a problem with any attempted analysis of this form familiar from attempts to provide cognitive accounts of the emotions: that is, the problem of integrating the bearer of value (the cognition) into the experience. A crude cognitivism construes emotions as follows. The agent forms a belief—for example, that they are faced with a snarling dog. This belief causes various other changes—a change in phenomenology (the agent will have a feeling of fear), and a change in the physiology (increased heart rate, release of adrenaline, and so on). Together, these three elements comprise the emotion. The problem lies in the final claim—what is the relation between the three elements?

The most significant aspects of cognition make it appear as if they could not be part of any account of experience. Consider three important features of the experience of wonder. First, experiences of wonder come and go. In other words, they have duration; they could be timed on a stopwatch. Bill Bryson's experience of wonder began when the clouds lifted, lasted for some while, and then ceased. Second, they have a phenomenology; in a phrase that has become standard in philosophy, "there is something that it is like" to have an experience of wonder. Third, the experience, if valuable, is non-instrumentally valuable. We do not value the experience of wonder because it is a means to something else that we value (as I value my five-pound note because it is a means to lunch). Beliefs have none of these three features. While it is true that my belief that Paris is the capital of France has duration in the sense that there was some time that I acquired it, and it will disappear when my mind does, it does not come and go in the way that experiences come and go. Second, contemporary philosophy of mind stresses that beliefs do not have a phenomenology: there is nothing that it is like to believe that Paris is the capital of France. Finally, it is implausible to think that beliefs have non-instrumental value. Rather, their value lies in their role in our motivational economy: it is valuable for me to have the belief that Paris is the capital of France, because if I want to go to the capital of France, I know to go to Paris. In short, we are trying to explicate a non-instrumentally valuable experience in terms of an instrumentally valuable non-experience. The cognitive content of the experience of wonder, construed as a belief, cannot provide the account of its value.

Practices of Wonder

This problem, as I have said, has been around for a while. Regrettably, the philosopher who has done most to explicate aesthetic experience (from which we could hope to get some enlightenment about wonder), Monroe Beardsley, fudges this issue. He lists "active discovery" as one of his five criteria for aesthetic experience, which he defines thus:

> A *sense* of actively exercising constructive powers of the mind, of being challenged by a variety of conflicting stimuli to try to make them cohere; a keyed-up state amounting to exhilaration in seeing connections between percepts and between meanings, a sense (which may be illusory) of intelligibility.[5]

In other words, Beardsley "solves" the problem by dropping talk of cognitions going on in favor of talk of a *sense* of cognition going on. However, a sense is only a sense; it is not the sense of thinking that is valuable, but rather the thinking itself. The cost of Beardsley's solution is, unfortunately, vacuity.

It is perhaps not surprising that we have reached this impasse given the implausibility of the model of the emotions with which we were working. I described it above as a conjunction of three states: the cognitive, the physiological and the phenomenological. However, this is clearly inadequate: we could have all those three states simultaneously and still not be experiencing an emotion. An adequate model of the emotions will cease treating these as discrete states; in particular, it will allow that our beliefs can change the nature of our experiences (the so-called cognitive penetration of experience). It is, for example, our belief that the dog is rabid that causes us to see the dog as threatening.

I claimed above that "there seems to be a conceptual link between feeling wonder towards something and that thing being in some way profound, and in some way impressive with respect to ourselves." Granting the cognitive penetration of experience, this opens the possibility that when we believe an object is in some way profound and impressive with respect to ourselves, that is how we experience it. That is, the experience of wonder is the experience of an object *as* in some way profound and impressive with respect to ourselves. We have reached the third of our three attempts to ground the value of wonder: that is, to construe it as an affective state, but of a complex and valuable kind.

What can be said in defense of the cognitive penetration of experience? It has been thought in the past that what we really perceive are

---

5. Beardsley, "Aesthetic Experience," 288–89.

splotches of color, which we then construct into a representation of the world. There might be some sense in which that is true, however there is another sense in which the content of our visual experience is not splotches of color—what we see are sheds, trains, and streetlights. In short, our concepts are already bought to bear on the content of experience. Hence, the real issue is not whether cognitive content is built into perceptual experience, but where to draw the line between content that is part of perceptual experience and content that is not. For example, when we look at a tree in March do we literally see the onset of spring, or do we see the buds and infer that spring is on its way? What is the general principle by which we decide whether something is part of the content of an experience, or an inference based on that experience?

The obvious form such a principle could take would be whether what we claim is part of our perceptual experience is, in fact, *perceptible*. However, any such principle will be question-begging, as we can see if we apply it to our problematic case. The principle would claim that we see the March buds as the arrival of spring only if the arrival of spring is perceptible. However, the question of whether the arrival of spring is perceptible is exactly what is at issue. Rather than look for such a principle, we can instead point to a contrast. That is, there are some beliefs we hold about things that nobody would claim affect our experience of those things. To quote Malcolm Budd:

> Most of us know that water is H2O, but this knowledge does not enable an enhanced aesthetic appreciation of water, in dew, mist, rain, snow, rivers, or waterfalls, for example. For knowledge of the nature of a natural phenomenon to be able to effect a transformation of the subject's aesthetic experience of it, the knowledge must be such that it can permeate or inform the perception of the phenomenon, so that what the subject sees it as is different from how it is seen by someone who lacks the requisite knowledge. We do not see water or copper differently from one who is ignorant of their nature: we do not see water as H2O or copper as possessing atomic number 29, for the knowledge we bring to our perception is not such as to integrate with the perception in such a manner as to generate a new perceptual-cum-imaginative content of experience.[6]

In place of a general principle, we will need to decide whether or not certain thoughts or beliefs "generate a new perceptual-cum-imaginative

---

6. Budd, *Aesthetic Appreciation of Nature*, 22.

content of experience" in a more piecemeal manner. Our belief that water is H2O will not affect our experience of water, but our belief that the dog is rabid will affect our experience of the dog. That we decide on whether or not something features in our visual experience by reflecting on the nature our experience is nicely illustrated in this example from Richard Wollheim.

> I look at a picture that includes a classical landscape with ruins. And now imagine the following dialogue: "Can you see the columns?" "Yes." "Can you see the columns as coming from a temple?" "Yes." "Can you see the columns as coming from the temple as having been thrown down?" "Yes." "Can you see them as having been thrown down some hundreds of years ago by barbarians?" "Yes." "Can you see them as having been thrown down some hundreds of years ago by barbarians wearing the skins of wild asses?" (Pause.) "No." At each exchange, what "Yes" means is that the prompt has made a difference to what has been seen in the scene, just as the "No" signifies that, for at least *this spectator here and now*, the limits of visibility in this surface have been reached.[7]

Although we make decisions in a piecemeal manner, we need not make them on a case-by-case basis. In particular, it might be thought that the belief that an object is in some way profound and impressive in relation to ourselves will always make a difference to our experience of it. At least, that appears to be part of our thinking about the sublime, the one-time companion to the beautiful that has since fallen out of common use.[8] Ronald Hepburn explicitly draws this link in the paper with which I began: ". . . the presence of wonder marks a distinctive and high-ranking mode of aesthetic, or aesthetic-religious, experience characterizable by that duality of dread and delight. So conceived, sublimity is essentially concerned with transformation of the merely threatening and daunting into what is aesthetically manageable, even contemplated with joy: and this achieved through the agency of wonder."[9]

Kant's discussion of the sublime—or rather, his discussion of two notions of the sublime—is what I had in mind in picking out the thought of an object being in some way profound or impressive with respect to ourselves. Kant described his two notions as "the mathematically sublime" and "the dynamically sublime." The mathematically sublime concerns the

7. Wollheim, "Pictorial Representation," 23–24.

8. Although it has enjoyed a vogue amongst philosophers, especially those interested in postmodernism. See Crowther, *Kantian Sublime*.

9. Hepburn, "Wonder," 152.

efforts of the imagination to estimate the magnitude of an object. In the words of a recent commentator, this involves imagery: "the choice of a certain unit of measure and an estimate by sight of the magnitude of the given object as a certain multiple of this unit." The dynamically sublime also relates the world to ourselves. Kant defines those parts of nature that are the object of the dynamically sublime as "a might (a power that is superior to great obstacles) that is not considered superior to oneself."[10] These are experiences of objects under a certain description: an object *as* being a certain multiple of a unit greater than ourselves, or an object *as* being of great might, but not superior to ourselves. Indeed, the experience is even more complicated than that; not only do we have an experience of something as answering a certain description, but this is tied to a "twofold hedonic reaction" of both pleasure and displeasure. That is, we take pleasure and pain *in* the immensity of the universe, or *in* the might of nature.

The case that Budd gives to contrast with his earlier examples of beliefs that do not affect experience provides a good example of the attitude of wonder.

> A correct understanding of what is visible in the night sky thus makes possible a transformation of your experience from a condition in which you are struck by a milky path running across the sky to one in which your position in the universe—your position and that of everyone else you care about—is manifest to you in a manner which encourages an awareness of the minute stage on which the history of humanity unfolds, the peripheral status of what happens on earth even in our own galaxy, the awesome immensity of the multitude of stars that compose that galaxy, and the realization that you are forever isolated from whatever civilizations, perhaps countlessly many, are present elsewhere in space and that you must remain ignorant of their different natures and histories, no matter how fascinating these might be. Such thoughts, harnessed to your perceptual experience, constitute an important change in your perspective, and are likely to produce one of those peculiar combinations of mental states that have been called experiences of the sublime—in this case a feeling of wonder combined with an experience of vulnerability woven together with a sense of the relative insignificance of your individual self . . .[11]

---

10. Budd, *Aesthetic Appreciation of Nature*, 74, 78.
11. Ibid, 21–22.

Practices of Wonder

Granting that this is an experience of wonder, we need to show that it is an experience of a "complex and valuable kind." It is certainly complex, but is it valuable? Let us return to the way that Hepburn set up the problem at the start of this paper. There, the threat to the value of wonder was that it was a barrier to, or a replacement for, understanding. However, on this construal of wonder there is no conflict. The experience Budd describes is one imbued with understanding—an experience he could not have were he not possessed with the requisite understanding. That is, the threat to the value of wonder that Hepburn describes vanishes; there is no conflict between wonder and understanding.

I shall conclude with one further thought about the value of wonder. According to Budd, our experience of the night sky is affected by various thoughts about "the minute stage on which the history of humanity unfolds, the peripheral status of what happens on earth even in our own galaxy, the awesome immensity of the multitude of stars that compose that galaxy, and the realization that you are forever isolated from whatever civilizations..."[12] Such thoughts manifest an understanding of the relation between ourselves and the universe. We can contrast this with another case in which we have thoughts that an object is profound and impressive with respect to ourselves, and those thoughts make a difference to our experience, but in which those thoughts are false. For example, someone might think a certain child is the reincarnation of former beings, who carries within him or her memories drawn from several lives across the ages. Such a thought makes a difference to their experience, and they regard the child with wonder. Would such an experience be valuable?

The question this raises is whether the value of wonder is a conditional one; that is, whether it is valuable only on condition that something else is the case. With wonder, the claim would be that it is valuable only if it is based on accurate understanding (that is, not based on false belief). There are other familiar cases that are potential instances of conditional value: pleasure is valuable only if it is taken in something good, or happiness is valuable only if it is merited. We do recognize a distinction here. Of course, it *seems* to the person who is having the experience that they are having a valuable experience. That, however, is only because they take it to be an experience of a certain sort. If the experience is not of that sort, then they will revise their claim. A marriage might seem valuable until it is discovered that one of the partners was only interested in the other for their money, which they spent on a succession of lovers. The wronged

---

12. Ibid., 22.

party's view of the value of the marriage is bound to change; although it seemed valuable, it was not. Similarly, the attitude of wonder towards the child is not valuable, given that the belief in reincarnation is false.

In summary, I have argued that the best defense of the value of wonder is that it is an affective state, but of a complex and valuable kind. What is complex and valuable about it is that it is affected by our beliefs; in particular, the belief that the object is profound and impressive in relation to us. Furthermore, wonder is only valuable if that belief is true. If the belief is false, then, although our experience seems to have value, in reality it does not.[13]

---

13. I would like to thank Jane Heal for comments on an earlier version of this paper, and the editor for her extensive and very helpful comments.

Bibliography

Beardsley, Monroe C. "Aesthetic Experience." In *The Aesthetic Point of View: Selected Essays*, edited by M. J. Wreen and D. M. Callen, 285–97. Ithaca: Cornell University Press, 1982.

Bryson, Bill. *The Lost Continent & Neither Here Nor There*. London: Secker & Warburg, 1989.

Budd, Malcolm. *The Aesthetic Appreciation of Nature*. Oxford: Oxford University Press, 2002.

Crowther, Paul. *The Kantian Sublime: From Morality to Art*. Oxford: Oxford University Press, 1989.

Hepburn, Ronald. "Wonder." In *"Wonder" and Other Essays*, 131–54. Edinburgh: Edinburgh University Press, 1984.

Kant, Immanuel. *The Critique of Judgment*. Translated by Werner S. Pluhar. Indianapolis: Hackett, 1987.

Walton, Kendall. "How Marvellous! Toward a Theory of Aesthetic Value." *Journal of Aesthetics and Art Criticism* 51 (1993) 499–510.

Wollheim, Richard. "On Pictorial Representation." In *Richard Wollheim on the Art of Painting*, edited by Rob van Gerwen, 15–27. Cambridge: Cambridge University Press, 2001.

7

The Microscopic Glance
Spiritual Exercises, the Microscope, and the Practice of Wonder in Early Modern Science

CLAUDE-OLIVIER DORON

IN AN ESSAY PUBLISHED in his study on ancient philosophy, *Exercices spirituels et philosophie antique*, Pierre Hadot used the term "spiritual exercise" to describe the physical part of Stoic philosophy, particularly as expressed in the work of Marcus Aurelius. In his view, the Stoics' study of nature had to be read as a technique of self-transformation, and as a means for the discipline and education of emotion, that is, as "a practice that aims to provoke a radical change in one's being."[1] Such a tradition, which understands the observation of the world, of its order and vastness, as a way of transforming one's experience of oneself, can easily be traced back to Plato, through books such as Seneca's *Quaestiones Naturales* or Cicero's *De Natura Deorum*. As Rémi Brague has remarked in his *La sagesse du monde*, during antiquity and the Middle Ages "the attitude that was thought to give a human being the means of realizing his humanity ... was linked to cosmology. The wisdom through which a human being is or should be what he is was a 'wisdom of the world.'"[2] And one of the most important

---

1. Hadot, *Exercices spirituels*, 271. All translations in this essay are my own unless otherwise indicated.
2. Brague, *Sagesse du monde*, 12.

experiences that was at stake in this ethical relationship between the wise and the world was a certain kind of *thauma*, of wonder before the order of nature, its regularity and its vastness.

What I will be arguing in this essay is that the microscope assumed a similar function subsequent to its initial development in the period of early modernity.[3] In many texts ranging from the end of the seventeenth century until at least the middle of the eighteenth it was described as an instrument that could be deployed for the practice and cultivation of such wonder. Wonder will not be understood here as an immediate emotion arising in response to strange or exceptional phenomena, such as extraordinary wonders or miracles. Rather, it emerges as a complex emotion produced through disciplined experience and by means of technical instruments and procedures of observation. As such, it is an emotion that requires practice and active effort to be maintained, and that may be derived from the most ordinary objects, even the smallest or most despised, such as insects, needles, raindrops, snowflakes, and so on. In this function, the microscope served as a means of producing an experience—the so-called "objective" experience of objects—that was of a very peculiar kind. It was not only an "objective" experience as we might understand this today, involving detailed observations and well-regulated procedures for producing truth and for preventing the observer's affects and subjective states from intruding. It was also a kind of "objective *mystical* experience" and a way of attaining wisdom and knowledge of God. It is a far from easy matter to distinguish between the experience produced by the microscope considered as a pure description of the world's phenomena, and considered in terms of its capacity to produce an inner transformation of the observer—"a radical change in one's being," in Hadot's words. In the latter capacity, it constituted a form of spiritual exercise in which the production of wonder in response to the ordinary, the despised and the minute, was decisive. And just as Hadot speaks of a "cosmic vision"—of a way of elevating oneself out of the world to regard it from a higher and more detached point of view—as an essential part of

---

3. The microscope was developed at the very end of the sixteenth century, notably by Zacharias Janssen and Galileo, but its use remained very rare until 1630. On this period, see Belloni, "Microscopia," 179–90. The first important texts on the microscope, such as Pierre Borel's *De vero telescopii inventores* (1655) and *Centuria observationum microscopiaricum* (1656), Henry Power's *Experimental philosophy* (1664), and Robert Hooke's *Micrographia* (1665), were not published until the second part of the seventeenth century. From this period on, the microscope enjoyed a real vogue in European high society and became a source of entertainment beyond its use as a scientific instrument. For more on this, see Bradbury and Turner, *Microscopy*, and Wilson, *Invisible World*.

physics as a spiritual exercise, we can speak of a "microcosmic vision," and analyze the microscope—as well as the telescope—as an instrument with great importance not only for the development of knowledge and of a scientific understanding of the world, but also, and through the same movement, for the transformation of the self.

Indeed, in saying that the microscope was deeply linked to a transformation of the self and carried important ethical and even "mystical" aspects, one could go even further. In many texts, the kind of spiritual exercises specified though the use of the microscope are not merely of the "loose" kind described by Hadot, but of the stronger and stricter kind we might associate with St. Ignatius of Loyola, in which a spiritual exercise includes "every way of examining one's conscience, of meditating, of contemplating, of praying vocally and mentally . . . every way of preparing and disposing the soul to rid itself of all its disordered tendencies and . . . to seek and find the Divine Will as to the management of one's life for the salvation of the soul."[4] One may find, correlated with the use of the microscope, exercises that serve for the humiliation of human pride—plunging it into an astonishment that yields the discovery of its nullity—or the celebration of God's almighty wisdom in each element of the world. And in each of these exercises, the production of wonder appears as the key element.

I must admit that it is not the usual way to do the history of science and I acknowledge that it is in some ways a risky one, one that needs to be carefully delimited. To use these terms in discussing the microscope and its development does not mean that we must neglect the more usual epistemological questions arising in this connection, such as those that concern the status of scientific experience, the connection between facts produced through experiments and theories, or the transition between occult qualities and empirical data, in which microscopic observations played a great part.[5] One may also have to consider the sociological context in which the claims concerning the usefulness of microscopic observations were produced, and especially the need for emerging natural scientists to legitimate their activities before religious authorities.

But there are several reasons why I believe we ought to study the development of the microscope, and of modern scientific experience in general, in the manner proposed here. The first is that, if we are now totally accustomed to the idea that the chief aim of science is (or should be) truth,

4. Ignatius of Loyola, *Spiritual Exercises*, 3.
5. On these questions, see Wilson, *Invisible World*.

or is (and should be) efficiency, usefulness, and so on, we tend to forget that for a long period of time, and even during the early development of what we now term "modern science," the quest for truth was deeply linked and intertwined with a quest for wisdom. Considered from this perspective, it implied a practice of the self and a project for the transformation of oneself and others. It is plain that this fact should be kept in mind when considering the period that preceded "modern science." As Lorraine Daston and Peter Galison have written: "This is why the rhetoric of the alchemists, Paracelsians, and other early modern reformers of knowledge and societies rings so strange to modern (and even eighteenth-century) ears. They sought wisdom, not just truth; enlightenment, not just knowledge."[6] But in fact, this continues to be true, to some extent, for many scientists, including some of the most important ones, until the second part of the eighteenth century, as this essay will show. The long tradition described by Hadot and others, in which knowledge of the world, wisdom, and self-transformation were intertwined, still provided the inspiration for many of the first "modern" scientific observations and indeed played a role in the very process of defining the notion of an "experimental science." To put it even more clearly, the distinction between the scientific and the religious self is more complex and harder to delineate than we might sometimes suppose.[7] And this is especially true in the last part of the seventeenth century and the beginning of the eighteenth century, a period that marked the development of the so-called natural theology,[8] which is closely linked with the development of modern science.

This remark should lead us to a second one. For a long period of time in the study of science, we have failed to pay adequate attention to the

6. Daston and Galison, *Objectivity*, 41.

7. Discussing the idea that the "scientific self" should be seen as part of a larger history of the self and that it can be usefully studied in analogy with the works of Hadot or Foucault on the practices of the self in antiquity or in a religious context, Daston and Galison write: "although the scientific self of objectivity of course arose in an entirely different historical context and aimed at knowledge rather than enlightenment, it, too, was realized and reinforced by specialized techniques of the self" (*Objectivity*, 38). It is far from certain that it arose in an "entirely different" context, as we will see.

8. "Natural theology" or "physical theology" can be described as a particular branch of theology that attempts to demonstrate the existence or the attributes of God through the investigation of nature, and more specifically through the exposition of its order and finality. It forms part of a longer tradition that goes back to Stoic and Aristotelian thought, and English natural science developed in close relationship to this tradition—as this essay should demonstrate, among other things—until the very middle of the nineteenth century. On natural theology and natural science in the first half of the nineteenth century, see Corsi, *Science and Religion*.

production of the scientific self as a phenomenon in its own right. This, as Daston and Galison suggest, has probably been because we have not clearly distinguished between science and the ideal of objectivity, where objectivity is understood in terms of the suppression of the self. Indeed, the great interest of their work is to study, through an analysis of the development of objectivity as a cardinal virtue of the scientific ethos, the way in which the scientific self has been produced through a complex of practices and technologies, and has been associated with a specific form of "discipline"—the cultivation of a particular kind of observation and manner of approaching phenomena, the trained effacement of individual personality, and so on—which aims at certain epistemological virtues that have evolved historically. This is an important methodology if one wants to study the history of wonder and of its valorization—which also involves considering the differences between the kinds of wonder valued in diverse historical periods—or its exclusion from what is thought to constitute the "legitimate" scientific self. As we will see, in the period that forms my focus, wonder—and a specific kind of wonder, very different from curiosity about extraordinary phenomena—is a fundamental element of the scientific self, and even a means of lending it legitimacy in the face of religious or other criticisms.

Objective and Mystical Experiences

In order to understand how the microscope could come to be described as an instrument productive of a type of "mystical objective experience," we first need to consider how the notion of "experience" was understood in early modernity, and the ambiguities that that term involved. Historians of science are well acquainted with the fact that "experience" was affirmed from several points of view in the seventeenth century as a legitimate guide to truth and wisdom; to many, it presented itself as a guide more legitimate and reliable than the scholastic tradition and the interpretation of texts, denounced as a vain "grammar" of discourses. We are familiar with the criticisms directed by Descartes or Bacon against the scholastic tradition, but what we should keep in mind is that these were in fact anchored in a much broader context. Similar criticisms are to be found, for instance, in what was emerging as "the saints' science" or, to use Surin's[9]

---

9. Surin, Jean-Joseph (1600–1665), French Jesuit and mystic who played an important part in the episode of possession at Loudun and authored several mystical essays. For further details, see De Certeau, *Mystic Fable* and *Possession at Loudun*.

words, "experimental science," that is, mystical knowledge of God, and of course in the Paracelsian tradition of the science of occult qualities. To us, it seems quite odd that, in the very same period, "experimental science" could both name the mystical way of relating to God and, as "new experimental philosophy," describe the development of a science based on facts and disciplined observations as this was inherited from Bacon's philosophy and represented in England by Power, Hooke, Boyle, and Grew, and was linked to the development of the Royal Society.[10] As Catherine Wilson puts it, "we need to ask how... the notion of a scientifically revealing experience became uncoupled from the broader notion of experience in general."[11]

To do so, we have to understand the complex relationships that existed between these different meanings of "experience," which were still far from clearly separated. When John Webster attacked the Universities in his *Academiarum Examen* in 1654,[12] he denounced scholastic teachings, studies of what he called mere "grammar" and "dead paper idols of creaturely-invented letters," and contrasted them with a certain kind of experimental study of worldly objects, "legible characters that are only written and impressed by the finger of the Almighty." And he described his experimental studies, which combined the works of Bacon, Kepler, and Descartes with those of English Paracelsians like Fludd and Croll, as mystical experiences,[13] that is, as a type of experience by means of which it was possible to grasp the occult principles of nature through the interpretation of God's imprint on things. In their reply, Seth Ward and John Wilkins could easily pour scorn on this confusion and stress that "there are not two ways in the whole word more opposite than those of L. Verulam [i.e., Bacon] and D. Fludd," the first based on "experiment," the second based on "mystical ideal reasons."[14] But in fact, the difference was not so easy to establish; firstly, because Paracelsians claimed their science was also grounded on experiment, and secondly, because the experience/experi-

---

10. Henry Power's *Experimental Philosophy* was published in 1664, whereas Surin's *La science expérimentale* dates from 1663. The Royal Society was granted its royal charter in 1662.

11. Wilson, *Invisible World*, ch. 3

12. *Academiarum Examen* (London, 1654) reprinted in Debus, *Science and Education*. Cf. Wilson, "Visual Surface," 93 and ff.

13. He contrasted also "the vulgar anatomy and dissection of the dead bodies of men" with "the vive [sic] and mystick anatomy" (*Academiarum Examen*, quoted in Wilson, *Invisible World*, 42).

14. *Vindiciae Academiarum*, in Debus, *Science and Education*, 46.

ment of the Baconian tradition, as we will see, was far from free from all mystical ideals.

This ambiguity runs through the very core of experience. As De Certeau puts it, there is a common element in this broad focus on "experience":

> whereas in medieval ontology, all treatment of language was in itself an experiment [*expérience*[15]] or a manipulation of the real, language would henceforth stand face to face with what "manifested itself" in it: it was separate from that real it intended . . . the experiment [*expérience*], in the modern meaning of the word, was born with the deontologizing of language . . . in Bacon and others, the experiment stood opposite language, as that which guaranteed and verified the latter. This split between a deictic language . . . and a referential experimentation [*expérience*] . . . structures modern science, including "mystical science."[16]

But mystical experience presents a number of characteristics that are highly problematic. First, it is rare: as Surin wrote, "experience is for the few,"[17] whereas faith and doctrine are for the common people. Second, it is necessarily an immediate, affective, and indeed subjective experience, even if the self is totally destroyed within it: its point of reference is an "I," be it a very fragile "I." Third and above all, it is fundamentally the experience of an excess, because it is considered to be an experience of the infinite, and, for this reason, it is impossible to communicate it or indeed to translate it into a shared language.[18] The same remark can, to some extent, be applied to the meaning of experience in the Paracelsian tradition. As Catherine Wilson notes, this refers "not merely to simple sensory familiarity, but to

---

15. The above quotations from De Certeau are drawn from the English translation of his work. But the translation misses the fundamental ambiguity of the French word *expérience*, which means both "experience" and "experiment" in English. It is very clear from De Certeau's text that both meanings are implied in his use of the word.

16. De Certeau, *Fable mystique*, 170; *Mystic Fable*, 123. All quotes and references that follow are drawn from the English translation unless otherwise indicated.

17. Unpublished draft of the preface to *La science expérimentale des choses de l'autre vie* (1663), quoted in De Certeau, *Mystic Fable*, 180.

18. As the Discalced Carmelite Diego de Jesus (1570–1621) wrote in his *Notes and Remarks* on the works of St. John of the Cross: "In matters so lofty and spiritual . . . in which experience triumphs over doctrine; in which he who knows cannot say; in which grace rather than language is mistress . . . we should not be governed by understanding nor by the rules of the masters. . . . how will we put order, or limits, or text, or means in the terms by which we must explain so lofty a thing, wanting everything that is immense and unsayable to be subject to the ordinary rules, without exceeding the common phrases and guarded terms" used by schools and masters? (de Jesus, *Notes and Remarks*, quoted in De Certeau, *Mystic Fable*, 138–39).

the cognitive identification with the object of knowledge achieved through insight" and "must be sought in ways that are occult, that is, in ways that cannot be directly taught."[19] It is an experience that is considered to occur by an immediate intuition that is very close to the knowledge of the angels as theologians describe it, and is the preserve of few.

Now, it is obvious that "experience," as a core element of "new experimental philosophy," has very different characteristics. First, because it requires effort and discipline, and is mediated by norms and processes that must (and can) be studied and applied by everyone—it is an experiment. Second, because it addresses reason. And third, because it requires as a fundamental element the possibility of comparing the data, of communicating and duplicating them, so as to confront reason with different kinds of evidence and thereby lead it to conviction, as in a tribunal. These are familiar considerations and I will not dwell on them here, but what should be pointed out is that the microscope seems to stand in an important relation to all of them. On the one hand, because it is closely linked with the understanding of "experience" as a disciplined process, that is, as one that is far from immediate and that requires the deployment of a larger number of procedural measures before truth can be grasped. The preface of Robert Hooke's *Micrographia* is very clear in this respect: the microscope proves how imperfect our senses are, and at the same time how they can be cured by the practice of "experimental philosophy," with its attention to observational procedures. In his treatise on the microscope, similarly, Henry Baker devotes many pages to dealing with what can be called the precepts for grasping truth, which constitute what we may call a kind of *askesis* of truth. "An examination of objects," he writes, "in order to discover truth, requires a great deal of attention, care and patience, together with some considerable skill and dexterity (to be acquired by practice chiefly), in the preparing, managing and applying them to the microscope."[20] The microscope, in Power's words, is a means of liberating us from mystical and occult considerations: "as the telescope freed us from futile speculation about the heavenly bodies by bringing what was remote near, so the microscope will demystify occult effects."[21] With the

19. Wilson, "Visual Surface," 92.

20. Baker, *Microscope Made Easy*, 52. Later in the text, Baker insists that truth has to be the only aim of research, one that requires a form of *askesis*: "When you employ the microscope, shake off all prejudice, nor harbour any favourite opinions... remember that truth alone is the matter you are in search after... let not vanity seduce you to persist in your mistake" (ibid., 62).

21. Power, *Experimental Philosophy*, preface.

microscope, one can produce clear and evident facts, at least if one follows correct procedures, and one can communicate them to others who can, following the same procedures, verify one's observations. Such an experience of truth becomes accessible to everyone who studies and applies the rules for producing it, and, far from being rare, it can be reproduced at will according to the same body of rules.

The following question may now be raised: does the experience produced by means of the microscope merely *demystify* objects, as Power suggested above? Or is it not also a way of producing a specific kind of "mystical" experience, one that shares the characteristics of "correct" experience as defined by the new experimental philosophy—that is, a disciplined observation one can verify and duplicate—but one that offers, by these means, something like an effective experimental proof of God's powers that is scientifically produced and necessarily compels reason to acknowledge it? And if it does, how does it achieve this goal?

How to Produce a Series of Revelations at Will?

The question may sound peculiar but it arises very naturally out of the works of the most famous microscopists of the period. In the words of Catherine Wilson: "some . . . found in the revelations of the microscope a way of reknitting the unravelling relationships between the natural and the supernatural, situating the knowledge of nature within a theological space." This kind of physical theology "even developed into a standard form of presentation of natural history in the first quarter of the eighteenth century."[22] Nothing was more common, in fact, than statements like the following: "The microscope, opening our eyes, enabled us to penetrate Nature's secrets and compelled us to glorify the One who commands Light to shine in the darkness";[23] or: such discoveries "furni[sh] a more just and sublime idea than mankind had before of the grandeur and magnificence of Nature and the infinite power, wisdom and goodness of Nature's almighty Parent";[24] or again: "whoever reads these things must be obliged to confess that the power of the Almighty cannot be known by clearer and more convincing proofs in any parts of his works than in those minute animalcules."[25] Many of the most important scientists of the Baconian

22. Wilson, *Invisible World*, 176.
23. Watkins, *Exercice du microscope*, 72.
24. Baker, *Microscope Made Easy*, xiii.
25. Swammerdam, *Book of Nature*, 78. All quotes and references are drawn from

tradition, such as Robert Boyle,[26] John Ray,[27] Nehemiah Grew,[28] or William Derham,[29] shared the same idea of a science that, far from reinforcing atheism, confirmed through experience—through the kind of experience about which Boyle acknowledged that he had "a great reverence for [it] in comparison to authority"—the belief in the revelation of the Scriptures. The disciplined experience of new experimental philosophy, when the scientist is "disposed to make use of the knowledge of the creatures to confirm his belief and increase his veneration of the Creator," "will furnish him with weighty and uncommon motives to conclude such sentiments to be highly rational and just."[30]

This entire tradition, from Bacon onward, drew its force from a sentence of St. Paul's Epistle to the Romans (1:20), which states that "the invisible things of God are clearly seen from the creation of the world as tokens and effects." It is obvious that, far from having lost its "mystical" value, the experience at stake in these texts is deeply linked to the revelation—an objective and reproducible revelation—of God's existence and power. But while the first part of the eighteenth century stressed the inner powers of nature, here, natural phenomena are deprived of their occult density to the benefit of a Divine design omnipresent in God's works.[31] And the governing idea at work is that through experience one may produce a kind of revelation without need for the mediation of texts and authorities. This experience is not a "subjective" one, but a regulated and objective one that everyone may reproduce, confirm, and verify by applying certain procedures and following a set of strict rules. In this way, scientific experience and microscopic experience in particular are transformed into "a new form of worship,"[32] one that garners an understanding of God through His creatures—and this, of course, is profoundly ambiguous—and is more efficient than any other proof because it is based on rational experimentation. As John Ray wrote in *The Wisdom of God Manifested in the Works of the Creation*, these experiences justify faith in God "by arguments drawn from

---

the English translation unless otherwise indicated.

26. See, for instance, Boyle, *Christian Virtuoso*, 508–40.
27. Ray, *Wisdom of God*.
28. Grew, *Cosmologia Sacra*.
29. Derham, *Physico-theology*.
30. Boyle, *Christian Virtuoso*, 514.
31. On this question and more broadly on the topic of this study, cf. Roger, *Sciences de la vie*, 206–54, to which I am deeply indebted in this essay.
32. According to the apposite expression of Wilson, *Invisible World*, 179.

Claude-Olivier Doron—*The Microscopic Glance*

the light of nature and works of creation . . . they are indeed supernatural demonstrations . . . but not common to all persons or times . . . but these proofs taken from effects and operations exposed to every man's view, not to be denied or questioned by any, are most effective for convincing all those who deny or doubt it,"[33] so that, as Derham would say, the ones who persist in their denial can justly be called unreasonable. The microscope and its (relative) diffusion enabled many to encounter experimentally the commonest miracles of creation and to see God's impress in all things.

Now how are we to understand this? Why did the microscope appear, as Leibniz would also remark, as the best way for corroborating the wisdom of God?[34] A central element in this serial reproduction of objective revelations was, in fact, the experience of wonder. Wonder, produced by the microscope when turned upon even the smallest and lowliest elements of the world, *necessarily* arose from microscopic investigations and *necessarily* compelled reason—indeed, overwhelming it—to acknowledge God and His perfections and, at the same time, induced man to perceive his nullity and vanity. The following sequence was a commonplace of microscopic descriptions. First, one produces a precise depiction of a small thing like a snowflake or semen, or of an insect as lowly as a louse or a worm. This depiction lays bare the perfection of God's design and reveals everything to be well ordained. As the Dutch naturalist Swammerdam (1637–1680) remarked: "if, while we dissect with care the larger animals, we are filled with wonder . . . to what a height is our astonishment raised when we discover all these parts arranged down to their least with the same regularity?"[35] Or it appears that, in a single drop of liquid, one can discover such an inexhaustible and "prodigious variety of small living creatures . . . that one can with reason call it a new world,"[36] and indeed an infinity of new worlds. Second, this discovery of unity and order, and infinity and variety, is necessarily productive of wonder; our authors insist on the fact that wonder arises always and invariably from these observations. And finally, such wonder necessarily compels one to admire and acknowledge the power and wisdom of God. What I wish to stress here is the fact that the microscopic investigation of natural things is taken to have a compulsive character, forcing the observer, by means of his wondering

33. Ray, *Wisdom of God*, preface.

34. "Now, nothing better corroborates the incomparable wisdom of God than the structure of the works of nature, particularly the structure which appears when we study them more closely with the microscope." Leibniz, "Concept of Justice," 566.

35. Swammerdam, *Book of Nature*, preface.

36. Watkins, *Exercice du microscope*, 39.

response, to an acknowledgment of God; it thus constitutes a way of linking human beings firmly and forcefully to religious truth. It is in this spirit that Robert Hooke would ask, "can any be so foolish as to think all those things the production of chance? Certainly, either their reasoning must be extremely depraved or they never in fact attentively considered and contemplated the works of the Almighty."[37] And later: "indeed if we consider the care of the Creator in the dispensation of his providence . . . we cannot choose but admire and adore him for his Excellencies."[38]

The Microscope and the Practice of Wonder

We can now turn our focus directly on the notion of wonder. What is particularly worth noting is that, through the strong link established by Boyle and others between the observation of natural objects and the worship of God, the most detailed natural investigations could now be encoded as an act of profound reverence toward divinity. This, in turn, was an important means of legitimating microscopic investigations (and science in general) before detractors, avoiding accusations of *vana curiositas*, mere time-wasting idleness, or sacrilegious penetration into the secrets of nature.[39] It is an oft-voiced claim that "nothing is more worth the attention of the wise man"[40] than the study of minute objects of nature; or, as Lesser puts it in his *Theology of the Insects*, "there is nothing in Nature, however abject it may appear, which is not a subject of wonder to the man who sets himself to consider it. Far from being unworthy of our regard, the study of Nature is not only useful but necessary to us since it furnishes as many occasions of praising our Creator as there are objects to contemplate."[41]

37. Hooke, *Micrographia*, 171.

38. Ibid., 190.

39. This was, of course, a familiar accusation leveled by the religious establishment. But one may recall other sources of criticism, such as the "satirically-minded popular culture" discussed by Catherine Wilson, of which we have an example in Thomas Shadwell's satirical treatment of the character of Sir Nicholas Gimcrack in *The Virtuoso* (1676), or, in France, in La Bruyère, who holds up curiosity to ridicule in the thirteenth book of his *Caractères*. Microscopists were usually depicted as wasting their time observing useless, sordid things such as insects, rotting cheese, and the like. One could indeed perform a narrow sociological reading of the texts I discuss here and construe them in terms of the microscopists' efforts to legitimate the practice of microscopic investigation, but I believe that to do so would be to miss the essential.

40. Watkins, *Exercice du microscope*, 1.

41. Lesser, *Insecto-Theology*, 1. All quotes and references are drawn from the English translation unless otherwise indicated.

More than that: following a well-established tradition that considers man duty-bound to contemplate God's works and glorify God for them, insofar as man is the only rational creature capable of contemplating the world and perceiving the Creator's existence behind it, many authors present microscopic investigations as a fundamental religious *duty*. Some may look upon these investigations "as an idle curiosity," claims Gedner, a student of the famous Swedish naturalist Linnaeus who endeavored to respond to these criticisms, "since they neither serve for food and physic: but if these are neglected, how many of the wonderful works of the Creator would be unknown?" So "I beseech you then, who ask me with a sneer to what end this or that stone, plant or animal serves, I beseech you to awake and open your eyes while you live in this world. All these things are not the works of man but of wisdom itself, which created both thee and me ... The Creator has so framed the world that man should everywhere behold the miraculous work of his hand."[42]

So wonder at the works of God is a duty and, as such, needs to be cultivated, even with regard to those works that seem not to deserve consideration but that, for that very reason, turn out to be the most wondrous. To the extent that the microscope provides us with a means for discovering a plethora of wonders where we formerly saw merely a contemptible reality, it is an instrument that extends the range of the works that serve for the glorification of God and that would otherwise have been ignored and wrongfully despised. One of the peculiarities of this development is the fact that it turns the commonest and most contemptible objects into wonders precisely at a time when the interest in exceptional curiosities and wonders, which had reached great intensity at the beginning of the sixteenth century,[43] has begun to come into criticism. This evolution is intimately linked to what might be called "a naturalization of miracles," that is, a wide-ranging critique of the idea that God intervenes—except on very rare occasions—in the order of nature to disturb its general laws,[44] and, at the same time, a diffusion of the idea that the true "miracles" lie in the order of nature itself, in its details and most familiar elements, which everywhere exhibit the same constancy, the same variety and the same governing laws.

---

42. Gedner, "Curiosity." Gedner has strong words against those who fail to contemplate nature, whom he compares to "brute beasts."

43. Cf. the famous book of Céard, *Nature*.

44. See for instance Emanuel Avelin, *Miracula insectorum*, where this student of Linnaeus criticizes the vulgar idea that miracles occur *sive contra natura* and develops a long analysis of insects as natural miracles.

Practices of Wonder

In the diffusion of these ideas, the microscope played an important part. In the first instance, that was because it presented itself as an instrument that helped manifest the infinite power of God in the most lowly and familiar things, and offered unlimited scope to the exercise of wonder. As Hooke remarked, echoing the words of many others, telescopes and microscopes had produced "new worlds and *terra incognita*'s to our view."[45] In the words of the French microscopist Louis Joblot (1645–1723): "the whole of nature turned out to be new . . . the microscope helped us discover on the face of the earth a small world that was entirely new, and gave us the opportunity to see in every single thing an infinity of beings no less wonderful than any we have hitherto known."[46] The microscope extended the power of our sight so deeply that we could discover new realms, new beauties and the "fingerprints of God" everywhere. Indeed, some professed to believe—though it would have been difficult to ascertain how seriously such professions were intended—that "by the addition of such artificial instruments and methods, there may be . . . a reparation for the mischiefs and imperfection mankind has drawn upon itself."[47] In other words, the use of the microscope was presented as a means of redeeming our senses from the imperfection and corruption that had come upon them as a consequence of original sin. And extending human vision also meant learning to see the power of the Creator in all things and extending the opportunities of glorifying Him. The most famous instance in this respect is, of course, the study of insects. As I have remarked, wonderment here was not understood as an immediate affect that arises spontaneously in response to extraordinary events; the microscope presented itself as a necessary mediation by means of which the wonderful aspects of any object could be revealed. "Every animal, flower, fruit and insect," said Baker, "nay, almost every particle of matter affords him [the observer] an entertainment. Such a man can never think his time hang heavy on his hands . . . each garden or field is to him a cabinet of curiosities . . . he considers the Universe as a magazine of wonders which infinite ages are scarce sufficient to contemplate and admire enough."[48]

All of this amply serves to illustrate the function of the microscope as a means for the exercise and practice of wonder, and for the discovery of the miraculous in every object—a practice closely connected with its

---

45. Hooke, *Micrographia*, preface.
46. Joblot, *Observations*, 2. On Joblot, see Lechevallier, "Louis Joblot."
47. Hooke, *Micrographia*, preface.
48. Baker, *Microscope Made Easy*, xiv.

effectiveness in establishing the power and reality of God. In the words of Swammerdam—echoing, in his own peculiar mystical prose, the thoughts of many who saw in the uniformity and beauty of the microscopic world a proof against those who believed beings could have arisen through spontaneous generation or chance—those who believe insects are a result of chance should "ascend in the paths of Nature and be led to the wisest of architects and by contemplating even the most minute of his works, be incited to prostrate themselves with a sacred reverence and most profound humility before Him, bidding adieu to their own opinions and former life, which, without the love of God, has been addicted only to the world."[49]

We must underline this point. Wonder is legitimate because it raises our thoughts from the creatures to the Creator. In this respect, microscopic vision can clearly be characterized as a spiritual exercise, one that traces out a path for elevating the observer's spirit from the world to the Deity and for profoundly transforming the observer in the process. There is no question of stopping on the path and confining one's admiration to created things. Hear, for instance, John Hill: "Even what the vulgar call the most abject things will show a wonderful utility and *lead the mind in pious contemplation higher than the stars.*"[50] Or again Hooke: "the more we magnify objects, the more excellencies and mysteries do appear; and the more we discover the imperfections of our senses and the omnipotence and the infinite perfection of the great Creator."[51] And finally, in the words of Lesser: "these minute animals raise our ideas to the knowledge of the Creator of the Universe."[52] This spiritual exercise consists in elevating one's spirit to discern the perfections of God, and in attaining—beyond mere and objective truth, and through the wonder experienced before the perfection and beauty of the new worlds discovered by the microscope—wisdom.

Such a train of progression will remind us of the progressive scale or path of ascent mystics claimed to be following in attaining the Divine. In some cases, it might even take the clear form of a surprising mysticism. Baker, for instance, insists on the fact that "as the microscope discovers almost every drop of water, every blade of grass, every leaf, flower and grain swarming with inhabitants; all of which enjoy not only life but happiness," "since the scale of beings advances with such regular step so high as man" we may suppose that it "still proceeds gradually upwards through

---

49. Swammerdam, *Book of Nature*, 47.
50. Hill, *Hypochondriasis*, 27 (emphasis added).
51. Hooke, *Micrographia*, 8.
52. Lesser, *Insecto-Theology*, 201.

numberless orders of beings of a superior nature to him."[53] He concludes his book with the remark: "The universe is so full of wonders that perhaps Eternity alone can be sufficient to survey and admire them all"; and perhaps this wonderment is what the soul feels in the other life, that affords her so much felicity: "when the soul shall become divested of flesh, the pleasures of sense can be no more" and those who were used to them will suffer in misery while "if [the soul's] principal delight has been [in this life] in the contemplation of the beauties of the Creation and in the adoration of their Almighty Author, it soars, when disembodied, into the celestial regions, duely prepared to the full enjoyment of intellectual happiness."[54] Such expression of mystical feeling, one that bears a clear Neoplatonic impress, is of course rare, but may not be so surprising if one considers all that has been said above. The microscope here is understood as a means of applying oneself to the pure sense of wonder that the soul will enjoy more fully in its afterlife. In other texts, and more frequently, it becomes a way of grasping the unity of the entire creation beyond time and space, the way one might see, for instance, contained inside a single drop of semen the concatenation of human generations that will eventually descend from it, and so *ad infinitum*. In the words of Baker, once again, this time in a Leibnizian tone: "every single berry that we find has really in itself whole forests of its kind . . . so Adam's loin contained his large posterity: all men that have been and all that ever shall be. Amazing thought! What mortal can conceive such wondrous smallness!"[55]

The climax of this mystical tone in microscopic investigations can be found in the idea expressed by Swammerdam—whose voice was by no means an isolated one—that, through the metamorphosis of butterflies, which rise out of the mud to spend their lives consuming the nectar of flowers in this terrestrial existence, we have "the most evident and palpable proofs drawn from nature" for "the resurrection of the dead." Here, mystical "experimental science" and the "new experimental philosophy" are brought together under one head in the most perfect partnership. As Swammerdam declares: "I can produce such manifest examples and such powerful arguments for the purification and succeeding glorification of bodies from the history of insects that I do not doubt but such unheard-of miracles will strike all mankind with the highest amazement. Natural truths are perfectly convincing and wholly divine; since what is

53. Baker, *Microscope Made Easy*, 306–7.
54. Ibid., 310–11.
55. Ibid., 251–52.

true proceeds from God . . . And what is more true than the books of nature and those visible things by assistance of which, as by sacred steps, we ascend . . . to divine and eternal truths?"[56]

"To Contract Our Vain Pride into as Small a Point"

These considerations, however, are far from the sole ground for characterizing microscopic investigation as a form of spiritual exercise. Wonder, as we have considered it up to this point, attached to the comforting aspect of order, and it satisfied reason by discovering a perfect order in all things. But there is another—and intimately linked—dimension of wonder produced by microscopic vision, in which this vision "strikes [the observer] with astonishment and terror."[57] Wonder here passes into the character of terrified astonishment, an experience that shares some elements with the experience of the sublime,[58] troubling and indeed humiliating human reason, human senses, and human pride. As we have seen, the microscope humiliates human senses by showing how limited they are in comparison to the infinite of creation.[59] But it also humiliates reason. Many of us will be familiar with Pascal's analysis of the infinite; in the terms of that analysis, we might describe the microscope as an effective exercise for human beings to learn how "the finite is annihilated in front of the infinite and becomes a pure nothingness."[60]

If wonder under the aspect we have analyzed so far was linked to what the tradition of spiritual exercises designated "consolation," with the contemplation of God's presence in natural phenomena and even an anticipatory view of the afterlife, here wonder is rather linked to "desolation," as expressed in the various exercises that aim to bring human beings to an awareness of their wretchedness and poverty without God. It should be stressed here that this analogy is by no means a distant one. One key element of spiritual exercises is the humiliation of human pride, as Ignatius remarks in his second exercise: I will "look at who I am, *lessening myself* by examples. First: how much I am in comparison to all men? . . . Third:

---

56. Swammerdam, *Book of Nature*, 146. This view is shared by others, such as Rodaert.

57. Watkins, *Exercice du microscope*, 4.

58. See on this point, Saint-Girons, *Fiat lux,* ch. 1, "Risques de la grandeur: vaste, infini, colossal."

59. See also Malebranche, *Recherche de la vérité*, ch. 6.

60. Pascal, *Pensées*, 435.

what all Creation is in comparison to God? Then, I alone, what can I be? Fourth, [I will] see all my bodily corruption and foulness."[61] We shall see that all these elements can be traced within the practice of the microscope.

One illustration of this can be found in the comparison of natural and artificial works when examined through the microscope, which has been a commonplace of microscopic observations from Hooke to Baker.[62] One submits to the infinite scrutiny of the microscope works of art and works of nature and observes, for instance, the most perfect needle or the finest and most expensive embroidery from Bruges. Under microscopic lenses, these works of art appear coarse, ugly, profoundly imperfect, while the works of God—a bee's sting, a spider's web—appear all the more perfect and wonderful the more they are magnified. "Such a comparison," writes Baker among many others, "must tend towards humbling the self-conceit and pride of man, by giving him a more reasonable and modest opinion of himself; and at the same time may in some degree conduce towards improving his imperfect conceptions of the Supreme Creator . . . every hair, feather or scale, even of the meanest insect . . . shews the abundant riches, munificence and skill of its Maker."[63]

But this exercise in humiliation and in the reduction of human pride to infinitesimal smallness appears with pervasive regularity in microscopic vision, leading to a very common baroque denunciation of *vanitas*. Let us hear Baker again, speaking from the last pages of his treatise, devoted to this kind of spiritual exercise. One will recognize here some of the themes of the "view from above" as studied by Hadot in the Stoics, as one finds it expressed, for instance, in Seneca's *Quaestiones Naturales*:[64]

> the minute size of microscopical animalcules and the little space they occupy, when compared with ourselves and the room we fill, may possibly increase our pride and folly and make us imagine ourselves of mighty consequence in the Creation; but if we carry our thoughts upwards and compare the body of a man to the bulk of a mountain, that mountain with the whole earth, the earth to the circle it describes round the sun [and so on until] the infinite space that is everywhere diffused about [the Creation], we shall find ourselves sink to nothing. . . . What then is the mightiest monarch that ever lived? What is the whole race

61. Ignatius of Loyola, *Spiritual Exercises*, 41 (emphasis added).
62. See Hooke, *Micrographia*, ch. 1; Ray, *Wisdom of God*, 40.
63. Baker, *Microscope Made Easy*, 292, 299.
64. On the "view from above," see Hadot, *N'oublie pas de vivre*, ch. 2, and Doron, "Vision cosmique."

of man? A mite upon a cheese is as large and considerable in proportion as a man upon the earth.[65]

The effect of the microscopic glance is to make human beings and all that is human appear dwarfed before the infinite; the length of human life and human time, the power of human senses, our familiar notion of space—all dwindle into nothingness before the infinite revealed before us by microscopic vision. This process departs from a sense of wonder that plunges human beings into perplexity and confusion and, in its final moment, leads to an experience of mortification before the grandeur of the Divine. It delivers a blow to human pride to witness the exquisite attention God has devoted to the paltriest creatures, lending them beauty, ornament, and so on. But it is even more humbling to consider, as Lesser says in a passage bearing the title "Motives of humiliation," that one is himself produced by a very small insect (the spermatozoon) and throughout his existence hosts the presence of so many insects (we may think of parasites) within his own body: "how ill it becomes us to be proud . . . A creature which perhaps derives from an insect so small as not be discoverable by our senses, and which serves as food to such myriads of others, cannot be too humble and too sensible of its own wretchedness." He goes on to scoff at the conceit of human beings, who inflate themselves with self-pride and yet are exposed to death from the attack of the smallest insects, and who, when they die, are devoured by "millions of enemies" that "no more respect the carcase of a lord, a prince or a king than the lowest of the human . . . Who, after this, does not feel his own wretchedness?"[66]

I would like to conclude this essay by returning for a final time to Swammerdam's *Book of Nature*. Many of the conclusions of the present study could have been just as easily demonstrated by drawing exclusively on a reading of Swammerdam's work. His work can be seen as a caricature

---

65. Baker, *Microscope Made Easy*, 340.

66. Lesser, *Insecto-Theology*, 86–87. One finds in Lesser another exercise of humiliation directed against the pride human beings take in ornaments and clothes, when he remarks that "velvet and silk which are the most precious of our [ornaments]" are "the excrement of a vile insect" (188). These images are reminiscent of Marcus Aurelius' famous exercises for grasping the "phantasia kataleptikê," that is, the adequate and objective representation of objects freed from the subjective feelings and evaluations we place in them, which is exemplified in descriptions like the following: "this phalernum, this excellent highly commended wine, is but a bare juice of an ordinary grape. This purple robe, but sheep's hairs, dyed with the blood of a shell-fish" (*Meditations*, 59); or again: "those other things that are so much prized and admired, as marble stones, what are they, but as it were the kernels of the earth? Gold and silver, what are they, but as the more gross faeces of the earth?" (114).

of the tradition that saw in the microscope an instrument for accessing a certain kind of mystical experience and producing a sense of wonder that raises human thoughts to God. Historians of science have sometimes felt embarrassed by his mystical tone, and sought to construe this in a variety of terms, whether as a personal disposition to melancholy or an excess of religious fervor. What the above can be taken to show is that Swammerdam is by no means exceptional in his views, and thus I would not agree with those who would see in his work merely the fanciful expressions of psychological malady. Placed in this light, it becomes possible to read his writings as offering some of the clearest illustrations of the microscopic glance as a spiritual exercise and of the intertwining of the quest for truth and the quest for wisdom in modern experimental science. Let us take, for instance, the chapter on the Louse, which consists of a letter addressed by Swammerdam to his friend Thévenot. In this "vulgar and loathed insect," he writes, "you will find miracles heaped on miracles and will be amazed at the wisdom of God most clearly manifested in a minute point."[67] And he concludes his detailed anatomy of the insect with a clear example of a spiritual exercise in the style of Ignatius:

> So many and such different miracles jointly proclaim in it the divine omnipotence. Wherefore though this animal is of no advantage to the body, yet it is able to raise our thoughts to God; so that by seriously contemplating the divine Majesty and the glittering rays of his miracles in this little animal, we may, with the most submissive humility, change and contract our vain pride into as small a point. . . . the miracles of God are magnificent in every thing he has created and even the smallest of them are the host of the Lord of Israel . . . [they] are open books whereby we are all reduced to our eternal origin, nor are we ever elevated above nature and created beings, until we constantly love God and renounce all that is not God.[68]

Here, more than ever, the scientific self and the religious self are totally indiscernible, and the link between the two is provided by what has been the centerpiece of the above discussion, and whose central place in the late seventeenth- and eighteenth-century understanding of the microscope I hope to have shown—a scientifically produced, universally replicable and ever-reproducible wonder.

67. Swammerdam, *Book of Nature*, 30.
68. Ibid., 37–38.

Bibliography

Avelin, Gabriel Emanuel. *Specimen academicum, sistens miracula insectorum*. Uppsala: Laur. Magn. Höjer, 1752.
Baker, Henry. *The Microscope Made Easy*. 2nd ed. London: Dodsley, 1743.
Belloni, Luigi. "Il primo ventennio della microscopia (Galilei 1610-Harvey 1628). Dalla microscopia alla anatomie microscopica dell'insetto." *Clio Medica* 4 (1969) 179–90.
Boyle, Robert. *The Christian Virtuoso*. In *The Works of the Honourable Robert Boyle*, 5:508–40. London: J. & F. Rivington et al., 1772.
Bradbury, Saville, and Gerard L'E. Turner. *Historical Aspects of Microscopy*. Cambridge: Royal Microscopical Society, 1967.
Brague, Rémi. *La sagesse du monde*. Paris: Fayard, 1999.
Céard, Jean. *La nature et les prodiges*. Geneva: Droz, 1996.
Certeau, Michel de. *The Mystic Fable*. Vol. 1, *The Sixteenth and Seventeenth Centuries*. Translated by Michael B. Smith. Chicago: University of Chicago Press, 1992.
———. *The Possession at Loudun*. Translated by Michael B. Smith. Chicago: University of Chicago Press, 2000.
Corsi, Pietro. *Science and Religion: Baden-Powell and the Anglican Debate, 1800–1860*. Cambridge: Cambridge University Press, 1988.
Daston, Lorraine, and Peter Galison. *Objectivity*. Boston: MIT Press, 2007.
Debus, Allen G. *Science and Education in Seventeenth-Century England*. London: Macdonald, 1970.
Derham, William. *Physico-theology: or, a Demonstration of the Being and Attributes of God from His Works of Creation*. 5th ed. London: Innys, 1720.
Doron, Claude-Olivier. "Le thème de la vision cosmique dans la littérature de consolation." Online: http://www.rehseis.univ-paris-diderot.fr/IMG/pdf/le_theme_de_la_vision_cosmique_dans_la_litterature_de_consolation.pdf.
Gedner, Christopher. "Of the Use of Curiosity." In *Miscellaneous Tracts Relating to Natural History, Husbandry and Physick*, edited by Benjamin Stillingfleet, 161–200. 3rd ed. London: Dodsley et al., 1775.
Grew, Nehemiah. *Cosmologia Sacra, or a Discourse of the Universe as it is the Creature and Kingdom of God*. London: Rogers, Smith & Walford, 1701.
Hadot, Pierre. *Exercices spirituels et philosophie antique*. Paris: Albin Michel, 2002.
———. *N'oublie pas de vivre. Goethe et la tradition des exercices spirituels*. Paris: Albin Michel, 2008.
———. *Qu'est-ce que la philosophie antique?* Paris: Folio, 1995.
Hill, John. *Hypochondriasis: A Practical Treatise on the Nature and Cure of that Disorder*. London, 1766.
Hooke, Robert. *Micrographia, or Some Physiological Descriptions of Minute Bodies Made by Magnifying Glasses*. London: Martin & Allestry, 1665.
Ignatius of Loyola, Saint. *The Spiritual Exercises of St. Ignatius of Loyola*. Translated by Elder Mullan. 1914. Reprint, New York: Cosimo, 2007.
Joblot, Louis. *Observations d'histoire naturelle faites avec le microscope*. Vol. 1. Paris: Briasson, 1754–55.
Lechevallier, Hubert. "Louis Joblot and His Microscopes." *Bacteriological Reviews* 40 (1976) 241–58.

Practices of Wonder

Leibniz, Gottfried Wilhelm. "Reflections on the Common Concept of Justice." In *Philosophical Papers and Letters*, edited and translated by Leroy E. Loemker, 561–73. 2nd ed. Dordrecht: Kluwer, 1989.

Lesser, Friedrich Christian. *Insecto-Theologia, Oder: Vernunfft- und Schrifftmäßiger Versuch, Wie ein Mensch durch aufmercksame Betrachtung derer sonst wenig geachteten Insecten zu lebendiger Erkänntniß und Bewunderung der Allmacht, Weißheit, der Güte und Gerechtigkeit des grossen Gottes gelangen könne*, Zweyte und vermehrte Auflage. Frankfurt: Blochberger, 1738. Translated *Insecto-Theology, or a Demonstration of the Being and Perfections of God from a Consideration of the Structure and Economy of Insects*. Edinburgh: William Creech, 1799.

Malebranche, Nicolas. *De la recherche de la vérité*. Paris: Galerie de La Sorbonne, 1991.

Marcus Aurelius. *Meditations*. Translated by Meric Casaubon. London: Dent, 1948.

Pascal, Blaise. *Pensées*. In *Pensées et opuscules*, edited by Léon Brunschvicg. Paris: Hachette, 1946.

Power, Henry. *Experimental Philosophy*. London: T. Roycroft, 1664.

Ray, John. *The Wisdom of God Manifested in the Works of the Creation*. London: Samuel Smith, 1691. Reprint, Hildesheim: G. O. Verlag, 1974.

Roger, Jacques. *Les sciences de la vie dans la pensée française au XVIIIe siècle*. 2nd ed. Paris: Albin Michel, 1993.

Saint-Girons, Baldine. *Fiat lux. Une philosophie du sublime*. Paris: Quai Voltaire, 1993.

Swammerdam, Jan. *The Book of Nature: or, the History of Insects*. Translated by Thomas Floyd and revised by John Hill. London: Seyffert, 1758.

Watkins, Francis. *L'exercice du microscope*. London, 1754.

Wilson, Catherine. *The Invisible World: Early Modern Philosophy and the Invention of the Microscope*. Princeton: Princeton University Press, 1995.

———. "Visual Surface and Visual Symbol: The Microscope and the Occult in Early Modern Science." *Journal of the History of Ideas* 49 (1988) 85–108.

8

Literary Wonder in the Seventeenth Century and the Origins of "Aesthetic Experience"[1]

ALEXANDER RUEGER

Introduction

AT THE BEGINNING OF the eighteenth century, English *literati* identified and analyzed the pleasurable experience of objects for its own sake, an experience that Joseph Addison named the "pleasures of the imagination" and that was later classified as "aesthetic experience."[2] Working in a different tradition, Alexander Gottlieb Baumgarten in 1735 called for the development of a new philosophical discipline, assigned to the analysis and perfection of such experiences, and gave it its name, *aesthetica*.[3] In contrast to the reception of the English theorists who did not make

---

1. Part of this chapter was previously published in "Aesthetics" by Alexander Rueger from "Oxford Handbook of Philosophy in Early Modern Europe," edited by Desmond M. Clarke and Catherine Wilson (2011). Used by permission of Oxford University Press.

2. For classic discussions of this development, see Monk, *Sublime*, and Stolnitz, "Beauty."

3. Baumgarten, *Meditations*, 78 (§116).

claims to upset philosophical taxonomies, recognition and acceptance of Baumgarten's project was slow and encountered obstacles. One of these obstacles, presented by Germany's foremost literary theorist, Johann Christoph Gottsched, is instructive, although it might easily appear in hindsight as a misunderstanding. In 1760, Gottsched claimed that the new discipline of aesthetics was a bombastic sham and that the "alleged new science" contained nothing else than what had been dealt with in textbooks of rhetoric and poetics, that is, the analysis of tropes and metaphors in poetical discourse.[4]

Gottsched's "misunderstanding" is instructive because it is a reminder that aesthetics, whether in the English or the Continental version, indeed developed out of the traditional framework of rhetoric.[5] In this essay I would like to follow one line in this process that leads from the seventeenth-century debates, framed in rhetorical categories, about the experience of wonder or the marvelous in literature[6] to the early eighteenth-century attempts to articulate aesthetic experience as separate and distinguished from the rich variety of emotions traditional rhetoric had been concerned with. This development was not smooth; it involved prolonged struggles about the legitimacy of the marvelous as an artistic tool and the subsequent neoclassicist transformation of wonder into the experience of the sublime. Only after the marvelous had undergone this transformation in the hands of Nicolas Boileau (1674) and become, as it were, respectable, could it figure as the subject of the theoretical efforts that we now classify as the first analyses of aesthetic experience. It was important in this process that the sublime initially was understood as the highest degree of beauty rather than as a contrast to beauty—a fact often overlooked in hindsight and under the impression of Burke's later characterization (1757) of this contrast. The late seventeenth-century efforts at characterizing the "marvelous in discourse" or the sublime as a kind of experience that is not adequately captured by the rhetorical framework—a separate "practice of wonder"—prepared the ground for a theory of the aesthetic that emancipated itself from that very framework.[7]

---

4. Reiss, "Naturalization," 656, quoting from Gottsched, *Handlexicon oder Kurzgefasstes Wörterbuch der schönen Wissenschaften und freyen Künste* (1760).

5. Cf. Dockhorn's somewhat polemical claim that "modern aesthetics" developed as an "interpretive exercise" on classical treatises of rhetoric (*Rhetorik*, 94). For Baumgarten's debt to rhetoric, see, e.g., Bender, "Rhetorische Tradition."

6. These debates, of course, did not start only in the seventeenth century. See, e.g., Weinberg, *Literary Criticism*, and Hathaway, *Marvels*.

7. For a more detailed discussion of the seventeenth-century background of

1. Rhetorical Wonder in *Rebus* and *Verba*

The so-called disinterestedness of aesthetic experience, its characterization as the pleasurable experience of an object for its own sake, not subservient to other ends or motives,[8] is as good a feature as any with which to illustrate the contrast between the early eighteenth-century theorizing and the rhetorical framework in which the treatises on poetics and other arts throughout the seventeenth century were written. In this framework, the aim of both, oratory and poetry, is to persuade the audience; rhetoric and poetics are classified, in a taxonomy that derives from Aristotle, as branches of *logica specialis*. Orator and poet, according to this view, design special forms of argument that persuade the audience to accept and apply some piece of moral knowledge. In the case of poetry, the characteristic form of argument is the *exemplum*, a special case of a moral rule, from which the audience is supposed to induce the general rule and apply it to their own situation. The use of figures and tropes—the familiar poetic techniques—are ways of making the *exempla* evident and appealing to emotion.[9]

Poetry—as the formula goes—aims at instructing, delighting, and moving the audience's mind, and the poet thus has to make his speech "beautiful, amiable, and probable so that he moves the reader's mind and stimulates it to pleasure and wonder (*Verwunderung*) about the things he talks about..."[10] Delight and movement were usually (though not always) seen as necessary conditions or means for achieving the aim of instruction. The rules for the artist and the critic that we find in the seventeenth-century treatises are therefore not understood as rules for producing or judging beauty in a work but rather as instructions for bringing about (and judging) more specific intended effects in the audience. Schematically, the rules are supposed to answer questions of this kind: Given the audience's opinions, expectations, and moral views, what are the optimal means for achieving a certain effect (delight, movement) that is conducive

---

aesthetics, see Rueger, "Aesthetics."

8. For Shaftesbury and Addison, see Stolnitz, "Beauty" and "Origins." In Baumgarten we can identify an analogous concern: the science of aesthetics is concerned with "perfecting" the workings of the lower faculty of the mind (sensibility); for Baumgarten this means that this faculty has a perfection of its own and is no longer conceived as merely contributing to the aim of the higher faculty, the acquisition of clear and distinct knowledge. Cf. Baumgarten, *Meditations*, 77f. (§115) and *Ästhetik*, 5f. (§8) and 11 (§14).

9. See Edwards, "Zabarella."

10. Buchner, *Anleitung*, 14ff.

to the aim of (moral) instruction?[11] The form of the question makes it clear that the emotional and instructional effects on the audience can be achieved only if the background of the audience's opinions is taken into account. Only if the artist can ensure that neither the instruction nor the means applied are in too obvious conflict with these background beliefs, can he hope to be successful in persuading the audience. If, for instance, the *exemplum* in a tragedy appears unbelievable to the audience because the tragic hero speaks in a manner inappropriate to her social status, then the chances of inducing the intended moral knowledge are decreased. The fable, the persons, their actions, etc., therefore have to be "probable"; the collection of rules that are designed to ensure agreement with the audience's views is the *decorum*. Though following decorum is not sufficient for an artist to succeed, violations of decorum result in failure to achieve the intended effect.[12]

The decorum-regulated framework in which the artist had to work contained obvious tensions. As important as a probable fable, person, etc.,—one that is in agreement with "what is believed by most"—might be for the instructional or emotional effect of a work, it is not always the most effective means for inducing emotions in the audience. Artists and authors of rhetorical treatises were well aware that the wonderful or marvelous in art is one of the most powerful tools for arousing the audience's emotions, and more specifically, the emotion of wonder or admiration. But the wonderful is also that which goes against "what most believe." Arcimboldo's "monstrous" portraits, trompe d'oeil architecture and painting, epics and plays with supernatural interventions by devils or angels, Giambattista Marino's poems with their far-fetched "conceits" (metaphors) and "witty" phrases, the works of the English "metaphysical" poets around John Donne are some examples of the kind of baroque art that placed emphasis on the marvelous. Early in the seventeenth century, Marino made it explicit that "the poet's aim is the marvelous [*maraviglia*]" and his task is to amaze the reader.[13]

---

11. Many of the views found in seventeenth-century treatises are, of course, commentaries on, or derived from, Aristotle's *Rhetoric* and *Poetics*, Horace's *Ars Poetica*, and various Hellenistic writers. For an especially pertinent survey, see Shuger, *Sacred Rhetoric*.

12. Cf. Patey, *Probability*, ch. 4.

13. Cf. Mirollo, *Poet*, 116–20; 167–74. One of the stylistic tools for achieving the intended effect on the reader was Marino's use of sequences of "conceited" epithets, e.g., when a rose and the sun are compared as "sun on earth" and "rose in heaven" or when love is called a "warlike peace" and a "tempestuous calm" (see Marino, *Adonis*, 82 and xxxiii). In such comparisons, as Gracián put it, "contrariety gives soul to the

Art theoretical debates in the seventeenth and well into the eighteenth century regularly touched on the tension between wonder and probability, that is, on the question whether the use of the marvelous could be justified within the constraints of decorum. To mention only a few famous examples from France: the *Querelle du Cid* (1637ff.), the *Querelle du merveilleux chrétien* (1657ff.), and the *Querelle des anciens et des moderns* (1687ff.) all contained discussions of the relation of the wonderful to decorum. Although the seventeenth century has been characterized with good reason as the "age of the marvelous,"[14] the existence of these debates clearly reveals the problematic status of wonder in art.

This ambiguous status has ancient roots. Wonders had been defined since Aristotle, and in more detail by Thomas Aquinas, as effects of which we do not know the cause.[15] Wonders thus depended on knowledge, or, rather, on a lack of knowledge. An obvious problem then was to explain our delight in wonders, given that we delight in knowledge and are displeased by ignorance. If delight comes from learning, from acquiring knowledge, as Aristotle held, the marvelous should be displeasing. Aristotle's claim that wonders entice us to learn their causes was not the most convincing answer to the problem because the delight in the marvelous did not coincide with the beginning of an actual investigation into the causes. There is a very apt formulation of the issue in *Parts of Animals*: We seem to desire to know those things most intensely of which we can, in principle, not acquire much knowledge because they are too distant from us, too high up in the hierarchy of beings—for which reason we admire them most: "although our grasp of the eternal things is but slight, nevertheless the joy which it brings is, by reason of their excellence and worth, greater than that of knowing all things that are here below . . ."[16]

One conclusion to draw (as, for example, Aquinas did) was that the highest objects of our desire for knowledge *require* obscurity; their dignity and superiority induces wonder and admiration in us and, as it were, outweighs our lack of knowledge. This "ancient dilemma of knowledge"[17] could thus lead to a defense of wonder against the requirement of probability by placing the emphasis on the intrinsic value of the objects rather than on their believability. But the defense requires or presupposes a distinction

---

similitude, which in itself would be dead" (cited in Smith, *Wit*, 53).

14. Kenseth, *Age*.
15. For the following, see Cunningham, *Essays*, 53–74, and Biester, *Lyric*, ch. 4.
16. Cited in Trimpi, *Muses*, 98.
17. Ibid., 97ff.

between objects worthy and not worthy of admiration. The most important result of the "dilemma," however, is that the pleasure in the marvelous cannot be classified with the pleasure that issues from knowledge (of the divine or of other things), no more than with the satisfaction connected with achieving non-cognitive aims. It is not the same as the delight in harmony or proportion of sensual items but rather a pleasure in something ineffable or inscrutable. This is echoed, at the turn of the eighteenth century, in John Dennis's attempt to identify the "chief Thing" in great poetry as "Enthusiastick Passion" whose characteristic it simply is to be a passion "whose Cause is not comprehended by us."[18]

The marvelous in poetry comes in two forms: with respect to the *res* and with respect to the *verba*. Representations of marvelous objects or occurrences (*res*) were obviously problematic if the requirement of probability was invoked. Poets from Torquato Tasso (1594) to John Dennis (1704), for example, tried to circumvent the difficulty by allowing such occurrences and creatures only if they could be shown to have a Christian, hence believable, pedigree.[19] But it might seem that an age that is famous for delighting in collections of marvels of nature and art—the baroque *Wunderkammern*—should not have had scruples about the "imitation" of wonders in poetry. There was, for example, an established trade in stuffed fabulous creatures like dragons, and the owners of cabinets of curiosities competed for the rarest and most spectacular possessions.[20] One might have thought that the actual existence of such marvelous objects implies that their artistic "imitation" should count as probable and satisfy the requirements of decorum. Nevertheless, the Aristotelian understanding of poetry as distinct from history provided an obstacle to poetic representation of natural marvels. Art was supposed to imitate not what was true (that would be the task of writing history) but what could or should occur, that is, the "verisimilar." In the words of Jean Chapelain, since real (true) events often result from chance, poets "agreed to banish truth from their Parnassus"; they "judged that because of the fortuitous and uncertain pattern of chance occurrences, the truth (which stems from chance) would spoil their efforts," that is, to achieve credibility or probability in the interest of moving the audience.[21] Since the marvelous specimens of the

18. Dennis, *Works*, 1:217.

19. On Dennis, see Patey, *Probability*, 274–80.

20. For sixteenth- and seventeenth-century trade in marvelous objects like hydras and basilisks, see Findlen, "Inventing"; for the collections more generally, cf. Bredekamp, *Antikensehnsucht*, and Daston and Park, *Wonders*, ch. 7.

21. Chapelain (1623), cited in Patey, *Probability*, 79. On the differences and

collections were generally understood as "freaks of nature," as deviations of nature from its lawful course, their artistic imitation would not have qualified as imitation of what is probable. Though this constraint could not prevent poets from presenting non-actual marvels, the supernatural rather than the freakish, the artistic focus on verisimilitude, especially in the second half of the seventeenth century, had a parallel in natural philosophy: the gradual rise to prominence of a distinction between "true" and "false" marvels and an associated differentiation between a respectable and a "vulgar" taste for such objects.[22]

The marvelous is also to be found in *verba*, in the stylistic means a poet uses, in figures of speech, in tropes, or metaphors. These "ornaments of speech" too can arouse admiration, and, given the rhetorical framework, they indeed fit the definition of wonder as that of which we do not know the cause. It was common to think of the (final) "cause" of a work of art as the moral lesson or the fable the author intends to relate, and all ingredients of the work, ideally, had to be related to this cause.[23] Ornaments, however, do not have such a relation, at least not in a straightforward sense, and are thus "uncaused" additions. This is just another way of saying that ornaments do not have content since the work's (final) cause, in the rhetorical understanding, and its content are intimately related, if not indeed identified. Because the rules of decorum are concerned with the adequacy of style to content, ornaments, having no content, are inherently difficult to regulate by such content-based rules. Thus ornaments can be marvelous precisely because they have no content and so tend to conflict with decorum. The problem was paradigmatically expressed by Dryden in his criticism of the "metaphysical" poets (1699): "in the heightening of Poetry, the strength and vehemence of figures [of speech] should be suited to the occasion, the subject, and the persons. All beyond this is monstrous: 'tis out of Nature, 'tis an excrescence, and not a living part of Poetry."[24] Such a comparison of stylistic marvels with monsters in nature, which is not original with Dryden, is deeply suggestive of the tendency towards the end of the seventeenth century to criticize a vulgar taste or curiosity for rare monstrosities as violations of decorum, whether in natural philosophy or in poetry.

---

ultimate identification of Aristotle's "verisimilitude" and "probability," see ibid., ch. 3.

22. Daston and Park, *Wonders*, chs. 8 and 9; Platt, *Wonders*.
23. Patey, *Probability*, 110ff.
24. Dryden, *Essays*, 247.

2. The Defenders of Wonder

The deviant or "monstrous" was an aspect of wonder that justified for one group of baroque art theorists the use of the marvelous as a necessary stimulant of the human mind. For Emanuele Tesauro—besides Baltasar Gracián the most important and ambitious of these theorists—humans, as opposed to animals and angels, have a natural tendency to develop "a certain nausea for ordinary affairs, however beneficial they may be," and hence they crave for stimulation by art, by ornament and "novelty of style" in particular.[25]

Tesauro, of Jesuit extraction, published in 1655 a voluminous contribution to rhetoric under the title *Cannocchiale Aristotelico*. From the frontispiece of the work, the *cannocchiale* (telescope) can be understood as alluding to Aristotle's *Poetics* and *Rhetoric*, which allow the discovery of the secrets of the arts; but the sun towards which the telescope is directed shows the spots that Galilei had interpreted, forty years earlier, as blemishes on the symbol of perfection. Tesauro thus presumably intended to identify and correct imperfections in the arts using the precepts of the "divine philosopher."[26] These corrections, however, were remarkable because they constituted a unified theory of the arts: artistic production, for Tesauro, was based on a faculty that unified intellect and imagination (*ingegno*); the nature of the work of art *in general* he found to lie in metaphorical expression; and the response to art he characterized by *one* dominant emotion, viz., admiration or wonder (*l'ammirazione*).[27]

Tesauro unhesitatingly compared the poet to God, and one is tempted to find in his work a theory of creative genius in the eighteenth-century sense. But this is mistaken because the very aim of the work was to assist the poet in finding surprising metaphors, for example by providing long lists of items that can be combined into "strange" conceits. More appropriately, Tesauro himself compared the poet's work with the tricks performed by jugglers (*Giocolieri*).[28] The basic principle for achieving the intended aesthetic delight—that is, surprise—was the invalid syllogism or enthymeme, built into metaphorical expressions, which is recognized as

---

25. Tesauro, *Cannocchiale*, 122.

26. See ibid., 633ff., and Mehnert, "Bugia," 198ff.

27. For these reasons Tesauro's work has sometimes been characterized as "the first great theory of aesthetics" (Tatarkiewicz, *History*, 391). For a critical view, see Smith, *Wit*, ch. 5.

28. Tesauro, *Cannocchiale*, 82ff.

such by the audience and hence is distinguished from sophistic deception.[29] Pleasure resulted from the audience's recognition of the initial deception and the ensuing admiration of the artist's *ingegno*.[30] Miraculously, the ingenious artist makes "mute things talk, insensate things alive, resurrects the dead: graves, marble reliefs, and statues are lent voice, soul, and movement."[31] The delight is thus ultimately based on the admiration of the artist's ability to give the false the appearance of the true. That the *ingegno* becomes especially pertinent and visible when the audience's mind is engaged in apprehending the artfulness of "lies" may seem perverted, as it did to neoclassicist critics. But this apparent perversion follows from the fact that the truth itself, the "*Ragioni vere*," is boring—"*senza novità, senz' acume*"[32]—and that what is to be represented here, the glory of the mind, cannot straightforwardly be presented in imitations of the truth.

Although the invalid syllogism is the highest manifestation of *ingegno*, for Tesauro art more generally consisted in finding metaphors. In fact, all arts—from poetry, painting, and dance to tournaments and masquerades[33]—are based on metaphorical expression. While metaphors, from an Aristotelian point of view, could be incorporated into the tools that assist poetic imitation because finding metaphors required the poet to recognize similarities between things, Tesauro's account emphasized metaphors based on *dis*similarities. Such *discordia concors*, though in a sense non-mimetic, he claimed to be especially effective because the tropes containing it were the most surprising and hence admirable. The *Cannocchiale*'s emphasis on wonder, which neglected the various other emotions traditionally considered as effects of art, thus provided a unification of the arts by ascribing one dominant emotional aim to them. This unification furthermore allowed a partial suspension of decorum as far as it pertained to the separation of genres in literature. While traditionally the genre adequate to a subject matter was determined by the subject matter, Tesauro (and other baroque theorists) subordinated the choice of genre to the overall aim of effecting *admiratio* through the display of *ingegno*. Under this perspective, lyrical elements could invade the epic,

---

29. For instance, if Achilles is portrayed as a lion, we can understand the metaphor as involving an invalid syllogism with two premises, "Achilles is courageous" and "lions are courageous." For more details, cf. van Hook, "Concupiscence."

30. Tesauro, *Cannocchiale*, 12.

31. Ibid., 2.

32. Ibid., 492.

33. Ibid., 13ff.; 731ff.

Practices of Wonder

comedy could be combined with tragedy, etc.[34] Marino, who had written an heroic epic which consisted, as a contemporary critic complained, of a collection of madrigals—a clear transgression of the boundaries between genres—figured as one of Tesauro's poetic paradigms.[35]

By turning metaphor into the constitutive feature of art, Tesauro changed the rhetorical framework in a significant way. Metaphor traditionally belonged to the ornaments of speech, by no means to the essence of a work of poetry; since ornaments, as I claimed before, have no content and thus can be admirable but also problematic under the aspect of decorum, Tesauro's elevation of metaphor was revolutionary. The tension of this account with the content-based rhetorical framework is brought out very clearly by another baroque theorist, who held views similar to Tesauro's, in the remarkable claim that "the more an expression has of appearance and the less of substance, the more admirable [*mirabile*] it will be."[36]

This astonishing view should be understood, however, in relation to the intense interest art theorists like Tesauro (and later in France, for example, Dominique Bouhours, the theoretician of the *je ne sais quoi* [see below]), took in the genre of "devices," that is, emblems and *impresa*.[37] This form of art had a relatively short but intense boom from the late sixteenth century to the end of the seventeenth, and the large number of treatises on it during those hundred years shows that the device was close to the heart of seventeenth-century aesthetic sensibility. Many of the doctrines on art are brought together in the discussion of emblems as in a microcosm. The emblem, one could say, is an intensified metaphor. Intensified, because the emblem combines two ingredients, the motto and the picture (and perhaps also an *inscriptio*), each of which on their own may appear like a metaphor but which achieve their intended meaning only in combination. The rules for constructing emblems, for instance, proscribed the use of proverbs, enigmas, or questions as mottos because these had meanings on their own, independently of their interaction with the picture.[38] The claim quoted above—that expressions with less substance are more admirable—is likely related to this doctrine: a device is the more perfect, the less pre-established meaning or content its ingredients carry. Less content

---

34. Cf. Schulz-Buschhaus, "Gattungsmischung."

35. Cf. Regn, "Fundierung."

36. Matteo Peregrini (1639), citied in van Hook, "Concupiscence," 29; cf. also Regn, "Fundierung."

37. I here ignore the otherwise important difference between these devices.

38. Klein, "Theory"; Gombrich, "Icones."

of this sort thus meant higher ingenuity of the device and therefore higher worthiness of admiration.

3. The Neoclassicist Response

Against poetry of the kind Marino and his followers wrote—and, by implication, against the justification of this literary practice in later theories like Tesauro's—a growing critical consensus had formed in France since the 1630s. It was, among other things, a response against the use of the marvelous in poetry and a defense of "naturalness" as a criterion of quality; a response that was based on a distinction between good and bad "taste"—a new art theoretical term—and "true" and "false" wonder. Guez de Balzac, in 1639, complained about contemporary comedies in a way that would be echoed in the writings of later neoclassicist critics like Boileau, Rapin, or Dryden: "We saw [on stage] unnatural men, borrowed passions, and artificial actions. . ." Only the vulgar could delight in such plays, Guez maintained: "the crowd likes prodigies [that is, the marvelous] and . . . comets receive more attention than the sun." These illegitimately successful works did not "stimulate the beautiful passions [*belles passions*] . . . [but] resemble the illusions of magic that astonish the imagination and satisfy only bad curiosity [*mauvaises curiositez*] . . ."[39] René Rapin, one of the most widely recognized literary theorists of the late seventeenth century, therefore counseled the poet that tragedy has to avoid supernatural, marvelous, or extraordinary events and should instead aim at making them "naturels et passionnés."[40]

Despite these attacks on the use of the marvelous as a means of instructing and delighting the audience, the neoclassicists were aware that wonder was a necessary ingredient in art without which it would lose much of its effectiveness. Pierre Nicole, who would write the Port-Royal *Logic* with Antoine Arnauld, insisted therefore in 1659 that metaphors must be used like discords in music—sparingly. They relieved, he thought, the "répugnance que causerait une harmonie parfait," the "dégout de la nature." This appeared to be in agreement with Tesauro's view, but Nicole's evaluation of the practice is radically different: that metaphors are needed for this purpose is a symptom of human nature's "faiblesse."[41] Corneille himself had to fend off such criticisms in the *Querelle du Cid* and

39. Guez de Balzac, "Réponse," 118; 129.
40. Rapin, *Réflexions*, 107.
41. Nicole, *Vraie Beauté*, 75.

developed complex distinctions within the concept of *vraisemblance* in order to show that the marvelous could be combined with the probable and the imitation requirement.[42] Such a balance of the decorum with the marvelous was the standard neoclassicist prescription: "The admirable [*le merveilleux*] is all that which is against the ordinary course of nature," defined Rapin, and the "probable is whatever suits with common opinion." But most poets, "by too great a passion they have to create admiration, take not sufficient care to temper it with probability."[43] This may sound as if a compromise was possible because one could take "the ordinary course of nature" to be distinct from "what suits common opinion" and thereby "temper" wonder with probability. An event violating the ordinary course of nature could become probable if, as Rapin put it, an agent is introduced "to whose power this change was possible."[44] Common opinion would be satisfied if the cause of the marvelous event (the agent) itself was beyond the ordinary course of nature. Although Corneille himself had adopted this maneuver, it had already been pointed out by Tasso that it succeeds only for supernatural agents with Christian pedigree in whose existence everybody had to believe; pagan deities or supernatural agents in the exemplary works of the ancient poets could not be rescued in this way.[45]

The neoclassicists developed a further strategy (also already found in Tasso) to justify poetic violations of what to common opinion *appears* to be the ordinary course of nature in the name of a "higher" truth. Imitating what is true (nature as it is or is commonly thought to be) is, as Aristotle's *Poetics* taught, not the aim of the poet because, as Rapin put it,

> truth represents things only as they are, but probability (*vraisemblance*) renders them as they ought to be. Truth is wellnigh always defective by the mixture of particular conditions that compose it. Nothing is brought into the world that is not remote from the perfection of its idea from the very birth. Originals and models are to be searched for in probability and in the universal principles of things, where nothing that is material and singular enters to corrupt them.[46]

---

42. Corneille, "Discours."
43. Rapin, "Reflections," 288.
44. Ibid.
45. Tasso, *Discourses*, 38ff. See also above, note 18.
46. Rapin, "Reflections," 288. For the Renaissance history of this theme, cf. Panofsky, *Idea*, who notes its significance for neoclassicist painters like Poussin.

The poet's imitation of "the probable," understood in the sense of the "idea" or "original" of ordinary, corrupt nature, thus could well produce marvelous effects because the originals, revealed to the artist, are not known to common opinion. The artwork could be marvelous by going against common opinion and still be probable in this modified sense.

But this compromise was, of course, deeply problematic. While probability at first, in Rapin's own definition, referred to common opinion, it now pointed to the world of ideas, an uncorrupted reality into which the poet has special insight. The traditional concept of *vraisemblance*, the accordance with the opinions of the audience, coexisted now with an, in principle, audience-independent notion that was claimed to be based on *raison* or nature.

4. The "Marvelous in Discourse" and Aesthetic Experience

The neoclassicist rejection of the baroque emphasis on wonder was intimately connected with the rise of the notion of "good taste" in the last quarter of the seventeenth century. One aspect of this criticism was an attitude of moderation towards the representation of passions in art and their evocation in the audience. This stance against "excesses" clearly agreed with views on the passions that Descartes had formulated in the 1640s. Although he classified wonder or admiration (*l'admiration*) as the first of the "passions of the soul" and indeed as a sort of disinterested pleasure,[47] he warned that when admiration turns into astonishment, it paralyzes reason and blocks the progress to knowledge.[48] Tesauro, the theorist of the marvelous conceit, by contrast had characterized precisely this state of paralysis or stupor as the effect the artist should aim at.[49]

A key document in which neoclassicist views about moderation appear to be codified is Nicolas Boileau's versified doctrine of criticism, the *Art poétique* of 1674. It has therefore often seemed paradoxical that Boileau, at the same time, published an annotated translation of a Hellenistic tract on "the sublime," the *Peri Hypsous*, attributed to (Pseudo-) Longinus. The aim of this rhetorical treatise seemed to be directly opposed to the

---

47. Descartes, "Passions," 350 (§53; AT XI 373). Cartesian wonder could be called disinterested because we can feel this passion "before we know whether or not the object is beneficial to us."

48. Ibid., 354–56 (§§73–78; AT XI 382–86).

49. For a more detailed comparison of Descartes and Tesauro's attitudes towards wonder, cf. Hanafi, *Monster*, 190ff.

call for moderation and for avoidance of excess that the neoclassicists, at least on one reading of the *Art poétique*, emphasized.⁵⁰ Longinus' sublime appeared more like an intense feeling, based on vaguely characterized stylistic features, than a rhetorical device that could be employed according to rules, more like an excess of emotion than a means of persuasion. It "produces ecstasy rather than persuasion in the hearer," said Longinus, "and the combination of wonder and astonishment always proves superior to the merely persuasive and pleasant. This is because persuasion is on the whole something we can control, whereas amazement and wonder exert invincible power and force and get the better of every hearer."⁵¹ This sounded very similar to the way in which the effect of "metaphysical" poems like Donne's had been described earlier in the century as committing "holy Rapes upon our [the readers'] will"⁵²—the sort of poetic production the neoclassicists later condemned.

Boileau's translation was published as the *Traité du sublime* in 1674, and with this work began the career of the sublime in Europe as a main topic of art theoretical discussion. The subtitle of the translation, however, suggests how Boileau intended to connect Longinus' praise of rapture and of the orator's powers of overwhelming and stunning the audience with the earlier debates about the legitimacy of the wonderful. "Du merveilleux dans le discours" makes it clear that his main objective was the transformation of the old concept of the marvelous into a legitimate artistic tool, that is, a tool acceptable to neoclassicists. This was to be accomplished in part by establishing an ancient pedigree for the notion of "the marvelous in discourse."

Boileau, of course, was far from making the marvelous the constitutive feature of poetry but, in the form of the sublime, he thought it could achieve especially intense effects that did not fall under the neoclassicist verdict against the "vulgar," baroque understanding of wonder. And the differences are plain: Boileau's sublime or marvelous was explicitly distinguished from the *genus sublime* (or *genus grande*), a style of writing rich in ornaments; the "marvelous in discourse" incorporated the feature of simplicity. Like the wonderful, however, the sublime could not be characterized in terms of its causes but only through its effects.

---

50. For a detailed study of Boileau's aims in publishing the *Traité*, see Cronk, *Sublime*.

51. Longinus, "Sublimity," 462 (1.4).

52. Thomas Carew (1633), cited in Biester, *Lyric*, 110.

Both of these aspects were important in giving legitimacy to the emotion of wonder, the response to the sublime. The dignity of the object (the content of the sublime thought) that causes the audience's rapture, and the opposition of the style to any bombast or superfluous ornament, could both be called marvelous, with respect to *res* and to *verba*, in the traditional sense. The object of the sublime response is wonderful because it is so grand, so elevated above our common knowledge that we do not really grasp the cause of the effect it has on us. Thus the "ancient dilemma of knowledge" that we encountered above in the debates about the wonderful surfaces again: we desire to have knowledge most of all of those objects that are highest in the hierarchy of things; but the distance of these objects from our own position prevents us from gaining accurate knowledge.[53] In the example used by Longinus and Boileau, such an object is the infinite power of God, expressed in the divine words *fiat lux* of the first book of *Genesis*. From the unapproachable nature of the object, it followed that a mimetic representation was not possible because such imitation would presuppose accurate knowledge. The unavoidable lack of similarity between object and representation, one might say, had to be substituted for by the adequacy of the effect of the representation to the status of the object. It was thus only superficially paradoxical that Bernard Lamy in his *Art de parler* of 1675—sometimes regarded as the rhetorical complement to the Port-Royal *Logic*—quoted the *fiat lux* as a case of perfect conformity of word and thing; the phrase, he explains, leads the reader's mind "directly to the end of the design," which is a "strong Idea of the power of God over his Creatures."[54]

The simplicity of the sublime expression, of the *verba*, furthermore was itself marvelous because it appeared to stand in contrast to the intensity of the effect achieved. The influential critic Bouhours maintained in 1687 that "the great and sublime are . . . not natural, nor can they be, for the Natural carries in it somewhat [sic] low, or less elevated,"[55] a remark that illustrates how extraordinary Boileau's combination of the sublime with simplicity of expression must have appeared. Given that simplicity was generally associated, at the time, with naturalness, he attempted to bring together what did not seem to go together: the *merveilleux dans le discours* and the natural.

---

53. See above, section 1.
54. Cited in Shuger, *Sacred Rhetoric*, 158.
55. Bouhours, *Art*, 156.

Practices of Wonder

The lack of resemblance between the sublime object and its representation and the associated emphasis on the intensity of the effect make it also possible to understand that the sublime delight could be occasioned by poetic discourse that violates the traditional standards of beauty, harmony, order, and proportion. Pindar's odes were mentioned in the *Traité* as examples of sublime writing and the *Art poétique* traced their effect to a "beau désordre" in the poetic diction.[56] Although this was an isolated remark in Boileau's poetics (nevertheless indicating a connection with the *Traité*), its importance and consequences were considerable. That disorder could bring about aesthetic delight of a perhaps more intense quality than the pleasure we find in order and proportion must have confirmed the view that the ultimate causes of this delight in the objects are inscrutable—for both, beauty and the sublime. "What is this sublime?" asked La Bruyère mockingly. "It does not appear to have been defined."[57] That the sublime could not be defined in terms of its cause but only characterized through its effects was indeed central to Boileau's message: "The Sublime is not properly a Thing to be prov'd and demonstrated; but . . . it is a certain Marvellousness [*un merveilleux*] which seizes us, strikes us, and makes it self be felt."[58]

This was, in fact, the reason—for Boileau as well as for later theorists like Hume—why the "test of time" had to play a central role in the theory of art: this criterion—the continued success of works of art with audiences over the ages—looks *only* at effects.[59] For the defender of a new form of the wonderful, however, the "test of time" presented an awkward challenge. The marvelous had traditionally been associated with novelty or the extraordinary;[60] but, as Longinus already noted, what is novel cannot remain so for long. The sublime, therefore, could not be linked to the experience of novelty even though it occasioned admiration or wonder. Boileau indeed recognized this problem and attempted to solve it by redefining novelty in a way that made it seemingly compatible with the timelessness of the sublime. "What is a new, brilliant, extraordinary thought?" he asked. "It is not at all . . . a thought that no one ever had or ought to have had. It

56. Boileau, *Oeuvres*, 164.
57. La Bruyère, "Caractères," 85ff.
58. Boileau, *Oeuvres*, 546 (the translation is from Boileau, *Longinus*, 62).
59. The test is already invoked by Longinus ("Sublime," 467 [7.4]) on behalf of the sublime. In the *Querelle*, the "Moderns" had insisted on the historical relativity of beauty; Boileau and the "Ancients" replied with the timelessness of the sublime. For Boileau's use of the test, see, e.g., *Oeuvres*, 1; 524 (Réflexion V); 546f. (Réflexion X).
60. E.g., Descartes, "Passions," 350 (§53; AT XI 373) and 353 (§70; AT XI 380).

is, to the contrary, a thought that ought to have occurred to everyone and that someone is [just] the first to express."[61]

In the last quarter of the seventeenth century, Boileau's respectable marvelous was not the only aesthetic notion characterized by inscrutable causes and by defiance of rules. The *je ne sais quoi*, defined Dominique Bouhours in the widely read *Entretiens d'Ariste et d'Eugène* of 1671, "is a pleasing effect which animates beauty."[62] The effect is immediate; it strikes us in the "shortest possible moment" and "evades reason" and the control of our will. If we think we know why art pleases because we are familiar with the rules that connect features of the artwork with the effect in the audience, we are mistaken, explained Bouhours. The great artists discovered "that nothing pleases more in nature than that which does so without our knowing why," and they "sought to make their works pleasing by concealing their art with great care and artifice." The connection between work and effect thus becomes mysterious and the audience's response is ascribed to an "occult quality," a term Bouhours himself uses. In the end, then, the *je ne sais quoi*, much like the slightly later notion of the sublime,[63] rephrased the traditional definition of the wonderful: its effect is the pleasure whose cause we do not know.

It seems plausible that the introduction of "occult causes" prepared, within the theory of art, the ground for the problem that would exercise Hume and others in the eighteenth century, viz., the question of how to account for the non-arbitrariness of judgments of taste, their dependence on a "standard," when we cannot specify the properties that prompt us to make such judgments. This problem, Hume claimed, became serious only after a new "species of Philosophy"—the "new way of ideas"—separated ideas or sentiments from their external causes.[64] And indeed when Addison discussed the pleasures of the imagination, he referred to "Mr. Lock's [sic] Essay on Human Understanding" and "that Great Modern Discovery, which is at present universally acknowledged by all the Enquirers into Natural Philosophy," the view that properties like colors and light "are only Ideas in the Mind, and not Qualities that have any Existence in Matter." This doctrine motivated Addison's resolve

---

61. Boileau, *Oeuvres*, 2.

62. Bouhours, *Entretiens*, 141; the following quotes are from pp. 143, 147, and 148.

63. See Marin, *Poussin*, for the claim that the sublime indeed is a species of the *je ne sais quoi*.

64. Hume, "Standard," 268ff.

to exclude the search for efficient causes of the pleasures of the imagination from his project:

> [W]e must own that it is impossible for us to assign the necessary Cause of this Pleasure, because we know neither the Nature of an Idea, nor the Substance of a Human Soul, which might help us discover the Conformity or Disagreeableness of the one to the other; and therefore, for want of such a Light, all that we can do ... is to reflect on those Operations of the Soul that are most agreeable ... without being able to trace out the several necessary and efficient Causes from whence the Pleasure or Displeasure arises.[65]

It should, however, be evident by now that this attitude, common to the early theoreticians of "aesthetic experience," derived not only from the "new philosophy" but also followed from a line of art theoretical discussions about a special sort of experience for which causes and rules could not be specified.

5. Beauty and Sublimity

With the acceptance of the sublime in art theory, a particular experience, primarily in response to works of poetry and oratory,[66] had been singled out as extraordinary and to be distinguished from other responses to art. No rules concerning the production and reception of the sublime were to be found in Longinus or Boileau, and virtually everybody agreed that it could not be analyzed in terms of its causes but could only be characterized through its effect. The theoretical efforts therefore focused on this experience, the effect, rather than on the inscrutable causes. It was thus not only the "new philosophy" that motivated Addison, Dubos, or Hume to give up on the search for the causes of aesthetic pleasure; the issue had already been prepared in the art theoretic discussions, especially of the sublime. The respectable marvelous set the stage for the eighteenth-century notion of a special aesthetic experience as well as for the problem of the

---

65. Addison, *Spectator*, 547 and 544ff. (no. 413). Cf. also the Abbé Dubos' admission that "[i]t would be to no purpose to ask me the physical reasons for these fitnesses or agreements [between properties of a work of art and the audience's response]; I can allege none but the instinct which suggests them to us, and the example of the great painters that have observed them. The same remark is applicable to poetry." (Dubos, *Reflections* 1:91ff.) Hume's discussion of the standard of taste relied heavily on Dubos.

66. But see already Longinus on oceans, rivers, and mountains: "Sublimity," 494 (35.4).

standard of taste. As we will furthermore see, the extraordinary emotional response to the sublime was, in this early phase, considered as continuous with the response to beauty.

The sublime in the second half of the eighteenth century, after Burke's *Philosophical Enquiry into the Origin of Our Ideas of the Sublime and Beautiful* (1757), was an ambivalent emotion, a pleasure mixed with terror and in this respect clearly distinguished from beauty. Significantly, however, the feeling of terror was not an ingredient in Boileau's notion of the sublime.[67] Although John Dennis, in his famous description of the experience of the Alps from 1688, referred to such an ambivalent emotion,[68] it ultimately did not play the dominant role in his theory of the sublime: "his sublime is simply the highest beauty, not a separate experience, different from one's perception of the beautiful."[69] Similarly, for the French theoretician of painting, Roger de Piles, the sublime was a more intense form of beauty: "in Painting there must be something Great and Extraordinary to Surprize, Please and Instruct . . . 'Tis by this that ordinary things are made Beautiful, and the Beautiful, Sublime and Wonderful . . ."[70] Addison's essays on Milton's *Paradise Lost* contain phrases like "some passages are beautiful by being sublime . . ."[71] Jonathan Richardson in 1725 took the sublime in painting "to be the Greatest, and most Beautiful Ideas, whether Corporeal or not," a "Kind and Degree of Beauty," and Ten Kate (1728) dealt with the sublime under the title "le Beau Ideal," and though his characterizations are not especially clear,[72] they show how the sublime was widely understood as potentiated beauty.[73] The later separation of beauty and sublimity became firmly established only through Burke.[74]

I have suggested that the sublime, in association with beauty, demarcated a special sort of experience that theoreticians like Boileau tried to characterize from within the rhetorical framework as a successor to the

---

67. Nor is terror regularly an ingredient of the sublime in the tradition Shuger traces (e.g., *Sacred Rhetoric*, 190).

68. Dennis, *Works*, 2:380–82.

69. Monk, *Sublime*, 54; similarly, Barnouw, "Morality," and Patey, *Probability*, 274–80.

70. De Piles (1699), cited in Monk, *Sublime*, 171.

71. Addison, *Spectator*, 392.

72. The sublime, he said, is "a real *Je ne scai quoi*, or an unaccountable Something . . . an harmonious Propriety, which is a touching or moving Unity . . . a true Decorum, a *Bienséance* . . ."

73. Richardson, "Sublime," 409ff., Ten Kate, "Ideal," 411.

74. Cf. Litman, *Sublime*, 241.

enjoyment of the marvelous. At the same time, the sublime experience pointed beyond the traditional framework because this feeling was singled out among all the other sorts of emotions that rhetoric and poetics considered as effects of works of art. The sublime thus is connected backwards with the traditional marvelous and forward to the eighteenth-century "aesthetic experience." To illustrate this Janus face of the sublime—and hence of the early aesthetic theories—I would like to contrast the interpretation I suggested with a frequent claim in the literature concerning the sense in which the sublime around 1700 emancipated itself from rhetoric.

According to this contrasting view, it is around this time that we can distinguish a "natural sublime"—the concept applied to objects in nature—from the traditional "rhetorical sublime," the sublime as a feature of poetic discourse. The "natural sublime," it is claimed, actually preceded in England (in the works of Dennis, Shaftesbury, and Addison) the reception of the "rhetorical sublime" (as represented by Longinus and Boileau) and, precisely because of its independence from the rhetorical tradition, represented the concept of "a new aesthetic experience."[75] This opposition within the notion of the sublime and the claim that the new aesthetic experience resulted from the non-rhetorical sublime, seem misconceived. Not only can the key document for this view—Dennis's letter of 1688, reporting his experience of the Alps[76]—be shown to have been arranged according to Longinian rhetorical precepts,[77] but furthermore the analysis of the "new experience" by Shaftesbury reveals the connection with the rhetorical tradition.

The early documents that report the sublime experience of nature are written against the background of physico-theological conceptions of the apparently harmful or terrible aspects of nature; according to the vogue of these accounts in the later seventeenth century, God's glory and benevolence could be seen even in those aspects: mountains as well as fleas were thus incorporated into a "deeper" view of God's creation. But this physico-theological view has to be understood as a subtext to the experience of the sublime in nature; this experience itself is, as it were, organized like an emblem, a picture (of nature) with a motto (the physico-theological story), a structure that is quite explicit in Dennis's letter about the Alps as well as in poetry from the early eighteenth century, like Barthold Heinrich Brockes' attempts to represent natural objects like the

75. Nicholson, "Sublime," 334.
76. Dennis, *Works*, 380–82.
77. See Zelle, "Geburt."

starry sky.[78] These early participants in the sublime experience still "read" the book of nature—an activity that is unlikely to have been completely independent of rhetorical precepts.[79] When Shaftesbury explained in 1709 why "the wildness pleases," why objects "how terrible soever or how contrary to human nature, are beauteous in themselves," he referred to our assurance—against our "short views"—that all this is part of an "economy ... in respect of which things seemingly deformed are amiable, disorder becomes regular, corruption wholesome ..." The delight in such "graces of the wilderness" therefore seemed due, in good part, to the contrast between the irregular or terrible appearance and the underlying order and "economy."[80] A *discordia concors* thus is the occasion of the pleasure, the realization of the meaning beneath the surface, just like the realization of the meaning behind the superficially puzzling ingredients of the baroque emblem or like the insight into a clever conceit that Tesauro described. Wild nature in Shaftesbury still seems like a conceit of the divine poet, perhaps not designed for our pleasure but able to delight us when we make an effort to grasp the poet's meaning.

To conclude: It is certainly objectionable, from a methodological perspective, to project the concept of "aesthetic experience," as understood in the early eighteenth century, into the art theoretical debates of the previous century and to claim that the Renaissance and baroque critic, "as he looked more and more closely into the meaning of the marvelous ... was increasingly confronted with questions of aesthetic effects" or that "the study of ways of achieving the marvelous became a substitute for classification of aesthetic categories."[81] But it can nevertheless be made plausible that from such concerns with wonder as an artistic tool and as an emotional response, the eighteenth-century analyses of the singular experience of beauty resulted. This process, however, did not lead straightforwardly from the old theories of wonder to the empiricist or rationalist analyses of aesthetic experience. As tempting as it may seem to find, for instance, in views like Tesauro's the "first great theory of aesthetics,"[82] baroque wonder and admiration had to go through the neoclassicist transformation of the marvelous into the sublime before Shaftesbury, Addison, or Baumgarten could construct the concept of aesthetic experience.

78. Spörl, "Berge."
79. Morris, *Religious Sublime*, 7.
80. Shaftesbury, "Moralists," 315 and 317.
81. Hathaway, *Marvels*, 59; cf. also 152.
82. See note 26 above.

Bibliography[83]

Primary Texts

Addison, Joseph. *The Spectator*. Edited by Donald F. Bond. Vol. 3. Oxford: Oxford University Press, 1965.

Baumgarten, Alexander Gottlieb. *Reflections on Poetry*. Translated by Karl Aschenbrenner and W. B. Holther. Berkeley: University of California Press, 1954.

———. *Theoretische Ästhetik*. Edited and translated by H. R. Schweitzer. Hamburg: Meiner, 1988.

Boileau, Nicolas. *Oeuvres completes*. Edited by A. Adam and F. Escal. Paris: Gallimard, 1966.

———. *Boileau on Longinus*. Translated by J. Ozell. Reprint of 1713 edition. Sheffield: University of Sheffield, Department of English Literature, 1972.

Bouhours, Dominique. *The Art of Criticism*. Translated by Philip Smallwood. Reprint of original translation of 1705. Demar, NY: Scholars' Facsimiles, 1981.

———. *Les Entretiens d'Ariste et d'Eugène*. Edited by F. Brunot. Paris: Colin, 1962.

Buchner, August. *Anleitung zur Deutschen Poeterey*. Reprint of 1665 edition. Tübingen: Niemeyer, 1966.

Corneille, Pierre. "Discours de la Tragédie." In *Oeuvres completes*, edited by G. Couton, 3:142–73. Paris: Gallimard, 1987.

Dennis, John. *The Critical Works of John Dennis*. Edited by E. N. Hooker. 2 vols. Baltimore: Johns Hopkins University Press, 1939.

Descartes, René. "The Passions of the Soul." In *The Philosophical Writings of Descartes*, vol. 1, translated by John Cottingham, Robert Stoothoff, and Dugald Murdoch, 326–404. Cambridge: Cambridge University Press, 1985.

Dryden, John. *Essays of John Dryden*. Vol. 1. Edited by W. P. Ker. New York: Russell & Russell, 1961.

Dubos, Jean Baptiste. *Critical Reflections on Poetry, Painting and Music*. 3 vols. Translated by Thomas Nugent. London: J. Nourse, 1748.

Guez de Balzac, Jean-Louis. "Réponse à deux questions, ou du caractère et de l'instruction de la comédie." In *Oeuvres diverses (1644)*, edited by Roger Zuber, 117–32. Paris: Champion, 1995.

Hume, David. "On the Standard of Taste." In *Essays Moral, Political and Literary*, edited by T. H. Green and T. H. Grose, 1:266–84. London: Longmans, 1875.

La Bruyère, Jean de. "Les caractères." In *Oeuvres completes*. Edited by Julien Benda. Paris: Gallimard, 1951.

Longinus. "On Sublimity." In *Ancient Literary Criticism: The Principal Texts in New Translations*, edited by D. A. Russell and M. Winterbottom, 460–503. Oxford: Oxford University Press, 1972.

Marino, Giambattista. *Adonis. Selections from "L'Adone" of Giambattista Marino*. Translated by Harold M. Priest. Ithaca: Cornell University Press, 1967.

Nicole, Pierre. *La vraie beauté et son fantôme* [*Dissertatio de vera pulchritudine et adumbrata*]. Edited and translated by B. Guion. Paris: Champion, 1996.

Rapin, René. *Les Réflexions sur la poétique de ce temps*. Edited by E. T. Dubos. Genève: Droz, 1970.

---

83. Translations into English are my own unless indicated otherwise.

———. "Reflections on Aristotle's Treatise of Poesy." In *The Continental Model*, edited by S. Elledge and D. Schier, 279-306. Rev. ed. Ithaca: Cornell University Press, 1970.

Richardson, Jonathan. "Of the Sublime." In *Art in Theory, 1648-1815*, edited by C. Harrison et al., 409-10. Oxford: Blackwell, 2000.

Shaftesbury. "The Moralists, a Philosophical Rhapsody." In *Characteristics of Men, Manners, Opinions, Times*, edited by Lawrence E. Klein, 231-338. Cambridge: Cambridge University Press, 1999.

Tasso, Torquato. *Discourses on the Heroic Poem*. Translated by M. Cavalchini and I. Samuel. Oxford: Oxford University Press, 1973.

Ten Kate, Lambert H. "The Beau Ideal." In *Art in Theory, 1648-1815*, edited by C. Harrison et al., 410-12. Oxford: Blackwell, 2000.

Tesauro, Emanuele. *Il Cannocchiale Aristotelico*. Reprint of 1670 edition. Edited by A. Buck. Bad Homburg: Gehlen, 1968.

Secondary Literature

Barnouw, Jeffrey. "The Morality of the Sublime: To John Dennis." *Comparative Literature* 35 (1983) 21-42.

Bender, Werner. "Rhetorische Tradition und Ästhetik im 18. Jahrhundert." *Zeitschrift für deutsche Philologie* 99 (1980) 481-506.

Biester, James. *Lyric Wonder: Rhetoric and Wit in Renaissance English Poetry*. Ithaca: Cornell University Press, 1997.

Bredekamp, Horst. *Antikensehnsucht und Maschinenglauben*. Berlin: Wagenbach, 1993.

Cronk, Nicholas. *The Classical Sublime: French Neoclassicism and the Language of Literature*. Charlottesville, VA: Rockwood, 2002.

Cunningham, James Vincent. *Collected Essays of J. V. Cunnigham*. Chicago: Swallow Press, 1976.

Daston, Lorraine, and Katharine Park. *Wonders and the Order of Nature, 1150-1750*. New York: Zone, 1998.

Dockhorn, Klaus. *Macht und Wirkung der Rhetorik*. Bad Homburg: Gehlen, 1968.

Edwards, William F. "Jacopo Zabarella: A Renaissance Aristotelian's View of Rhetoric and Poetry and Their Relation to Philosophy." In *Arts Libéraux et Philosophie au Moyen Age*, 843-54. Montreal: Institut d'études médiévales, 1969.

Findlen, Paula. "Inventing Nature." In *Merchants and Marvels: Commerce, Science, and Art in Early Modern Europe*, edited by Pamela H. Smith and Paula Findlen, 297-323. London: Routledge, 2002.

Gombrich, Ernst. "Icones Symbolicae: Philosophies of Symbolism and Their Bearing on Art." In *Symbolic Images*, 123-91. Chicago: University of Chicago Press, 1972.

Hanafi, Zakiya. *The Monster in the Machine*. Durham, NC: Duke University Press, 2000.

Hathaway, Baxter. *Marvels and Commonplaces*. New York: Random House, 1968.

Kenseth, Joy, editor. *The Age of the Marvelous*. Hanover, NH: Hood Museum of Art, 1991.

Klein, Robert. "The Theory of Figurative Expression in Italian Treatises on the Impresa." In *Form and Meaning*, 3-24. New York: Viking, 1979.

Litman, Theodore A. *Le Sublime en France (1660-1714)*. Paris: Nizet, 1971.

Marin, Louis. *Sublime Poussin*. Stanford: Stanford University Press, 1999.

Practices of Wonder

Mehnert, Herbert. "'Bugia' und 'Argutezza.'" *Romanische Forschungen* 88 (1976) 195–209.

Mirollo, James V. *The Poet of the Marvelous: Giambattista Marino*. New York: Columbia University Press, 1963.

Monk, Samuel H. *The Sublime*. New York: Modern Language Association, 1935.

Morris, David B. *The Religious Sublime: Christian Poetry and Critical Tradition in Eighteenth-Century England*. Lexington: University Press of Kentucky, 1972.

Nicholson, Marjorie H. "Sublime in External Nature." In *Dictionary of the History of Ideas*, edited by Philip P. Wiener, 4:333–37. New York: Scribner's, 1973.

Panofsky, Erwin. *Idea: A Concept in Art Theory*. Translated by J. J. S. Peake. Columbia: University of South Carolina Press, 1968.

Patey, Douglas L. *Probability and Literary Form*. Cambridge: Cambridge University Press, 1984.

Platt, Peter G., editor. *Wonders, Marvels, and Monsters in Early Modern Culture*. London: Associated University Presses, 1999.

Regn, Gerhard. "Metaphysische Fundierung und ästhetische Autonomie." In *Diskurse des Barock*, edited by J. Küpper and F. Wolfzettel, 359–82. Munich: Fink, 2000.

Reiss, Hans. "The 'Naturalization' of the Term 'Aesthetik' in Eighteenth-Century German: Alexander Gottlieb Baumgarten and His Impact." *Modern Language Review* 89 (1994) 645–58.

Rueger, Alexander. "Aesthetics." In *Oxford Handbook of Philosophy in Early Modern Europe*, edited by Desmond Clarke and Catherine Wilson, 201–23. Oxford: Oxford University Press, 2011.

Schulz-Buschhaus, Ulrich. "Gattungsmischung—Gattungskombination—Gattungsnivellierung." In *Epochenschwellen und Epochenstrukturen im Diskurs der Literatur- und Sprachhistorie*, edited by H. U. Gumbrecht et al., 213–33. Frankfurt: Suhrkamp, 1985.

Shuger, Deborah K. *Sacred Rhetoric*. Princeton: Princeton University Press, 1988.

Smith, A. J. *Metaphysical Wit*. Cambridge: Cambridge University Press, 1991.

Spörl, Ulrich. "Berge, Meer und Sterne als Erhabenes in der Natur?" *Deutsche Vierteljahresschrift für Literaturwissenschaft und Geistesgeschichte* 73 (1999) 228–65.

Stolniz, Jerome. "'Beauty': Some Stages in the History of an Idea." *Journal of the History of Ideas* 22 (1961) 185–204.

———. "On the Origins of 'Aesthetic Disinterestedness.'" *Journal of Aesthetics and Art Criticism* 20 (1961) 131–43.

Tatarkiewicz, Wladyslaw. *History of Aesthetics*. Vol. 3. The Hague: Mouton, 1974.

Trimpi, Wesley. *Muses of One Mind*. Princeton: Princeton University Press, 1983.

Van Hook, J. W. "'Concupiscence of Witt': The Metaphysical Conceit in Baroque Poetics." *Modern Philology* 84 (1986) 24–38.

Weinberg, Bernard. *A History of Literary Criticism in the Italian Renaissance*. 2 vols. Chicago: University of Chicago Press, 1961.

Zelle, Carsten. "Die Geburt der Natur aus dem Geiste der Rhetorik." In *Erschriebene Natur*, edited by M. Scheffel, 145–67. Frankfurt: P. Lang, 2001.

9

The Conception of *Camatkâra* in Indian Aesthetics

MICHEL HULIN

BEFORE ANALYZING THE NOTION of *camatkâra* and investigating its possible links to the general theme of wonderment, it seems appropriate to give a brief sketch of the so-called Indian aesthetics. This respectable branch of learning goes back to a rather voluminous treatise of dramaturgy, the *Nâtya-shâstra*, ascribed to a certain Bharata who flourished sometime around the junction of the fourth and fifth centuries AD. While dealing especially with the problem of theatricality (stage, costumes, acting, etc.), it is also concerned with dancing and music. Within two to three generations, its theories had been extended to the field of poetry (both lyric and epic) and, a few centuries later, to the plastic arts: architecture, sculpture, painting. It was abundantly commented upon over a millennium[1] and we may consider it as the fountainhead of all later developments. Its very first—and most important—aphorism (*sûtra*) runs as follows: "From the union of Determinants, Consequents and Transitory Mental States, the birth of *rasa* takes place." The notion of *rasa* is so central in this context that Indian aesthetics very often goes by the name of *rasavâda* or "doctrine of *rasa*." But what does the word *rasa* actually stand for?

1. By far, the most important of its commentators was the Kashmiri Abhinavagupta (flourished circa 980–1015 AD), famous not only as a poetician, but also as a metaphysician and tantric master.

Practices of Wonder

According to the Monier-Williams Sanskrit-English Dictionary, *rasa* can be translated as "the sap (of a plant) . . . the juice (of a fruit)" and, by extension, "the best or finest part of anything, its essence." That is why aesthetic experience is frequently referred to as *rasâsvâda* or the "tasting of *rasa.*" But where does *rasa* come from? What sort of fruit has to be crushed for it to flow abundantly and quench the thirst of theatre-goers? According to Bharata, there are eight fundamental feelings (*sthâyi-bhâva*) that are never absent from any human soul whatsoever. They are pleasure (*rati*), exhilaration (*hâsa*), sorrow (*shoka*), anger (*krodha*), enthusiasm (*utsâha*), fear (*bhaya*), disgust (*jugupsâ*) and, most significantly, wonder (*vismaya*). They are supposed to permanently reside in the minds of all people, in the form of latent impressions or tendencies, either derived from experiences of the present life or inherited from past lives, according to the all-Indian notions of transmigration and *karman*. As such, they are ready to emerge to consciousness on every occasion. Now, these very basic feelings or emotions will give birth, once "processed" by the whole theatrical apparatus, to the different *rasas*. That is, each of them undergoes a sort of transmutation that enables it to reappear, in the sensibility of the spectators, in a new, sublimated form. The audience feels them intensively but in the paradoxical mode of the "as it were," without being impelled by them to any action or reaction. So, the *rasas* will also be eight in number, namely the Erotic, the Comic, the Pathetic, the Furious, the Heroic, the Terrible, the Odious and the Marvelous. Moreover, in everyday experience, the *sthâyi-bhâvas* are excited by the proper causes of their manifestation: the various situations and encounters of life. They produce their proper effects, in terms of trembling of the voice, paleness, tears, and so on. They are associated with various transient moods, such as anxiety, briskness, etc. Once on the stage, the causes will become the Determinants (*vibhâva*), the effects the Consequents (*anubhâva*), and the moods the Transitory Mental States (*vyabhicâri-bhâvai*).

In order to be relished, the *rasas* have to be pleasurable. In other words, they are experienced as different ways for the imagination of the spectator to play freely, miles away from the dreariness and dullness of common life. The underlying idea is that the dichotomy between positive or joyful *sthâyi-bhâvas* (pleasure, exhilaration, enthusiasm, wonder) and negative or painful ones (sorrow, anger, fear and disgust) is overcome at the level of *rasas*. All of them have to be pleasant, even the Pathetic or the Odious. So what is the secret of that alchemy, capable of transforming the vilest or most sinister human feelings into sources of moral and spiritual

Michel Hulin—*The Conception of* Camatkâra *in Indian Aesthetics*

delight? In other words, how could spectators otherwise accept to attend (for up to four or five days according to old Indian standards!) theatrical performances brimming over with evocations of human misery? That is where *camatkâra* comes in, because it primarily characterizes the experiencing of *rasa*, the very process of tasting it.

Camatkâra can be analysed as *camat-kâra*: the fact of "making" (i.e. uttering) the sound *camat*. *Camat* itself is "an exclamation of surprise." Thus it can be interpreted on the famous model of *aham-kâra*, (literally "making of I," then "I-utterance" and finally "ego-consciousness"). So it does not come as a surprise to come across the dictionary definition of *camatkâra* as "astonishment" or "surprise." On the other hand, the term seems to be derived from the verbal root *cam* with the sense of "sipping" or "tasting." But, how to reconcile these two meanings: being surprised or struck with wonder *and* quietly enjoying? Vasudev Raghavan, an Indian critic of the twentieth century, gives us a hint in this respect:

> It's a striking coincidence that, like the concept of Rasa, the concept of Camatkâra also came . . . from the Pâka shâstra (i.e. the science of cooking). Its early semantic history is indistinct and dictionaries record only the later meanings, the chief of which are "astonishment" and "poetic relish." It appears to me that originally the word Camatkâra was an onomatopoeic word referring to the clicking sound we make with our tongue when we taste something snappy, and in the course of its semantic enlargements, it came to mean a sudden fillip relating to any feeling of a pleasurable type.[2]

First of all, we need to avoid an all too easy misunderstanding. *Camatkâra*, in the present context, does not stand for any passive wondering, any dazed gaping—for instance, at the fantastic exploits of gods or demons, at astounding miracles performed by saints, at the incredible physical or mental achievements of yogis. Indian religious literature in general, especially the great epics, the Mahâbhârata and Râmâyana, from which the Nâtya draws the majority of its motifs, is, of course, replete with such fanciful stories. But, quite symptomatically, the Indian, especially the Kashmiri treatises on *rasa*, pay very little attention to what should otherwise have been their main topic, the *Adbhuta-rasa* or the Marvelous. The reason for this is that they understand *camatkâra* in a completely different way. To put it briefly, they tend to picture it as the sudden and unexpected rediscovery by the human mind of its own infinite freedom.

2. Raghavan, *Some Concepts*, 268–69.

Practices of Wonder

A proper understanding of that "introverted" wondering would require a conceptual reconstruction of the main religious, psychological and metaphysical presuppositions from which those thinkers, like Abhinavagupta for instance, depart. In brief, we can say that they are interpreting the all-Indian notion of servitude (*bandha*)—as opposed to liberation: *moksha* or *nirvana*—not so much in terms of ignorance as in terms of passivity, resignation, consent to one's position in society and one's lot in life in general. Practically all of us are presumed to lead a gloomy, joyless existence. Ordinary human consciousness is described, metaphorically, as stiff, crouched, shriveled, curled up, half-heartedly trudging along the path of destiny.

Let us now concede, at least for a while, that they are right. The vocation of dramatic or lyric poetry—not to speak of art in general—becomes more or less evident: it offers the reader or spectator a respite from the dreariness of his or her everyday life, giving them at the same time an opportunity to reconsider their past and future life in a new perspective. In the words of Abhinavagupta:

> When we go to the theatre, we do not have any inclination to think: today, I will have to accomplish something real. Rather we feel: I will listen to and see something beyond my everyday experience, something worthy of my attention, whose innermost essence is pure joy. I will share this experience with the whole audience. One's heart becomes then like a spotless mirror; for all one's preoccupations have been completely forgotten and one is lost in aesthetic rapture, listening to the fine singing and music. At this moment, we can identify ourselves with joy, with sorrow, in fact with any one of the feelings evoked in us by the performance of the actors. Listening to the dramatic text, looking at the different figures on the stage, we get an intuitive knowledge of what Râma or Râvana, for instance, are. And such a knowledge is not circumscribed by a definite time or place. Our mind, carried away by wondering (*camatkâra*), takes for a couple of days the very form of its own Self and sees the whole world through it.[3]

There are actually two reasons why an experience of wondering can be expected here. First, the absence of any gradual transition between the social world outside the theatre and the hall where the dramatic representation takes place. Abhinavagupta, and many authors before and after him, in

---

3. *Abhinavabhâratî*, I, 107, quoted in Masson and Patwardhan, *Aesthetic Rapture*, I, 33.

Michel Hulin—*The Conception of* Camatkâra *in Indian Aesthetics*

fact devote much time to justifying the role of theatrical conventions: the space separating the audience from the stage, the curtain, the burning of incense, the need for the actors to wear masks (in order not be recognized as this one or that one by the spectators), the role of music in the prelude (to stress the solemnity, even the sacral character of the performance), etc. All these devices serve, on the one hand, to ward off the obstacles that could spoil the relishing of *rasas* and, on the other hand, to mark the discontinuity between an outer "profane" space and a "holy" inner area.

But there is still another, more essential, reason. In the perspective of these schools, *camatkâra* is not just a rare and precious experience, accessible to a few chosen minds in favorable circumstances; it should be, and in a way it *is*, the natural state of the soul. According to them, it belongs to the very essence of the soul to disentangle itself immediately from any content, never to allow itself to get trapped in some particular thought. Insofar as it cannot help perpetually dissociating itself from its own representations, the soul is basically Wondering, even when it is busy ascertaining the presence or absence of external realities: "Even the unreality of things will be the object of [some kind of] wondering. When we say: 'There is no pot here,' that alleged non-existence is itself a thought and, as such, completely different from an inanimate object, like a wall."[4] That's why insentience (*jadatva*) is currently assimilated to the absence of any wondering.[5] True, a wall is insentient inasmuch as it cannot think; but its very incapacity to think is itself rooted in a more fundamental incapacity to wonder.

Still another feature of consciousness, obviously connected to its essential freedom, is its innate serenity or joyful essence. The soul suffers—in hatred, fear, envy, disgust, and so on—to the extent that it does not realize that nothing in the world has the power to restrict its independence. Its freedom is indeed indestructible, so that it persists unharmed through the negative affects that overwhelm the soul in ordinary circumstances. Now, the theatrical or, generally speaking, literary conventions, make all these negative affects (along with the positive ones) appear as such in a universalized form, without any reference to the particular case of this or that spectator, and so they enable these people to "look through them," understand the way they work and the way in which they ensnare every soul. They partly and temporarily lift the veil, allowing the innate joy of the soul to radiate more freely. In this way, *camatkâra* can be defined as

---

4. Abhinavagupta, *Tantrâloka*, 91 (I, 53).
5. Abhinavagupta, *Paratrimshikâvivarana*, 49.

"an immersion in an enjoyment which can never satiate and is thus uninterrupted . . . That enjoyment, in so far as it characterizes the experience of *rasa*, consists of an otherworldly wonder (*alaukika-camatkâra*) and is decidedly different from ordinary mundane (*laukika*) knowledge, such as the one produced by memory and inference."[6]

As an example of that difference Abhinavagupta quotes a famous verse by Kalidâsa, from his *Shakuntalâ*, the most famous play of the whole Sanskrit theatre (translated into English by W. Jones at the end of the eighteenth century). That verse can be literally rendered thus: "Often a man, though happy, becomes uneasy of mind on seeing beautiful objects and hearing sweet music. Surely, he remembers in his soul, though vaguely, associations of former births, deeply implanted in him" (V, 2). But there is a more literary, almost as accurate translation by the American poet W. S. Merwin: "Even a man who is happy / glimpses something / or a hair of sound touches him / and his heart overflows with a longing he does not recognize / then it must be that he is remembering / in a place out of reach, shapes he has loved, in a life before this / the print of them still there in him waiting."[7] This verse is considered a fine illustration of the *Shringara-rasa*, the Erotic, and is put into the mouth of King Dushyanta, Shakuntala's lover. But at that moment, due to some malediction, Dushyanta has lost Shakuntala and he is not even sure that she is still alive. He cannot therefore be considered to be experiencing any kind of love pleasure. But the Determinants (*vibhâva*)—in this case some air played by the court musicians, some pictorial renderings of the forest hermitage where he had once met her—call up some hazy memories within him. These in turn arouse a kind of longing in him. The remembrance involved here is not an ordinary one, insofar as it does not bear on a definite object. It is nothing more than an obscure revival of certain latent impressions (Sanskrit: *vâsanas*) left in his unconscious by former love-experiences, either in his present life or in former births. These latent impressions are brought back to life by his hearing the music and they give him some intimations of pleasures he formerly tasted. But the delight is no longer a direct one. It has undergone a process of purification, through which it has risen well above the original. And this is *Shringara-rasa*, a pure vibration of love, completely cut off from worldly preoccupations.

---

6. *Abhinavabhâratî*, I, 279 and I, 284.

7. "Even the man who is happy" by Kalidasa, translated by W. S. Merwin. Copyright © 1998 by W. S. Merwin, used by permission of The Wylie Agency LLC; excerpted from Merwin, *East Window*, 31.

Michel Hulin—*The Conception of* Camatkâra *in Indian Aesthetics*

Nevertheless, the essence of *rasa*, and consequently of *camatkâra*, will stand out better still if we turn our attention towards *rasas* like the Terrible (*Bhayânaka*) or the Pathetic (*Karuna*), whose counterparts in life (respectively fear and sorrow) are unpleasant or even painful. In the *Abhinavabhâratî* we come across another quotation from that very same play, *Shakuntalâ*, that serves as an illustration of the Terrible. The passage (I, 2) depicts a hunting scene. Some sort of deer, or buck, is being chased by King Dushyanta: "Gracefully bending its neck, [the deer] looks now and then at the chariot chasing it. Its rump unceasingly moves forward as if afraid of the arrow ready to swoop down on it. The animal is strewing the path with half-chewed herbs and drops of saliva falling from its mouth kept wide open by exhaustion. Oh! Look how its mighty jumps make it move in the air, while it barely skims the ground!" Then follows the aesthetic interpretation:

> Once the [literal] meaning of the sentences has been grasped there arises in the mind of every spectator an intuitive representation, freed from all divisions of time, etc., contained in the text. In such a perception, the young deer, for example, appears as devoid of all particularity. And the actor [representing it], that imparts fear to the spectators, is [as such] not absolutely real. Then arises something like Fear as such, a fear that is no longer circumscribed by time and space. It is altogether different from ordinary experiences of fear, like "I am afraid" or "my friend, my enemy is afraid," because all those experiences are full of obstacles [to the relish of *rasa*] inasmuch as they inevitably result in unpleasant reactions, like the desire of chasing or of running away, and so on. On the contrary, this perception is free from obstacles and it directly penetrates the heart. Now, the *rasa* of the Terrible is, so to speak, spinning around before our eyes. In such a type of fear, the [individual] self is neither engulfed nor clearly manifested.[8]

The spectator, here, has personally nothing to fear. And there is no question for him of "trembling for the deer," as might be the case with someone strolling in a forest and happening to witness a hunting party. That does not mean that he remains indifferent. On the contrary: while "vibrating" in sympathy with the chased animal, he is lifted up by a mighty emotional wave, but in such a way that no confused, egoistic feeling, no temptation of interfering would creep into his mind. At the same time, this kind of pure emotion is actually tinged (Sanskrit: *uparakta*) by a faint

---

8. *Abhinavabhâratî*, I, 278.

remnant of fear, and so it remains completely distinct from other types of pure feelings, like depersonalized forms of sorrow, anger, etc. *Rasa* is thus nothing else than that type of paradoxical experience that manages to preserve the whole intensity of ordinary emotions but in a purified form, free from any reference to the private ego of the experiencing subject. And so it seems to me that the ultimate reason why the relish of *rasa* is called *camatkâra*, wondering, is linked to the very puzzle it embodies, namely the "impossible" and yet real association of an extreme emotional intensity *and* a sense of aloofness from the quagmire of human passions.

This interpretation receives confirmation by looking at yet another *rasa*, the Pathetic (*Karuna-rasa*), which is the literary transfiguration of sorrow. The *Abhinavabhâratî* introduces its reflection on this *rasa* by quoting quite a number of anonymous stanzas to the effect that sorrow appears, at least to an Indian sensitivity, chiefly as that dark side of love which is the pain of separation. Here are some examples:

> As two wooden logs happen to bump into each other on the surface of the vast ocean, and immediately go asunder, carried away by waves and currents, so brief is in this world every love-encounter.
>
> As birds alight at dusk, in huge numbers, on the branches of a lofty tree, only to scatter at dawn, so brief is in this world every love-encounter.
>
> If you have decided to go, then leave you must. But why such a hurry? Stay two or three minutes more, while I gaze at your face. In this world, our life is like water swiftly rushing out of a cracked jug. Who knows if we shall meet again?[9]

According to Abhinavagupta, the reader or auditor of such short poems, far from feeling dejected, experiences a strange sense of elation. Why? Because, he says, of the similes and of the hidden teaching deposited in them: the logs, the birds, the jug, they all point to some kind of law or order (*dharma*) presiding over the course of the universe, the law of the so-called *dvandvas* (pairs of opposites). It states that contraries, like day and night or like the recto and the verso of a coin, belong together in their very opposition, so that you cannot elect one term, clasp it and reject the other one. Thus, it is only foolish to cling to one's present good fortune, refusing to anticipate its unavoidable disappearance. Most important: in talking of "anticipation," Abhinavagupta does not have in mind some grim, masochistic

---

9. Quoted in Masson and Patwardhan, *Aesthetic Rapture*, I, 30.

way of spoiling one's present happiness with gratuitous evocations of misfortunes to come. He merely wants to stress that the very idea of a constant, indefinitely prolonged mundane happiness is self-contradictory. And that is what the *Karuna-rasa* is all about: it helps the reader or spectator to realize that earthly joys, "like flashes of lightning standing out in the background of gloomy monsoon clouds," owe their value precisely to their momentariness. True, the Pathetic is "tinged with sorrow," the same way the Terrible is "tinged with fear." Here, sorrow could even be considered, in a way, to be more intense than it is in "real" life, due to the exclusion of any "cheap" consolations. Hence the *camatkâra* of an intensified pain that instantaneously switches to an almost mystical bliss, once the magic of poetic expression allows it to be viewed in the light of universal necessity.

Let us finally read yet another text of Abhinavagupta where this paradoxical view finds its most striking formulation:

> And this wondering (*camatkâra*) is present in the very heart of suffering: some sort of internal joy, made of energy, that a wife or a son used to give us in former times blossoms out once again at the view of people who look like them, or on hearing some moaning. We think: "They will never come back," and that is the very essence of suffering: a particular wonderment made up of despair. As it has been said: "... Even confronted with pain, there is a possibility, thanks to the blossoming forth of consciousness, of gaining access to serenity."[10]

Just *because* he realizes: "They will never come back"—and not *in spite of* this thought—the subject feels a "blossoming forth," that is an unlimited expansion of his consciousness. In other words, he feels the vanity, almost the blasphemous character, of rebelling against the law of the universe and, consequently, he breaks out of the all too natural, ego-centered perspective. That would not have been the case if he had retained even the slightest hope of seeing again those people he has lost. This opens the possibility of an almost superhuman wondering: the laying down of every kind of human hope (let us think of the inscription at the entrance of Dante's *Inferno*: "*Ô voi che entrate qui lasciate ogni speranza . . .*") as the very condition of gaining access to an otherworldly serenity. At this point, however, we are already leaving the field of aesthetics and penetrating into the sphere of religious experience and indeed of mysticism.

---

10. Somânanda, *Shivadrishti*, 185 (V, 9), quoted in Abhinavagupta, *Paratrimshi-kâvivarana*, 49.

Bibliography

Abhinavagupta. *Tantrâloka*. Vol. 1. Kashmir Series of Text and Studies 23. Srinagar, 1918.

———. *Paratrimshikâvivarana*. Kashmir Series of Text and Studies 18. Srinagar, 1918.

Bansat-Boudon, Lyne. *Pourquoi le théâtre? La réponse indienne*. Paris: Mille et une nuits, 2004.

Bharata Muni. *Nâtyashastra of Bharatamuni with the Commentary Abhinavabhâratî*. 4 vols. Edited by R. S. Nagar. Parimal Sanskrit Series 4. Delhi; Ahmedabad: Parimal, 1981–1983.

Gnoli, Raniero. *The Aesthetic Experience According to Abhinavagupta*. 2nd ed. Chowkhamba Sanskrit Studies 62. Varanasi: Chowkhamba Sanskrit Series Office, 1968.

Masson, Jeffrey Lloyd, and Madhav Vinayak Patwardhan. *Shântarasa and Abhinavagupta's Philosophy of Aesthetics*. Bhandarkar Oriental Series 9. Poona: Bhandarkar Oriental Research Institute, 1969.

———. *Aesthetic Rapture: The Rasâdhyâya of the Nâtyaśâstra*. 2 vols. Poona: Deccan College Postgraduate and Research Institute, 1970.

Merwin, W. S. *East Window: The Asian Translations*. Port Townsend, WA: Copper Canyon, 1998.

Raghavan, Venkatarama. *Studies on Some Concepts of the Alamkâra-shâstra*. Adyar Library Series 33. Adyar: Adyar Library, 1942.

Somânanda. *Shivadrishti*. Kashmir Series of Text and Studies 54. Srinagar, 1934.

10

Wonderment Today in the Abrahamic Traditions[1]

DAVID B. BURRELL, CSC

REFLECTIONS AMONG JEWS, CHRISTIANS, and Muslims associate the experience of wonderment with the question of creation and the contingency of being, where it can be explored in connection with philosophical accounts of this contingency, but certainly also as a lived experience that is both expressed in such accounts and is in turn cultivated by them. We shall explore the lived experience of creation and the contingency of being, as well as its ostensible eclipse in our "secular age," by calling upon participants from each Abrahamic tradition, as those often quite disparate traditions concur in believing in the mystery of free creation. Moreover, they each locate wonderment primarily with respect to human being, whose privileged yet hybrid origin baffled the angels yet also reveals a privileged divine image to those who can detect it. For Sufi Islam, the fact that "on the day of *Alast*, the primordial revelation was placed in the human heart"[2] gives primacy to the creation of Adam: "other creatures

---

1. Part of this chapter earlier appeared in *Learning to Trust in Freedom: Signs from Jewish, Christian, and Muslim Traditions* by David B. Burrell, published by University of Scranton Press (2010). Used by permission of the publisher.

2. From Keeler, *Sufi Hermeneutics*, 139: Maybūdī, *Kashf* III, b571; see also *Kashf* VIII, 545, where Maybūdī states that human beings alone among creatures are privileged with the "look of love" from God (*Sufi Hermeneutics*, 146, n. 54).

came by way of creation, Adam by way of love."³ Reflecting on the biblical expression that human beings are made in God's "image and likeness," the Jewish philosophical theologian, Moses Maimonides, reinforces similar views on the primacy of human beings in God's intent in creating, though he will resist regarding human beings as culminating creation in the sense that all was created for their sake.⁴ Christian thinkers will link their anthropology directly to the Genesis texts on which Maimonides comments, yet identify the divine "image and likeness," in which human beings are said to be made, with the Word of God "through whom the world is made" (John 1:10), incarnate as the Christ.

Yet even here affinities with Sufi Islam abound, as the preexistent Muhammad provides the paradigm for the created universe, much as the preexistent Torah supplies the pattern for the order of the world:

> The first essence to receive the robe of honour of the command *kun* ["Be!"], and the first upon whom the sun of God's grace shone was the pure spirit of that master.⁵ This 'pure spirit' of Muhammad has come to be known in Islamic mysticism as the Muhammadan light [*nūr Muḥammadi*]. . . . Not only was Muhammad the first in creation, but he was the purpose for which the universe was created.⁶

To be sure, the preexistent Prophet is better compared with biblical Wisdom, as the "firstborn of all creation," than with the uncreated Word of God as elaborated in Christian trinitarian belief. Yet multiple affinities remain among all three Abrahamic faiths as they attempt to elaborate the insistence of their respective revelations that the origin of the universe comes by way of free creation on the part of the One.

What is at stake here? The principal implication of the teaching of free creation by the One: that the order of the universe, which Aquinas identifies with the creator's primary intent, cannot be impersonal, even if the way it is "personal" will escape us. For if the metaphysics of free creation requires that everything that is come forth continuously from the One bestowing existence to all, then (as Aquinas notes) the very being of each will be a being-to-the-creator (*esse ad creatorem*), giving existence itself the metaphysical valence of a *relation*.⁷ And since the One to whom

---

3. Anawati and Gardet, *La mystique musulmane*, 131.
4. Maimonides, *Guide for the Perplexed*, 3.13.
5. *Kashf* IX, 375, in Keeler, *Sufi Hermeneutics*, 130, 145 n. 36.
6. Keeler, *Sufi Hermeneutics*, 130.
7. *Summa theologiae* 1.45.3.

it is in relation is paradigmatically intentional, so will the relation be. Yet since the "emanation of all things from the very cause of being" (*ST* 1.45.1) will be unlike any causal relation that we know, the relation may be asserted yet never adequately articulated, since it will escape the terms of causality as we know it. Yet in the case where the beings so related are themselves intentional as well, emanation will elicit a complementary dynamic of *return*, all of which will be thoroughly intentional. And while this dynamic will indeed elude articulation in categories tailored to created things, the fact that created existence is in itself a *relating* to a transcendent source will serve to elicit a correlative sense of wonder. As Aquinas puts it, creatures are suspended between two knowings: the divine knowing bringing them into being and the created knowing seeking to understand them.[8] Now this very scheme demands that the founding relation outreach our articulation, since "the distinction" (Sokolowski) of creator from creatures embodies a unique mode of causality that free creation requires. So realizing the presence of this founding relation that is constitutive of each thing lends an aura of mystery to every existent.[9]

Now Charles Taylor contends that this aura of mystery has been eclipsed by "the secular age," introduced in the West by "the Enlightenment," yet in which much of the world increasingly finds itself.[10] Let me warn at the outset, however, that his immensely articulate description of the shift in consciousness that a "secular age" demands, persuasive as it is, exudes a Hegel-like presumption—that the transition is at once inevitable and irreversible—that may or may not be accurate. So like many Hegelian *tours de force*, this presumption needs to be challenged by fine-grained narratives offering a surprising dénouement to the main lines of his perceptive analysis. How describe this crucial transition to "a secular age"? Taylor's description is dialectical and multi-layered, in a conscious "polemic against what [he calls] 'subtraction stories,'" which seek to explain *modernity* and *secularity* "by human beings having lost, or sloughed off, or liberated themselves from certain earlier confining horizons, illusions, or limitations of knowledge" (22). Such stories foster the positive valence in the term *Enlightenment*, of course, whereas Taylor attempts to show how "Western modernity, including its secularity, is the fruit of new inventions, newly constructed self-understandings and related practices and can't be

---

8. Ibid., 1.14.8.3.

9. See Sokolowski, *God of Faith and Reason*.

10. Taylor, *Secular Age*. Some of the material on Taylor has been adapted from my *Learning to Trust*, 61–65.

explained in terms of perennial features of human life" (22). Rather, these novel features have "been coterminous with the rise of a society in which for the first time in history a purely self-sufficient humanism came to be a widely available option" (18). The result is a new set of "social imaginaries" that effectively disembed society from cosmos, replacing inherent hierarchies (or "sacred orders") with "the mutual respect and mutual service of the individuals who make up society" (165), "agents who through disengaged, disciplined action can reform their own lives, as well as the larger social order" (171). This psychic transformation results in a "public sphere [as] an association which is constituted by nothing outside of the common action we carry out in it: coming to a common mind, where possible, through the exchange of ideas" (192). This "social imaginary," embodying the "crucial fiction of 'we, the people' . . . articulates into a new understanding of time" (208), itself central to that understanding of secularity into which Taylor would introduce us.

Having already reminded us how Walter Benjamin had made "'homogeneous, empty time' . . . central to modernity" (54), Taylor can delineate this feature of the social imaginary that has overtaken us: "Our encasing in secular time is also something we have brought about in the way we live and order our lives. It has been brought about by the same social and ideological changes which have wrought disenchantment. In particular, the disciplines of our modern civilized order have led us to measure and organize time as never before in human history. Time has become a precious resource, not to be 'wasted.' The result has been the creation of a tight, ordered time environment. This has enveloped us, until it comes to seem like nature" (59).

Benedict Anderson then exploits this novel sense of *time* to explain "the new sense of belonging to a nation, [with] society as a whole consisting of the simultaneous happening of all the myriad events which mark the lives of its members at that moment. These events are the fillers of a kind of homogeneous time. This very clear, unambiguous concept of simultaneity belongs to an understanding of time as exclusively secular" (208–9), in stark contrast to Augustine's sense of the elusive present moment imaging eternity in time, and celebrated liturgically by punctuating continuous chronological time. Theological readers will be reminded of the way Catherine Pickstock delineates modernity's "mathematicization of time," in her persuasive argument that nothing short of incorporating the *kairos* ("acceptable time") of liturgical practice into philosophical discourse will enable it to articulate transcendence.[11]

This persuasive description of "a uniform, univocal secular time, which we try to measure and control in order to get things done" reminds us instantly of Max "Weber's famous description of . . . an iron cage. It occludes all higher times, makes them even hard to conceive" (59). Yet ironically enough, Taylor's potent prose also tends to replace the "option" in his original description of the project—to show how "for the first time in history a purely self-sufficient humanism came to be a widely available option"—with an ineluctable and encompassing "cage," reinforced by a set of "social imaginaries" without alternative. I have identified this penchant with a Hegel-like presumption that takes the transition to be inevitable and irreversible. Much like Karl Marx's trenchant critique of capitalism his 1844 *Manuscripts*, Taylor's analysis can hardly be gainsaid, yet reflective persons made aware of subsisting within the "cage" may well be led to search for spiritual antidotes. Freedom can intimate responses to confining situations, much as "social imaginaries" once made explicit can suggest hitherto hidden ways to dissolve their constraining power. The standing contribution of Marx, and now of Taylor, will be to remind us how many forces conspire to reinforce "a secular age," yet Taylor's prescient use of the "social imaginary" construction reminds us that however powerful these constraints may be, as "imaginaries" they cannot be ineluctable. Indeed, learning how to articulate the constraints our age imposes may also open ways for us to feel them as constraining, and so begin to appreciate what we are missing. May our spontaneous "wonderment" at the very *presence* of a universe that need not be, not have led people in diverse situations from varied backgrounds to sense the need for "something more," to feel the constraints of an ideology that pretends to assert that there can be nothing more?

Taylor himself notes "certain contemporary modes of postmodernism which deny, attack or scoff at the claims of self-sufficient reason" which he has identified as the hallmark of "a secular age," yet finds "they offer no outside source for the reception of power" (10), by which he characterizes an authentically religious outlook (8). I would plump for a more benign variety of postmodern reflections, exemplified by John Henry Newman or Bernard Lonergan, which can nudge us into a more properly medieval ethos where critical reason will have to be tempered with conscious faith to realize its own inherent goals. And indeed something of this sort will

---

11. Pickstock, *After Writing*.

provide the dénouement for Taylor's sinuous journey, as the last part of the work elaborates "Conditions of Belief" in five stages, culminating in a set of narrated "Conversions." As their provocative titles suggest, the stages detail fissures in the prevailing "social imaginaries" sustaining or resulting from "a secular age": "the Immanent Frame," "Cross Pressures," "Dilemmas 1 and 2," and "the Unquiet Frontiers of Modernity." So the point of this complex apologetic work becomes an Archimedean point: one that will serve as the fulcrum on which a "return to self" will hinge, a reversal gaining special poignancy as it is executed in the face of the "social imaginaries" that had purportedly eliminated such moves. So the "drama of atheistic humanism," to purloin the title of Henri de Lubac's earlier *tour de force*, can issue in a dramatic resurgence of faith, capturing the death/resurrection motif of Taylor's own faith. Yet what gives the Archimedean point its leverage is precisely what we are calling "wonderment."

Taylor supplies the fulcrum, ironically enough, in his illuminating chapters identifying "The Turning Point," where he delineates the modernist Western gutting, if not trivialization, of the Christian story (largely sanitized of its roots in Jewish sensibility) under the titles of "Providential Deism" (ch. 6) and "Impersonal Order" (ch. 7). It is this deliberate "naturalization," if you will, of Christian tradition, abetted by its political ascendancy, that turns out to leave an increasingly manifest void there where faith had offered "fullness" or "wholeness." Moreover, it must be noted (which Taylor does not) that the void—or dark underbelly—of Western political ascendancy has been starkly mirrored in slavery and cognate forms of exploitation, first in Ireland and then in Africa and Asia. Once we realize how "the Enlightenment" offered a prime justification for colonization (*mission civilisatrice*), as it was bankrolled by it, we can show even more how

> the narratives of modernity have been questioned, contested, attacked, since their inception in the eighteenth century. . . . Running through all these attacks is the specter of meaninglessness; that as a result of the denial of transcendence, of heroism, of deep feeling, we are left with a view of human life which is empty, cannot inspire commitment, offers nothing really worthwhile, cannot answer the craving for goals to which we can dedicate ourselves (717).

And to recall the dimension of political hegemony, we should add "self-congratulatory"; it is *we* who offer the paradigm for what is human, even while our actions towards others unlike us were hardly humane!

David B. Burrell—*Wonderment Today in the Abrahamic Traditions*

Yet Taylor could never draw such a convincing picture of the cognate movements of "Enlightenment" and "Reform" were he to regard their results as simply debilitating; in fact, he will always remind us of the capacity of these movements, with their "social imaginaries," to empower human beings to achievement, especially in their struggle for human freedom, however chauvinistic that may turn out to be. In fact, his resolute refusal to indulge in "subtraction stories" allows him to unveil the ambiguities latent in what he dubs the "Modern Moral Order," which he can celebrate for "its endorsing of universal human rights and welfare as one of our crucial goals . . . as our stepping out into a wider, qualitatively different sense of inter-human solidarity . . . analogous to certain precedent ones in history: inaugurated, for instance, by Buddha, by Stoicism, by the New Testament preaching ('in Christ is neither Jew nor Greek, slave or free, male or female') and by Muhammad" (608). For despite all that, something has been felt to be missing, specifically "the aspiration to wholeness, particularly as it emerges in the reaction to the disciplined, buffered self in the Romantic period. The protest here is that the rational, disengaged agent is sacrificing something essential in realizing his ideals. What is sacrificed is often described as spontaneity or creativity, but it is even more frequently identified with our feelings, our bodily existence" (609).

So he reminds us "that this understanding of wholeness which has to include a crucial place for the body is a legacy of our Christian civilization" (610), yet insisting that restoring it to our "social imaginary" will involve re-appropriating that tradition across several baffle plates of distortion on the part of Christianity itself (chs. 17–18: "Dilemmas 1 and 2"). So if the journey to "a secular age" has ever been a dialectical one, so will be the move beyond its "iron cage." Here there can be no substitute for narratives of "conversion" out of "the immanent frame," though as we have suggested, these narratives should also prompt us to ask what might move individuals to sense the constraints of the "iron cage," so as to begin to undertake a journey that holds the promise of freeing them from it?

Taylor focuses on strategic figures like Bede Griffiths, Vaclav Havel, Dostoyevsky, Flannery O'Connor, T. S. Eliot and Jacques Maritain, Thomas Merton and Ivan Illich, along with groundbreaking poets Charles Peguy and Gerard Manley Hopkins, to illustrate how such "conversions" will seldom be a simple "return to religion," but will each variously exemplify what Taylor nicely describes as "the future of the religious past." I shall focus on the reflections—at once spontaneous yet carefully structured—of a young Jewish woman in Holland during

Practices of Wonder

German occupation, Etty Hillesum. Published in English as *An Interrupted Life*, they were celebrated in *The New York Review of Books* as a "masterpiece of spirituality," a term one might not have expected in that sophisticated literary journal. These diaries did not appear in English until 1985, requiring painstaking efforts to render an account composed under the crabbed conditions of Nazi occupation into legible Dutch. Later combined with her "Letters from Westerbork" into a single edition (1996), the extended narrative offers an intimate account of spiritual awakening on the part of an expressly bohemian, hence "secular," Jew, faced with imminent extermination.[12] These evocative entries reveal a person seeking to center and order her life, who one day finds herself "forced to the ground by something stronger than myself. . . . I suddenly went down on my knees in the middle of this large room . . . almost automatically" (76). And that action unfolds, through her interaction with Julius Spier, her psychoanalyst and intimate friend, to lead her to the point where she can say—in the midst of the misery of Westerbork, a staging area for transport to Auschwitz—"time and again it soars straight from my heart—I can't help it, that's just the way it is, like some elementary force—the feeling that life is glorious and magnificent" (247).

Nor is that feeling ephemeral, but a power making her over from within: "[as] the threat grows ever greater, and terror increases from day to day, I draw prayer round me like a dark protective wall, . . . and then step outside again, calmer and stronger . . ." (139). "It always spreads from the inside outwards with me . . ." (146). This courage is displayed by one who confesses: "I have never been able to 'do' anything; I can only let things take their course and if need be suffer" (249). An apt remark from a woman who sought therapy shortly after her twenty-seventh birthday, sensing a void in herself and her relationships: "I am . . . just about seasoned enough I should think to be counted among the better lovers, and love does indeed suit me to perfection, and yet . . . deep inside me something is still locked away" (1). So runs the opening paragraph of her diaries, plausibly the task given her by the man whom she had sought out, Julius Spier, as a catalyst to their inner work.

What follows can usefully be divided into three roughly even parts: her discovery of herself through the relationship with Spier that ensues (1–82), a period of preparation for serving others (82–160), and the actual crafting of her life as gift (160–243). The final phase begins at the point

---

12. Hillesum, *Interrupted Life*, and more recently, *Letters from Westerbork*; now combined in a single edition, from which page references here will be taken.

where all illusions are torn away: "What is at stake is our impending destruction and annihilation" (160), and is focused by the death of the guide whom she had come to love: "You taught me to speak the name of God without embarrassment. You were the mediator . . . and now . . . my path leads straight to God. . . . And I shall be the mediator for any other soul I can reach" (209–10). These remarks were written after she had volunteered to accompany the first group of Jews being sent to Westerbork. Yet they are rooted in the second, preparatory phase, as she discovers, encountering a former lover, that "everything is no longer pure chance . . . an exciting adventure. Instead I have the feeling that I have a destiny, in which the events are strung significantly together" (91). Less than two months later she will assert: "I have matured enough to assume my 'destiny', to cease living an accidental life" (138).

What happens in her happens in a scant two-and-a-half years as the restrictive legislation bars "Jews from the paths and the open country [yet] I find life beautiful and I feel free. The sky within me is as wide as the one stretching above my head. I believe in God and I believe in man and I can say so without embarrassment" (151). It is at the end of this period that she begins to formulate expressly theological dicta, in the face of "the latest news . . . that all Jews will be transported out of Holland . . . to Poland" (157).

> And yet I don't think life is meaningless. And God is not accountable to us for the senseless harm we cause one another. We are accountable to Him! I have already died a thousand deaths in a thousand concentration camps. . . . And yet I find life beautiful and meaningful. From minute to minute. (157)

The capacity for gratitude and praise that she finds within herself moves her in this period of formation beyond humiliation or hate to a newfound peace and freedom: "despite all the suffering and injustice I cannot hate others" (89). "One day I shall surely be able to say to Ilse Blumenthal, 'Do not relieve your feelings through hatred, do not seek to be avenged on all German mothers. . . . Give your sorrow all the space and shelter in yourself that is its due . . . then you may truly say: 'Life is beautiful and so rich . . . that it makes you want to believe in God.' " (100–1).

Yet in an earlier diary entry that takes the form of a prayer, Etty had already introduced us to the God in whom she will come to believe:

> Dear God, these are anxious times . . . but one thing is becoming increasingly clear to me: that you cannot help us, that we must help you to help ourselves . . . Alas, there doesn't seem to be

> much You Yourself can do about our circumstances, our lives. Neither do I hold you responsible. You cannot help us but we must help You and defend your dwelling place inside us to the last. (186–87)

She feels responsible to what has happened within her, and so to the world to which she has come to relate with all that she has. As she writes from Westerbork in an epilogue to her diaries: "I see more and more that love for all our neighbors... must take pride of place over love for one's nearest and dearest" (251). The turning point is expressed in a prayer from her diary shared with her friend Tide:

> You have made me so rich, oh God, please let me share out Your beauty with open hands. My life has become an uninterrupted dialogue with You, oh God, one great dialogue. (255)

Recording what God is accomplishing in her gives Etty's account its authenticity: not only what she finds herself able to do—in the midst of indescribable misery (245)—but for capacities continuing to emerge as a surprise to herself. Etty Hillesum's spontaneous diaries celebrate the unlocking of "what is truly essential, and deep inside me" (1), and the consequent transformation of a "miserable, frightened creature" (2) into a "soul . . . forged out of fire and rock crystal" (241). A soul, moreover, shaped by "an uninterrupted dialogue" that allowed her to make us the gift of her "interrupted life."

What Etty celebrates is a real alteration testifying to a real power at work in the world, granting her a transformed vision: "It still all comes down to the same thing: life is beautiful. And I believe in God—right in the thick of what people call 'horror'" (238). And she addresses these words to her friend Jopie, by way of insisting that such a reality is accessible to her as well. Indeed, what one finds startling about Etty's diaries is the precise way they articulate a conviction shared by Jew and Christian alike: that life itself, indeed the universe, is a gift. Her Marxist friend, Klaas, whom she introduces as a "dogged old class fighter," was indeed "dismayed and astonished at the same time," and challenged her: "But that—that is nothing but Christianity!" Her response is one we will by now have come to expect: "And I, amused by your confusion, retort quite coolly: 'Yes, Christianity, and why ever not?'" (222–23). Given the historically pockmarked relations between Judaism and Christianity, this response touches a profound nerve, but for present purposes we can simply note how she comes to offer witness to a shared conviction: that life is a gift. And her acute sense of wonder at that gift will allow us some fruitful reflections on the way in which such convictions function in transforming lives.

If one focuses on "the experience itself"—whatever that might be—of transformation, then the accounts may be contingently related to what it is that we cannot help but remark in the person before us. But when we are privileged enough to have access to the narrative account, we come to appreciate how these narratives are shaped by sets of convictions that can otherwise be expressed as doctrines of specific religious traditions, where the fact that doctrines shape narratives reminds us that they do not play a theoretical but a *grammatical* role in the lives of the faithful.[13] They do not, in short, offer explanatory access to the One to whom individuals like Etty respond, but rather provide a way of expressing how their respective responses offer us access to the reality revealed in their transformations. Doctrine, in other words, both comes to life and is embodied in the response of those whom we cannot but recognize to be saints.

It is obvious enough how doctrine "comes to life" there, but how can we say that it is *embodied* in such lives? The argument here is at once simple and subtle: it turns on the fact that we will always be forced to speak of religious matters in a language that is inherently analogous. The term *transformation* offers a handy example. Any formula we give for it will contain terms of a like quality—terms whose "open texture" or "systematic ambiguity" will demand that we offer an example to establish our "frame of reference" or "benchmark" usage.[14] And it is precisely individuals who provide the living examples to anchor our usage—a commonplace yet remarkable situation that accounts for the fact that we can recognize such exemplary individuals without always being able to *say* what it is that makes them such. Yet their narrative accounts, when available, can be found to be structured in such a way as to be shaped by what we otherwise call doctrinal statements. That is the way in which their lives embody doctrine.[15]

What, then, are we to do with the further fact that different lives will embody diverse doctrines, and yet each exhibit a comparable transformation? (We may even presume that their respective accounts can be shown to embody different doctrinal positions.) Celebrate it, I contend, for so far we have no way of placing ourselves in the position of comparing or

---

13. A synoptic exploration of this sense of doctrine has been fruitfully carried out by George Lindbeck in his *Nature of Doctrine*.

14. See Ross, *Portraying Analogy*, and for the history of these matters, my *Analogy and Philosophical Language*.

15. See Barron, *And Now I See*.

ranking religious traditions. I am not pontificating, insisting that we cannot do so; in fact, I suspect that we must. I am only remarking that we are not *yet* in a position to do so. We must acquire a set of intellectual skills allowing us to compare cultural frameworks. In fact, nothing, so effectively displays the cultural particularity of Christianity as the emergence of a post-colonial world, in which Western Christians found themselves facing other religious traditions yet no longer able to presume an accustomed superiority. And how might we respond conceptually to such novelty? By reminding ourselves, I would suggest, that responses are structured by traditions whose doctrinal patterns provide the grammar of the response. Insofar as those doctrinal patterns shape and give direction to a lived response in such a way that it issues in an authentic transformation, then we must acknowledge them to be true, much as the aim and correlative skills of an archer allow his arrow to find its mark.

This strategy keeps us from directly comparing statements lifted out of different traditions, and reminds us that such statements—if they be religious statements—subserve that transforming relationship which we have noted through Etty's narrative. Yet *within* each functioning tradition, there will be a set of shaping beliefs or doctrines, the truth of which will (or will not) be exhibited in the life of the community, especially in its notable exemplars. And where those exemplary individuals tell their story, as Etty has, astute critics will be able to discern the doctrinal patterns that give their narratives a structure distinctive to the community in which they partake. Such is the grammar of the matter: lives are rendered in narratives that display a structure; we are compelled by the lives, inspired and illuminated by the narratives, and guided by what we can discover of their structure.

What have we given up, in trying to respond to the new situation of religious and cultural diversity? *Not* the "truth claims" of particular religious traditions, but rather a presumptive way of ranking them. *Not* the certitude that Newman attributes to faith, whereby we freely give "real assent" to what is offered us as liberating and life-giving, but a monocultural attitude of *certainty* in which we know that we are right.[16] What we have recovered is an attitude of critical modesty towards our modes of expression, which could help us recover a modesty not unlike that displayed by medieval thinkers, using it to profit from a situation that appears so unsettling. In fact, we have long overlooked just how intercultural and

---

16. Newman, *Grammar of Assent*, with perceptive introduction by Nicholas Lash.

interreligious the medieval world really was.[17] Take Aquinas' account of religious language, for example, in which he used a sophisticated semantics to clarify and extend Moses Maimonides on attributing perfections to divinity. The portion of that account pertinent here is Aquinas' insistence that phrases like "God is just" can be said properly but imperfectly of divinity.[18] By exploring how expressions might "imperfectly signify" divinity, we can be led to see how one tradition may complement another, and so use the encounter with alternative conceptualities to enrich our own. That is, I believe, the sense of Etty's cool retort: "Yes, Christianity, and why ever not?" Far from a call to syncretism, that response appreciates a power peculiar to the gospels by appropriating them to her situation. These complementarities work quite well in practice, as the faithful in distinct traditions find themselves drawn to incorporate prayer patterns from one another, much as Jung remarked (in 1948) in reference to a divided Western European Christianity: that every cultured European he knew was either a Catholic Protestant or a Protestant Catholic.[19]

But what of that further assessment, to which we seem inevitably drawn, which would compare traditions by ranking them? I have already noted that we are not yet in a position to do that, and I emphasize the "yet" not because I believe we may one day be able to, but to remind us how unskilled we are in comparing across cultural and conceptual frameworks. The immediate alternative of accepting the picture of religious traditions as several ways up one mountain begs the central question by incorporating an answer. It offers a useful antidote, of course, to the need for pre-emptive certainty, as does our strategy of locating doctrines as the grammar structuring accounts of personal transformation. I find Wilfrid Cantwell Smith's programmatic suggestions in his *Towards a World Theology* helpful by pointing to ways in which we could develop the skills required for fruitful comparative study: a seminar composed of articulate believers from distinct traditions, in which communication would be deemed to be achieved when each person could understand the other's account as one in which they could plausibly participate.[20] Exercises of this sort, carried out regarding specific doctrines-cum-practices, might well be able to help those participating develop skills of comparative assessment. We might

---

17. See my *Knowing the Unknowable God*.
18. See Herbert McCabe's appendix, "Signifying Imperfectly," in *Knowing and Naming God*.
19. Jung, *Psychology of the Transference*, 30.
20. Smith, *World Theology*, 98–101.

discover, for example, that the "distinction" of God from the world is more ably secured in a tradition that was also forced to articulate how two natures functioned in one person (Christ) than in the other two faiths that avow creation, even though we can find analogues of that "distinction" in all three Abrahamic faiths.[21] In virtue of live encounters, however, we in the West are becoming more and more aware of the threshold on which we stand, which allows us to inquire into our own traditions (in the spirit of "faith seeking understanding") as they now face other major religious traditions with palpable histories of holiness.

Indeed, this "convergence-in-difference" that characterizes interfaith exchange today, and is so abundantly exemplified in the lived narrative of Etty Hillesum, offers a fresh appreciation of a "conversion" from the social imaginaries of our "secular age" to which Charles Taylor's rigorously convoluted journey carries us. Our exploration is much indebted to his historical and analytic skills, especially as they incisively delineate our "secular age," indeed celebrating the openings this "age" has extended to us all, only to suggest how exemplary individuals have discovered ways beyond its confining parameters. At the same time, I have attempted to make more explicit what his analysis does note and presume, in identifying what may move those individuals to find the parameters of the age confining, and so to seek for ways beyond them: that "wonderment" which embodies our sense of the radical contingency of the universe, prompting us to orient what we see and feel towards "something more." Moreover, the plethora of ways in which that orientation may be intimated hardly weakens but rather enhances our need to discover it.

---

21. See my "The Christian Distinction" for an attempt to extend Robert Sokolowski's "Christian distinction" in his *God of Faith and Reason* (note 8) to all Abrahamic faiths.

Bibliography

Anawati, Georges, and Louis Gardet. *La mystique musulmane.* Paris: Vrin, 1961.

Aquinas, Thomas. *Summa theologiae.* Vol. 3 (1a.12–13), *Knowing and Naming God.* Translated by Herbert McCabe. New York: McGraw-Hill, 1964.

Barron, Robert. *And Now I See.* New York: Continuum, 1998.

Burrell, David. *Analogy and Philosophical Language.* New Haven: Yale University Press, 1973.

———. "The Christian Distinction Celebrated and Expanded." In *The Truthful and the Good,* edited by John Drummond and James Hart, 191–206. Dordrecht: Kluwer, 1996.

———. *Knowing the Unknowable God: Ibn-Sina, Maimonides, and Aquinas.* Notre Dame: University of Notre Dame Press, 1986.

———. *Learning to Trust in Freedom: Signs from Jewish, Christian, and Muslim Traditions.* Scranton: University of Scranton Press, 2010.

Hillesum, Etty. *An Interrupted Life.* New York: Simon & Schuster, 1985.

———. *An Interrupted Life and Letters from Westerbork.* New York: Henry Holt, 1996.

———. *Letters from Westerbork.* New York: Pantheon, 1987.

Jung, Carl G. *Psychology of the Transference.* Princeton: Princeton University Press, 1966.

Keeler, Annabel. *Sufi Hermeneutics: The Qur'an Commentary of Rashīd al-Dīn Maybūdī.* Oxford: Oxford University Press and Institute of Ismaili Studies, 2006.

Lindbeck, George. *The Nature of Doctrine.* Philadelphia: Westminster, 1985.

Maimonides. *Guide for the Perplexed.* Translated by M. Friedländer. New York: Dover, 1956. Translated by Shlomo Pines. Chicago: University of Chicago Press, 1963.

Newman, John Henry. *An Essay in Aid of a Grammar of Assent.* Notre Dame: University of Notre Dame Press, 1979.

Pickstock, Catherine. *After Writing: On the Liturgical Consummation of Philosophy.* Oxford: Blackwell, 1998.

Ross, James. *Portraying Analogy.* Cambridge: Cambridge University Press, 1982.

Smith, Wilfred Cantwell. *Towards a World Theology.* Philadelphia: Westminster, 1981.

Sokolowski, Robert. *God of Faith and Reason.* Notre Dame: University of Notre Dame Press, 1982. Reprint, Washington, DC: Catholic University of America Press, 1995.

Taylor, Charles. *A Secular Age.* Cambridge: Belknap Press of Harvard University Press, 2007.

Index of Authors

Abhinavagupta, 225, 228, 229, 231, 232, 233
Abrams, Meyer H., 5, 57
Ackerman, Brian, 78
Addison, Joseph, 57, 201, 203, 204, 205, 217–18, 219, 220, 221
Aeschylus, 88
Anderson, Benedict, 238
Aquinas, Thomas, 205, 236, 237, 247
Arendt, Hannah, 145–46, 153, 154, 163
Aristotle, 2, 3, 7, 27, 36, 37, 39, 41, 51–52, 89, 145, 146, 203, 208, 212
Arnauld, Antoine, 211
Atran, Scott, 71
Augustine, 37, 39, 238
Avelin, Emanuel, 191

Bacon, Francis, 38, 183, 188
Baker, Henry, 186, 187, 192, 193–94, 196–97
Barnouw, Jeffrey, 219
Barron, Robert, 245
Baumgarten, Alexander Gottlieb, 201–2, 203, 221
Beardsley, Monroe, 172
Belloni, Luigi, 180
Bender, Werner, 202
Benjamin, Walter, 238
Ben-Ze'ev, Aaron, 66
Bergson, Henri, 75
Bernard of Clairvaux, 39
Bharata Muni, 225
Biester, James, 205, 214
Boileau, Nicolas, 57, 59, 202, 211, 213–18, 219, 220
Borel, Pierre, 180
Bouhours, Dominique, 210, 215, 217

Boyle, Robert, 40, 184, 188
Bradbury, Saville, 180
Brague, Rémi, 179
Bredekamp, Horst, 206
Brockes, Barthold Heinrich, 220
Brown, Deborah, 28
Bryson, Bill, 168–69, 170, 171
Buchner, August, 203
Budd, Malcolm, 173, 175–76
Burke, Edmund, 57, 202, 219
Burnyeat, Myles, 97
Burrell, David, 245, 247, 248

Carew, Thomas, 214
Carlson, Stephanie, 84
Carlyle, Thomas, 5
Cavell, Stanley, 6, 30–31
Céard, Jean, 191
Certeau, Michel de, 183, 185
Chapelain, Jean, 206
Charlesworth, William, 73
Cicero, 26, 179
Clark, Candace, 68
Coleridge, Samuel Taylor, 5, 57
Corneille, Pierre, 211–12
Corsi, Pietro, 182
Cosmides, Leda, 18, 65
Croll, Oswald, 184
Cronk, Nicholas, 214
Crowther, Paul, 174
Cunningham, James Vincent, 205

Dante, 233
Darwin, Charles, 18, 19
Daston, Lorraine, 8, 34, 35–49, 57–59, 182–83, 206, 207
Davidson, Richard, 66

251

Index of Authors

Dawkins, Richard, 7, 53–54, 66–67, 79, 82
Debus, Allen, 184
De Jesus, Diego, 185
Dennis, John, 57, 59, 206, 219, 220, 221
Derham, William, 188, 189
Descartes, René, 8, 25–26, 28, 40, 44, 51, 145, 146, 183, 184, 213, 216
Diamond, Cora, 139–41
Dockhorn, Klaus, 202
Donne, John, 204, 214
Doron, Claude-Olivier, 196
Dostoyevsky, Fyodor, 241
Dryden, John, 207, 211
Dubos, Jean Baptiste, 218

Edwards, Michael, 94
Edwards, William, 203
Ekman, Paul, 19
Eliot, George, 140
Eliot, T. S., 241
Elkind, David, 72
Elster, Jon, 20
Emerson, Ralph Waldo, 5
Empedocles, 106, 110, 112–14, 116
Evans, Richard, 72

Findlen, Paula, 206
Fisher, Philip, 8, 16, 27–28, 48, 52
Flavell, John, 72
Fludd, Robert, 184
Fredrickson, Barbara, 67
Freud, Sigmund, 89
Frijda, Nico, 19–21, 33
Fromm, Erich, 82
Fuller, Robert, 18, 33, 35, 46

Galilei, Galileo, 180, 208
Galison, Peter, 182–83
Gardner, Howard, 78
Gedner, Christopher, 191
Goldie, Peter, 22, 24
Gombrich, Ernst, 210
Gordon, Robert, 23
Gottsched, Johann Christoph, 202
Gracián, Baltasar, 204–5, 208
Grew, Nehemiah, 184, 188
Griffiths, Bede, 241
Guez de Balzac, Jean-Louis, 211

Hadot, Pierre, 26, 179, 180, 181, 196
Haidt, Jonathan, 18, 68–70

Hanafi, Zakiya, 213
Harris, Paul, 74
Hathaway, Baxter, 202, 221
Havel, Vaclav, 241
Haviland-Jones, Jeannette, 66
Heidegger, Martin, 54–56, 94, 121–30, 144–64
Hepburn, Ronald, 25, 32, 166, 167, 174, 176
Heraclitus, 110, 114
Herrero, Miguel, 90
Hesiod, 95
Hickling, Anne, 83
Hill, John, 193
Hillesum, Etty, 241–48
Hobbes, Thomas, 39
Homer, 90–91, 96, 104
Hooke, Robert, 180, 184, 186, 190, 192, 193, 196
Hopkins, Gerard Manley, 241
Horace, 204
Hume, David, 39, 45–46, 162, 217, 218

Ignatius of Loyola, 181, 195–96
Illich, Ivan, 241
Inwood, Brad, 26–27
Izard, Carroll, 65, 66, 78

James, Henry, 140
James, William, 80–81, 84
Janssen, Zacharias, 180
Jaspers, Karl, 151
Joblot, Louis, 192
Johnson, Carl, 74, 75
Jones, W., 230
Jung, Carl, 247

Kalidâsa, 230
Kant, Immanuel, 8, 27, 56, 59–60, 148, 170, 174–75
Keeler, Annabel, 235, 236
Kegan, Robert, 76
Keltner, Dacher, 18, 68–70
Kendall, Walton, 168
Kenseth, Joy, 205
Kepler, Johannes, 184
Kierkegaard, Søren, 53
Klein, Robert, 210

La Bruyère, Jean de, 190, 216
Lahn, Bruce, 70
Lamy, Bernard, 215
Lazarus, Bernice, 66, 79

Index of Authors

Lazarus, Richard, 22, 25, 66, 79
Lear, Gabriel, 102, 108, 115
Lechevallier, Hubert, 192
LeDoux, Joseph, 65
Leibniz, Gottfried Wilhelm, 189
Lesher, James, 96
Lesser, Friedrich Christian, 190, 193, 197
Lewis, Michael, 66
Lindbeck, George, 245
Linnaeus, Carl, 191
Litman, Theodore, 219
Lonergan, Bernard, 239
Longinus, 57, 59, 213–18, 220
Lubac, Henri de, 240

MacIntyre, Alasdair, 1–2
Maier, Henry, 75
Maimonides, Moses, 236, 247
Malebranche, Nicolas, 42, 195
Marcus Aurelius, 179, 197
Marin, Louis, 217
Marino, Giambattista, 204, 210, 211
Maritain, Jacques, 241
Marx, Karl, 239
Matsumoto, David, 19
Maybūdī, Rashīd al-Dīn, 235, 236
McCabe, Herbert, 247
McDougall, William, 19–20, 34
Mehnert, Herbert, 208
Merton, Thomas, 241
Merwin, W. S., 230
Mill, John Stuart, 167
Milton, John, 219
Mirollo, James, 204
Monk, Samuel, 59, 201, 219
More, Thomas, 58
Morris, David, 221
Mossman, Amanda, 69
Mulhall, Stephen, 30, 31

Nemeroff, Carol, 83
Newman, John Henry, 239, 246
Newton, Isaac, 38
Nicole, Pierre, 211
Nicolson, Marjorie, 57–59, 220
Nightingale, Andrea, 89, 90–91, 109–10, 115
Nussbaum, Martha, 22–23, 25, 33, 43, 77, 85

Oatley, Keith, 22
O'Connor, Flannery, 241

Ortony, Andrew, 19, 22, 33

Panofsky, Erwin, 212
Park, Katharine, 8, 34, 35–49, 57–59, 206, 207
Parmenides, 103–6, 113–14, 116–17
Pascal, Blaise, 53, 195
Patey, Douglas, 204, 206, 207, 219
Patrizia, Pinotti, 96
Peguy, Charles, 241
Peregrini, Matteo, 210
Peterson, Christopher, 18
Piaget, Jean, 69, 72–76, 83
Pickstock, Catherine, 238–39
Pieper, Josef, 52
Piles, Roger de, 219
Pindar, 216
Plato, 2, 3, 8, 49–52, 88–117, 122, 135, 145, 146, 154–63
Platt, Peter, 207
Plutarch, 96
Plutchik, Robert, 65, 66
Polo, Marco, 36
Poussin, Nicholas, 212
Power, Henry, 180, 184, 186
Prier, Raymond, 91

Raghavan, Venkatarama, 227
Rapin, René, 211, 212, 213
Ray, John, 188–89, 196
Regn, Gerhard, 210
Reiss, Hans, 202
Richardson, Jonathan, 219
Roger, Jacques, 188
Rorty, Amelie, 43
Rosengren, Karl, 83
Rösler, Walter, 88
Ross, James, 245
Rousseau, Jean-Jacques, 6
Rozin, Paul, 83
Rubenstein, Mary-Jane, 8, 17, 49–55
Rueger, Alexander, 203

Safranski, Rüdiger, 151
Saint-Girons, Baldine, 195
Schachtel, Ernest, 76
Schopenhauer, Arthur, 56
Schulz-Buschhaus, Ulrich, 210
Sedley, David, 97, 99, 112
Seligman, Martin, 18
Seneca, 26, 179, 196
Shadwell, Thomas, 190
Shaftesbury, 57, 59, 203, 220, 221

Index of Authors

Shiota, Michelle, 19, 68, 69
Shklovksy, Viktor, 5
Shuger, Deborah, 204, 215, 219
Slingerland, Edward, 64
Smith, Adam, 42–48, 51–52, 54, 166
Smith, Albert J., 205, 208
Smith, John E., 81–82
Smith, Wilfrid Cantwell, 247
Sokolowski, Robert, 237, 247
Solomon, Robert, 26
Somânanda, 233
Spinoza, Benedict, 40
Spörl, Ulrich, 221
Stolnitz, Jerome, 201, 203
Surin, Jean-Joseph, 183, 185
Swammerdam, Jan, 187, 189, 193, 194–95, 197–98
Szlezák, Thomas, 97, 99, 104

Tanner, Tony, 5
Tasso, Torquato, 206, 212
Tatarkiewicz, Wladyslaw, 208
Taylor, Charles, 237–48
Taylor, Marjorie, 84
Ten Kate, Lambert, 219
Tesauro, Emanuele, 208–11, 221
Tooby, John, 18, 65

Tremlin, Todd, 71
Trimpi, Wesley, 205
Turner, Gerard, 180
Turner, Terence, 19, 33

Van Hook, J. W., 209, 210
Vidal, Fernando, 76
Vincent of Beauvais, 36

Wagner, Richard, 134, 136
Ward, Seth, 184
Watkins, Francis, 187, 189, 190, 195
Weber, Max, 41, 239
Webster, John, 184
Weinberg, Bernard, 202
Wilkins, John, 184
Wilson, Catherine, 180, 181, 184, 185–86, 187, 188, 190
Wittgenstein, Ludwig, 6, 8, 27, 28–34, 121, 130–42
Wollheim, Richard, 174
Wordsworth, William, 5, 57

Xenophanes, 96, 103

Zeitlin, Froma, 88, 111
Zelle, Carsten, 220

www.ingramcontent.com/pod-product-compliance
Lightning Source LLC
Chambersburg PA
CBHW050436240426
43661CB00055B/2405